W9-AJU-074

The

PARENTING
COOKBOOK

The
PARENTING
COOKBOOK

Kathy Gunst

with the editors of *Parenting* magazine

Henry Holt and Company
New York

Henry Holt and Company, Inc.
Publishers since 1866
115 West 18th Street
New York, NY 10011

Library of Congress Cataloging-in-Publication Data
Gunst, Kathy.
The parenting cookbook / Kathy Gunst and
the editors of Parenting magazine.—1st ed.
p.   cm.
Includes index.
1. Cookery.   2. Children—Nutrition.   I. Parenting (San
Francisco, Calif.)   II. Title.
TX714.G88   1996   95-49042
641.5—dc20   CIP
ISBN 0-8050-3783-7

Henry Holt books are available for special promotions and
premiums. For details contact: Director, Special Markets.

First Edition—1996

Designed by Paula R. Szafranski

Printed in the United States of America
All first editions are printed on acid-free paper.∞
1   3   5   7   9   10   8   6   4   2

For my daughters,
Maya and Emma

Acknowledgments

This book is the result of a nearly decade-long relationship between *Parenting* magazine and myself. Over the years I have worked with their editors and have found them all to be dedicated to producing a magazine that speaks to parents in an honest and straightforward manner. This book was written with that same spirit in mind. In particular, I'd like to thank Bruce Raskin, Nan Wiener, Bonnie Monte, and Anne Krueger. Thanks also to Rik Boyd, who helped me learn to use my computer properly. I'd also like to thank all the other staff members who contributed their favorite family recipes.

Thank you to Dierdre Davis, who tested many of the recipes and helped to fine-tune them. And thanks to Larisa Yaskell for all her suggestions and fine edits. Many thanks to Hill Associates for the nutritional analyses that follow each recipe.

My agent, Robert Cornfield, was always there when I needed him. And many thanks to my editor, Elizabeth Crossman, who was attracted to this project from the very start and who nurtured it along the way.

My own family shares in my work in the most intimate and joyous ways. My children, Maya and Emma, are endlessly curious about food. I thank them both for their love and energy and boundless enthusiasm. My husband, John, is my editor, my tastebuds, my partner. None of this would be possible without him.

Contents

Introduction

"Do people really cook anymore?" the mother of two young boys asked me when I told her I was writing a cookbook devoted to parents and families. "I get up every morning at six, take my kids to school, go to work all day, pick them up at the sitter's, and stop somewhere for something to eat," she explained. "In our house cooking means opening a can of soup or zapping something in the microwave."

This woman and millions of other parents like her are the reason I collaborated with the editors of *Parenting* magazine to write *The Parenting Cookbook*. The truth is, there has never been a time when so many parents have needed guidance in cooking for and feeding their families. We are working incredibly long hours, carpooling, volunteering, juggling schedules, running households, and trying our best to raise happy children we can be proud of. Meanwhile, sitting down together as a family to share a home-cooked meal has become less and less of a priority. Despite the abundance of cookbooks on bookstore shelves and our national obsession with health and fitness, most families rarely eat together. Unfortunately, many American children are being raised on frozen, processed food—either heated up in a microwave oven or bought at the neighborhood fast-food joint. As one father told me, "There just doesn't seem to be time for real meals anymore."

But if we don't make time to eat well and teach our children about the joys of preparing delicious, fresh foods, who will? I attended a conference several years ago at which a group of food experts discussed the realities of family life and food. "Why is it," one woman asked, "that a 'Happy Meal' has become something to get in a place other than home?"

The Parenting Cookbook is a comprehensive guide for parents who believe that preparing and enjoying good, healthy food should be an important part of family life. This book offers recipes for every meal of the day, as well as for special occasions, meals that are nutritious, delicious, and in most cases quick to prepare. But this is more than just a collection of recipes. In these pages you will find ideas and strategies for dealing with many of the biggest food-related challenges parents face—satisfying children who are picky eaters, finding alternatives to sugary snacks, avoiding the hazards of grocery shopping with your child, dining out with children, and perhaps the biggest challenge of all, making time for meals at which the whole family sits down together.

I am a working mother with two young daughters. My husband and I share the work of raising our children, and yet we have made cooking and eating together a priority in our home. The recipes that fill these pages were designed with one thought in mind: you have a hundred things to do in a day, but given the right attitude, information, and, of course, a good set of recipes, you, too, can find the time for healthy eating.

You'll notice that none of the recipes are designed exclusively as "kid's foods." A woman I met said, with more than a hint of sarcasm in her voice, "Oh, a parenting cookbook! You mean lots of green food and smiley faces?" (Adding coloring to food and transforming it into a happy face or a clown is *not* what this book is about.) My belief is that fresh and simple food appeals to family members of all ages—from toddlers to grandparents. That's the philosophy behind every recipe you'll find in these pages.

While the emphasis here is on fresh ingredients, this is not a "health food" cookbook. The recipes range from low-fat, low-sugar dishes to richer, more elaborate ideas for special occasions—such as Sunday brunch, a Saturday night dinner party, or a birthday celebration. A wide variety of ethnic cooking styles has been incorporated, mirroring both current cooking trends and the diversity of American families.

These recipes were not developed in a corporate test kitchen. I cooked all of them in my home kitchen, working with our old G.E. range, a typical family refrigerator, and some basic cooking equipment.

You'll have greater success if you always read a recipe from beginning to end before you start cooking. The last thing you want in a recipe is a surprise. These recipes, like those found in *Parenting* magazine, are designed to make your job as a cook as easy as possible. The exact amount of preparation and cooking time is listed at the beginning of every recipe. Many also indicate how much of the dish can be prepared and cooked ahead of time. And because so many of us are concerned with a healthy diet, at the end of each recipe you'll find a nutritional analysis outlining the calorie, protein, fat, carbohydrate, sodium, and cholesterol content.

This book is organized to reflect your life. There are the pressing realities of getting food on the table Monday through Friday, and then there are weekends, when everything slows down to a manageable pace and mealtime becomes more relaxed. *The Parenting*

Cookbook takes you through each meal of the day, offering hundreds of recipes that are feasible for the hectic, activity-packed lifestyles most parents have these days.

While writing this book, I spoke with dozens of parents and children about food and the role it plays in their lives. I heard stories about picky eaters, children who insist on eating nothing but two or three different foods day after day. There were tales of families in which everyone demanded something different to eat at every meal. And frustrated stories about taking the kids out to a nice restaurant or doing the grocery shopping with an out-of-control toddler.

The general consensus from all the parents I spoke with—single mothers, couples, working parents, and stay-at-home moms and dads—was that feeding their families was rarely easy or simple. Everyone wished for a better way. It is our hope that this book will make food and eating a joyful, simple, and delicious part of your life.

—Kathy Gunst

Chapter One

The Parenting Pantry

🐝

The information and tips in this chapter will enable you to choose the best foods to keep around the house. It details a wide variety of ingredients that keep well and can be used to put together last-minute meals for those days when you just can't make it to the store. The first section, "The Well-Stocked Pantry," introduces a collection of interesting staples, condiments, spices, and flavorings that can make a huge difference in the flavor of your cooking. Next, you'll find tips for using your freezer most efficiently. And when you find that you are out of an ingredient, "Smart Substitutions" (page 9) will show you how to successfully substitute one ingredient for another.

The Well-Stocked Pantry

If you find yourself making the same dishes night after night, maybe it's time to explore some new ingredients. Keeping the following items on hand will transform an ordinary pantry into one full of exciting and healthful possibilities. Most of these ingredients will keep for several months or more. And on those hectic days when you can't make it to the market, these foods will be on hand to help you put together delicious, impromptu meals.

Consider this guide as a master list; try to pick up something new to add to your pantry shelves each time you go shopping.

Balsamic *and other vinegars:* A dark, richly flavored vinegar imported from Italy, balsamic is made by fermenting grape juice in wooden casks. It has a tangy flavor that is just right for salad dressings, marinades, barbecue sauces, poultry and fish dishes—even fruit salads. Balsamic vinegar can vary widely in price and quality; better products usually say "aged in wood" and "made in Italy" on the label.

I also keep a jar of cider vinegar around for making quick pickles in the summer and a few jars of red or white wine vinegar for vinaigrette dressings and sauces. Always look for a vinegar with at least 5 to 5½ percent acidity. All vinegars should be stored in a cool, dark spot.

Beans: Dried beans (white, black, kidney, etc.) are great to have on hand for soups, stews, and side dishes. They do, however, take quite a while to cook, so cooked canned beans (look for low-sodium varieties) are invaluable for last-minute preparations.

Broths *(chicken, beef, or vegetable):* A low-sodium, low-fat broth or stock is one of the most valuable things you can stock in your pantry. Canned broth makes nearly instant soup, sauces, and stews.

Capers: These mysterious little green seasonings are actual flower buds of the caper plant; they have been pickled in vinegar or brine. Many kids like their pungent flavor in salads, sauces, and stews. For a quick tartar sauce, add a few teaspoons of capers and a dash of lemon juice to a cup of mayonnaise. Store in the refrigerator.

Cheese: There are always a few varieties of cheese in my refrigerator for sandwiches, sauces, pasta dishes, fondue, quiches, and more. I like to keep a few hard cheeses—Cheddar, Swiss, and Parmesan—around for grating into sauces, pasta dishes, and casseroles. I also like to have a soft goat cheese, Brie, cream cheese, and a mild cheese like Muenster for the kid's sandwiches. For more information on cheese, see "Skimming the Fat: A User's Guide to Cheese" on page 118.

Chinese chili paste: Look for this bright red, fiery condiment in the specialty or Asian food section of your store. You may need to go to a gourmet or Asian market. There are several varieties available, but they all contain crushed hot chili peppers in a thick red paste. The chili paste is often combined with crushed garlic and/or Chinese black bean paste. This is a quick, easy way to add the heat of chili peppers to sauces, stews, stir-fries, and more.

Chinese fermented black beans: Small soybeans are fermented and preserved with salt and ginger. Before they are used, fermented beans should be rinsed under cold running water to remove the saltiness and then chopped. They can be added to sauces, marinades, and stir-fries. Available in specialty food markets and Asian food stores, they can be kept in a cool, dark spot for several months.

Chocolate: Bars of dark, semisweet, and milk chocolate can be invaluable for putting together last-minute desserts. The chocolate can be melted into sauces, or grated or chopped and served over fresh fruit salads, ice cream, sorbet, or cakes.

Chutney: Use this thick, sweet-and-spicy fruit sauce to enliven everything from grilled chicken to curries. Try a cream cheese and chutney sandwich on thinly sliced bread, or make a dip by mixing chutney, softened cream cheese, and a dash of Worcestershire sauce. Refrigerate after opening.

Clam broth: Look for a good-quality clam broth for making instant sauces for fish dishes, or use as the base for a quick fish soup or stew.

Crème fraîche: This thickened cultured French cream has a tart, sour flavor that is delicious added to everything from mashed potatoes to cakes. It has a high butterfat content and is similar to a rich sour cream. It can be used to thicken and add a rich, creamy flavor to sauces and is also delicious served over fresh berries or slices of ripe nectarines and peaches. Crème fraîche is now available in many supermarkets, as well as specialty food shops.

Dried fruit: Figs, apricots, prunes, and other fruits add a sweet taste and chewy texture to stuffings, sauces, and salads.

Dried mushrooms: Dried porcini, shiitake, and morel mushrooms can be pricey, but their rich, earthy flavor and meaty texture go a long way. Reconstitute by soaking in hot water for 25 minutes, then add to soups, stews, sauces, pizzas, salads, and sandwiches. Be sure to save the soaking liquid (which becomes a rich mushroom broth) to flavor sauces and soups.

Flavored mustard: Mustard is made with a wide range of seasonings, from tarragon to peppercorns. Add to salad dressings, sauces, and favorite sandwiches, or slather on chicken before baking. Refrigerate after opening.

Ginger: If you've never tasted fresh ginger, you're in for a real treat. It's a beige, knobby-looking root that is full of the powerfully fresh flavor of ginger. Store ginger, unpeeled, in the refrigerator for several weeks. When it begins to feel mushy and the skin shrivels up, it's time to get rid of it. To use fresh ginger, simply peel off the outer skin and either chop the fresh root or grate it.

Herbs and spices: Contrary to popular belief, dried herbs and spices don't keep forever. Buy a variety of dried herbs and spices every 6 months or so to guarantee freshness. Never store spices and herbs over the stove or in direct sunlight. Experiment with different herbs and spices and watch how interesting the same old dishes can taste. Keep the basics around—basil, thyme, sage, oregano, rosemary, and dill—but also try ginger, marjoram, mustard and coriander seeds, dried chile peppers, curry powder, cumin, cayenne pepper, allspice, and more.

Hoisin sauce: A thick, mahogany-colored sauce made from mashed and fermented soybeans, garlic, chilies, spices, and flour, hoisin has a slightly sweet, almost smoky flavor that is excellent in stir-fries and barbecue sauces. Or mix it with a touch of soy sauce and sesame oil and use as a dip for chicken, pork, or fish. You can also spread hoisin directly on foods before grilling or broiling for a sweet, flavorful glaze.

Honey: There are hundreds of varieties of honey available in health and gourmet food shops. Try to keep a few types on hand. A light, flowery honey is ideal for baking, for stirring into tea and hot drinks, and for soothing sore throats. A more expensive herb-flavored honey adds a distinctive flavor to special dishes in which the flavor of the honey really matters.

Hot pepper sauce: You can find hot pepper sauces in virtually every color and texture imaginable. What they all have in common is their ability to add a spicy punch to a wide variety of foods. Even kids who don't like "spicy" dishes will appreciate a dash to flavor a soup, stew, or casserole. A little goes a long way. A dash brings out the natural flavors in other foods and is a great way to season food without adding a lot of sodium.

Hungarian paprika: Despite popular misconceptions, this common red spice does more than add color to a dish. It can contribute a subtle sweetness that helps bring out the natural flavors in foods. Always store paprika in the refrigerator.

Nuts: Keep a variety of nuts—walnuts, almonds, pine nuts, pistachios, pecans—in the freezer. Chopped raw nuts add flavor and texture to stir-fries, sauces, pesto, and salad dressings. Sautéed in a touch of butter, they're a delicious topping for chicken breasts, fish fillets, even soups and stews. Nuts keep best when tightly wrapped and stored in the freezer. You can simply use what you need and keep the rest frozen for several months at a time.

Oils: Vegetable oils are excellent to have on hand for sautéing and cooking with high heat. They add no discernible flavor and can be used with a wide variety of foods. However, I prefer olive oil for almost all my cooking. I keep a mild, pure olive oil around for basic sautéing and for soups and sauces, and a good-quality extra virgin olive oil for cold sauces, pesto, and salad dressings. Olive and canola oil, which are monounsaturated, are more healthful than saturated animal fats like butter.

Olive paste: Black olive paste, also called *tapenade*, is made by pureeing black olives with olive oil, spices, and sometimes anchovies. It has a rich, strong flavor that can transform pasta sauces, salad dressings, sandwiches, and casseroles. Add just a touch, though, as too much can be overpowering. Make a tangy dip by mixing 1 cup of low-fat sour cream with 3 tablespoons of olive paste and a dash of lemon juice.

Pasta: Dried pasta is the ultimate pantry food: it keeps forever and can be put together with any number of foods at the last minute to make a wonderful meal. The more shapes and sizes you have on hand, the more possibilities you have for a quick meal.

Peanut butter: This may seem obvious, but peanut butter can be used not only in classic PB&J sandwiches but also to make sauces (for Chinese cold noodles, Thai curries, and more), cakes, pies, or even soup. Keep jars of smooth and chunky on hand.

Pie crusts: There are now many good brands of frozen pie crust sold in supermarket freezers. These crusts can be invaluable for putting together a quick quiche or sweet or savory pie. Use one pie crust for the bottom, add a fruit or other filling, and invert another frozen pie crust on top for a quick, simple covered pie. Be sure to make several slashes in the crust with a small, sharp knife to release steam while the pie bakes. Also keep a package of phyllo dough in the freezer for making spinach pie and desserts.

Pimientos: Spanish for peppers, pimientos are sweet red peppers that have been roasted, seeded, and preserved in water or oil. They are a great topping for pizzas and sandwiches. Make a colorful pasta sauce by pureeing a small jar of drained pimientos with 2 to 3 tablespoons olive oil, a clove of garlic, ⅓ cup pine nuts, and ⅓ cup grated Parmesan cheese.

Potatoes, onions, and garlic: No kitchen should ever be without these three "staple" foods. All keep well unrefrigerated. When potatoes begin to sprout (and grow "eyes") and become soft, they should be discarded. Garlic and onions get mushy and soft after several weeks.

Rice: Rice is one of the most versatile foods imaginable. I always keep several varieties around for making into side dishes, stuffings, risottos, puddings, salads, and more. There are more varieties of rice available than you could imagine; for an overview of the most common varieties, see "A Primer on Rice" on page 167.

Rice wine: Made from fermented rice, this colorless Chinese wine adds good flavor to marinades and sauces and can be added to stir-fried foods to make an "instant" sauce.

Salsa: There are now dozens of varieties of salsa sold on supermarket shelves—hot, medium, and mild. Keep a few jars around for making a quick sauce or dip or for snacking on with chips and raw vegetables. Or make your own salsa (see recipe on page 444) and can a few extra jars.

Sesame oil: Traditionally used in Asian dishes, this golden brown oil gets its distinctive flavor from toasted sesame seeds. Try a few drops in stir-fries, salad dressings, soups, stews, and noodle dishes.

Shredded coconut: A bit of this dried tropical fruit adds a crunchy texture and sweet flavor to milkshakes, desserts, curries, stews, and sauces. Make a fruit salad with thinly sliced oranges, strawberries, apples, and a sprinkle of shredded coconut. Always look for an unsweetened variety. Store coconut in the freezer after opening.

Soy sauce or tamari: These fermented soybean seasonings are generally interchangeable, although tamari tends to be thicker and contains no wheat. Both add a rich, salty flavor to marinades, barbecue sauces, salad dressings, and stir-fries, and both are available in low-sodium versions. Try marinating chicken pieces in a few tablespoons of soy sauce or tamari with a touch of sesame oil and lime juice, then broil until golden brown and crisp.

Sun-dried cranberries: These small, maroon berries have been dried to concentrate their flavor. They add an intensely tart, sweet flavor to sauces, muffins, cakes, and other dishes. They are especially nice to use around the holidays when fresh cranberries are abundant; the combination of the fresh cranberry mixed with its more intense dried cousin is memorable. And obviously they can be substituted for fresh cranberries in the spring and summer when cranberries are out of season.

Sun-dried tomatoes: When fresh tomatoes are in short supply, sun-dried tomatoes are a real bonus. They have a slightly sweet, concentrated flavor and come either marinated in olive oil or dried. The dried variety lasts longer and can be reconstituted by soaking in hot water for about 10 minutes or by boiling for 2 minutes. Drain the tomatoes and dry well on paper towels before using. Add them to pasta sauces, salads, and stews. For an instant pizza, place chopped sun-dried tomatoes on half of an English muffin, top with black olives and grated cheese, and broil for a few minutes.

Tahini (sesame paste): This thick paste is made by grinding roasted hulled sesame seeds. Tahini adds a nutty flavor to salad dressings, sauces, and dips. It is the base of cold Chinese noodles and many Middle Eastern dishes, such as hummus.

Tortillas: Keep a few packages of corn and wheat tortillas in the freezer for putting together last-minute meals. Good varieties that are not loaded with preservatives are now available at most grocery stores or specialty food shops, either fresh or frozen.

Tuna: Choose a less fatty, healthier water-packed tuna and keep several cans around at all times. Use for salads and sandwiches, or add to antipasto platters, sauces, and casseroles.

Wine, dry sherry, rum, Cinzano: Several recipes in this book call for wine, a splash of rum, or a cup of dry sherry to marinate foods in. I am not advocating that you get in the habit of serving your children liquor. None of the recipes call for a large quantity of alcohol—from ¼ to ½ cup. However, according to Sharon Tyler Herbst in her authoritative book, *The Food Lover's Tiptionary,* "Though it has long been thought that alcohol evaporates when heated, a USDA study has disproved that theory. In fact, from 5 to 85 percent alcohol may remain in a cooked dish, depending on various factors including how the food was heated, the cooking time, and the source of alcohol." Keep in mind that all the recipes in this book that contain alcohol are cooked for quite some time.

Worcestershire sauce: For a deliciously smoky flavor, add this thin, pungent sauce to marinades, soups, stews, poultry, and meat. A dash intensifies cheese sauces and makes a wonderful seasoning for steamed vegetables.

Some Thoughts About . . .

Frozen Assets: How to Use Your Freezer

It's time to bring your freezer out of the ice age. Instead of regarding it as a repository for unmarked containers of ancient mystery food, consider it a tool for providing your family with nutritious, less expensive meals. Buying food in bulk or on sale and then freezing the extra can yield significant savings. Freezing also lets you enjoy peak produce out of season. But in order to use a freezer properly, it's helpful to learn a few basics.

Safety First

To ensure that food stays fresh, make sure the freezer is cold enough to stop bacterial growth. The temperature should be between 0° and 8° Fahrenheit. (Hardware stores sell inexpensive freezer thermometers.) To freeze a large quantity of food at once, many experts suggest turning the freezer to the coldest setting a day ahead, then returning it to its normal setting once the food is thoroughly frozen.

Place food in the back and on lower shelves, where it's coldest. Once the food is thoroughly frozen, it can be moved toward the front. Don't store meats and poultry on the shelves in the freezer door; that's the warmest spot. The freezer door is best used for frozen juices and smaller items, or foods that have already been frozen in the back of your freezer. Freezers work most efficiently when they're 75 percent full, so if yours is too empty, stock it with water-filled milk cartons or bulky items like bread.

The safest way to thaw food is in the refrigerator—thawing foods at room temperature can encourage the growth of bacteria. In general, most meats and poultry take 5 hours per pound to thaw in the refrigerator.

To minimize the chances of contamination and keep out excess moisture, always thaw food in its wrapper. Place it on a large plate to catch any drippings. If you prefer to use a microwave for defrosting, check your manual for exact times and be sure to cook the food immediately after it's thawed.

Flavor Savers

Freeze leftovers when they're cool in order to minimize the amount of ice crystals that condense on the surface. (Allow leftovers to cool in the refrigerator rather than on a counter so that bacteria can't begin to multiply.) Although ice crystals don't interfere with the food's wholesomeness, they do affect the flavor. So does freezer burn, the gray or white surface that forms on food when it's exposed to cold air. To prevent condensation and freezer burn, it's crucial to wrap foods properly, says Elinor Klivans, author of *Bake and Freeze*. Double-wrap all foods—first in a tight seal of plastic wrap and then in heavy-duty foil, freezer paper, or a tightly sealed plastic freezer bag, container, or metal tin. When using self-sealing plastic bags, always squeeze out the air before storing.

No matter how good a memory you might have, be sure to label foods. It's surprising how unrecognizable the contents of a container become once they're frozen. Attach a freezer label or a piece of masking tape with the name of the food and the date clearly marked.

To prevent mini-explosions when liquids expand, leave about an inch of room at the top of containers. Always freeze foods in small portions and in a single layer. Not only does the food freeze more quickly, which prevents spoilage, but you can thaw just what you need.

Some Thoughts About . . .
Smart Substitutions

You decide to make brownies with the kids after school, only to discover that you're out of baking chocolate. You start mixing a batch of biscuits and find that you have no buttermilk. Or you're making a sauce and find that there's no chicken broth left in your pantry. Can you simply substitute another ingredient? Often you can, but not always.

"If you need to substitute one ingredient for another," cautions Lora Brody, author of *The Kitchen Survival Guide* and *The Entertaining Survival Guide*, "think it through before you just throw it in. You'd be amazed how many disasters you can avoid by just taking an extra minute or two."

The following guidelines should help you make successful substitutions.

• *Consider the role of the missing ingredient.* Is its flavor critical to the dish, or is it designed more for texture or color? Try to replace it with an ingredient that has similar properties. For instance, if a recipe calls for fresh green beans, you'll ruin the texture by using canned ones. You'd be better off using another fresh vegetable; the taste will be different, but the consistency will be right. In a salmon mousse, on the other hand, the distinctive flavor of the fish is essential. Canned tuna just won't work; its flavor is too different. But because all the ingredients are pureed together, texture is less of a consideration, and canned salmon would be satisfactory in place of fresh.

• *Don't substitute junk.* When an ingredient of equivalent quality is lacking, it's best to start over with a different dish. "Use common sense," says Brody. "You can't add your kid's old Halloween candy to a cake batter in place of quality baking chocolate and expect to have a fabulous dessert."

• *Be precise when baking.* In general, it's much easier to improvise substitutions when you're cooking savory dishes rather than sweet ones. Baking is more of an exact science, where using white flour instead of cake flour can ruin the texture. (If you're desperate, though, see the chart below for a reasonable equivalent.) Other baking taboos: switching to skim milk in place of whole milk; using peanut, sesame, or olive oil for everyday vegetable oil; substituting oil for solid shortening; and using sugar substitutes, which have chemical properties that are completely different from those of sugar.

• *Expect some difference.* Most stews, soups, and casseroles will tolerate a lot of flexibility, but the final dish won't taste exactly like the original. For instance, you can almost always substitute dried herbs for fresh, but the dried variety won't impart the same lively flavor. And most cooks would agree that nothing can replace the taste of fresh garlic; when you're in a bind, though, garlic powder will work.

Sometimes a judicious substitution can actually improve a dish. Once, when I was making a quiche and discovered mold on the mushrooms in my fridge, I substituted dried mushrooms and just used half as many. The result was a pie so rich and earthy that I've altered the recipe.

Here are a few substitutes to save a recipe.

IF YOUR RECIPE CALLS FOR:	SUBSTITUTE:
1 tablespoon fresh herbs	1 teaspoon dried herbs
1 chopped clove fresh garlic	⅛ teaspoon garlic powder
1 cup buttermilk	1 cup warm milk plus 1 tablespoon vinegar or lemon juice
Lemon or lime juice	Equal quantity orange juice
1 teaspoon baking powder	¼ teaspoon baking soda plus ½ teaspoon cream of tartar
1 cup cake flour	1 cup less 2 tablespoons white flour plus 2 tablespoons cornstarch
1 ounce semisweet chocolate	3 tablespoons cocoa mixed with 2 tablespoons butter and 3 tablespoons granulated sugar
Sour cream	An equal quantity of plain yogurt, but use only in cold dishes; will have a tangier flavor
Chicken, beef, or vegetable broth	An equal quantity of boiling water with one or more chicken, beef, or vegetable bouillon cubes, according to package directions

—————————— ❖ ——————————

Grocery Shopping:
Taking a New Approach

Grocery shopping in America has become a routine exercise that has almost nothing to do with culinary inspiration and almost everything to do with necessity. Many of us walk through the supermarket aisles, lists and coupons clutched in our hands, gathering food for our families in a zombie-like manner. "I just do it, week after week after week," a friend of mine admitted. "I never actually enjoy grocery shopping. It's just something that needs to be done, like going to the dentist."

Yet the first step to creative, healthful cooking is shopping. Every recipe really begins in the market as you choose the ingredients you'll be cooking with. Believe it or not, there are ways to make shopping, even in huge mega-supermarkets, a more inspired event. A few simple strategies can help you find the best, freshest food and break the routine of choosing foods with your eyes closed.

For many parents the first obstacle to grocery shopping is their kids: should they take them along or not? Most of us don't have a choice in the matter; we simply have to bring our children with us. However, if you have the option, it's often wise to leave them at home. When you shop by yourself, you control which foods do, and don't, end up in your kitchen.

Children and supermarkets can be a difficult combination. Supermarkets and food manufacturers spend a lot of time, money, and effort enticing children to buy products that are not particularly nutritious or good for them. For example, the most sugary breakfast cereals are generally stocked on the lower shelves, right at a child's eye level. And then, of course, there is the candy at the check-out counter. Grocery shopping with children is far too often a tug-of-war between "Mom, can we get this?" and "No, I don't want you eating that junk."

When you do take your children to the supermarket, be sure to lay down a few ground rules ahead of time. Talk to them about what they can and can't buy. Some parents let their kids pick out one special treat at the supermarket, which ensures that the adult chooses the rest of the groceries. One woman I know wants her children to feel "part of the shopping experi-

ence," so she allows them to select dinner—from main course to dessert—
for one night of the upcoming week.

Making a detailed grocery list can also be incredibly helpful. You tend
to spend less money when you're focused on getting only what you need
and don't roam around the store trying to remember which foods you already have at home.

But lists can also be a crutch. Let's say your list includes chicken,
pasta, cucumbers, and asparagus. You arrive at the store and the asparagus
are limp and unattractive, the cucumbers have soft brown spots on the
sides, and the brand of chicken you prefer is out of stock. However, the
store is having a sale on salmon fillets, and there are some really great-
looking avocados. Unfortunately, some shoppers are so "addicted" to following their lists that they don't even notice which foods are really fresh
(and cheap) when they go to the store. Try not to be a slave to your list.
Keep an open mind about trying new foods and be willing to change your
menu.

If you can't find the foods you want at your local store, ask the manager
to stock them. Alice Waters, owner of Chez Panisse restaurant in Berkeley,
California, tells a story about her local supermarket. "I kept asking them
for organic carrots and they didn't do anything about it," she recalls. "So, I
went into the store with ten friends, and we all asked for organic carrots.
Believe me, when a grocery store sees that there's a demand for something,
they'll carry just about anything."

But there are instances when you won't find everything you need in one
shop. It's worthwhile to take the time to visit a farm stand, a farmer's market, a bakery, or an ethnic food shop occasionally. These smaller shops give
you the opportunity to find new, generally fresher foods in an atmosphere
where you don't feel like a robot buying food from other robots. And shopping at smaller, neighborhood shops can give you and your children a
sense of community that you won't find in most large grocery stores.

At our local produce shop, my children love to see the variety of fruits
and vegetables that appear with the seasons. They march around carrying
the colorful plastic baskets the shop provides and help me pick out all sorts
of fresh foods they wouldn't ordinarily see in the supermarket. Here they
have learned about fresh figs and had their first taste of local fiddlehead
ferns (a springtime specialty in northern New England).

My husband remembers accompanying his mother to the local butcher when he was a young boy and claims he learned the difference between various cuts of meat by listening to his mother place her orders with the butcher over the years. The closer you get to the source, the more connection you'll feel to the food you buy.

Of course, most of us don't have the time to visit a butcher, a bakery, and a fish store each time we shop. That's why mega-supermarkets were invented. But there are ways to use these large, impersonal stores for what they do best: providing bulk items, speed, and convenience. The bottom line: if you're not excited by the ingredients you're bringing home, your cooking is bound to suffer.

———————— ⌀ ————————

How to Make the Most of Grocery Shopping

• Don't take your child shopping when she is tired, hungry, or cranky. You're bound to have a difficult time. Try to plan trips to the supermarket after a nap or a snack.

• Remember that you are setting an example when you go grocery shopping with your child. If you fill your cart with junk foods, your child gets the message that these foods are OK to eat.

• Always look for fresh, seasonal foods.

• Watch for daily or weekly specials (which usually indicate that a store has bought too much or that the food is seasonal and therefore perishable).

• Try not to shop on Sunday nights, when fresh shipments of food have been depleted and the new food for the week has yet to arrive.

• Always look—and feel and smell—to make sure that food is truly fresh. If fruits or vegetables are wrapped tightly in plastic, ask if you can open one to see if it's ripe.

• Try not to go to the same market every time you go shopping. Every few weeks visit an ethnic market or a special fruit and vegetable stand to vary the foods you buy—and ultimately cook with.

• Farmer's markets are great places to find the very freshest produce. Call your local agriculture department to find out about when and where markets are held in your area.

Buy Something New Every Week and Watch Your Family's Eating Patterns Change for the Better

I am quite convinced that most of us get into cooking ruts because we buy the same food every time we go shopping. And then we wonder why we can't think of anything new to make for dinner. If you have chicken every Monday night, pizza on Tuesdays, and your kids bring ham and cheese sandwiches to school five days a week, it's no wonder you don't feel inspired about your shopping—or your cooking.

But if you alter the routine by doing something as simple as buying one new ingredient each time you go shopping, it might inspire your cooking, jar your thinking, and change your family's diet for the better. Here are just a few suggestions.

• A jar of Chinese chili paste can add a rich, deep, spicy flavor to a wide variety of foods. Just a dab can transform an ordinary hamburger or a sauce for stir-fried vegetables into an exotic dish.

• A simple can of coconut milk can transform a regular chicken, beef, or vegetable stew into a Thai-flavored dish or add a fresh coconut flavor to vanilla or chocolate pudding.

• Sun-dried tomatoes can enliven a winter pasta sauce with the fresh flavor of tomatoes or add a tomato flavor to winter pizza.

• Dried mushrooms add a woodsy, earthy flavor to soups and stews. Simply soak a few dried mushrooms in a cup of warm water, drain, chop, and add to a simple soup to make it taste like it's been simmering for hours.

• Buy a few spicy sausages (chorizo or linguica) or a fresh Italian sausage and sauté with a can of white beans, a few chopped tomatoes, a chopped onion, and some thyme. A quick, instant stew can be served within 10 minutes.

• Look for a good-quality clam juice and make a quick fish stew using a chunk of white fish, a few chopped cloves of garlic, sweet peppers, tomato, beans, thyme, and some clam juice.

How to Use the Nutritional Data in This Book

The recipes in this book contain nutritional information based on the most current data available from the U.S. Department of Agriculture for calorie count; grams of protein, fat, and carbohydrate; and milligrams of sodium and cholesterol. This analysis is given for a single serving, based on the average number of servings listed for the recipe. (If a recipe says "Yield: 4 to 6 servings," the analysis was done for 5 servings. If a recipe calls for 2 to 3 cups of juice, the analysis was done using 2½ cups.) The nutritional analysis does not include optional ingredients or those for which no specific amount is stated (salt to taste, for instance). If an ingredient is listed with an alternative, the figures are calculated for the first choice only. (For instance, if a recipe lists ½ cup low-fat milk, sour cream, or heavy cream, the analysis was done for ½ cup low-fat milk only.) All recipes listing low-fat milk refer to 1 percent milk. All recipes were analyzed by Hill Nutrition Associates.

Chapter Two

Quick Weekday Breakfasts

Finding the time to eat a good, healthy breakfast on weekdays can be a challenge. But in this chapter you'll find dozens of recipes that are nutritious and pleasing for kids—and, best of all, can be made in minutes. For instance, you'll find fruit and yogurt drinks that can be whisked together in a blender in about 5 minutes. There are several quick egg dishes, a variety of interesting spreads for bagels and toast, and a fabulous muffin recipe that is assembled in less than 10 minutes and baked while you hop in the shower!

Fresh Fruit with Yogurt-Nut Topping

Breakfast Yogurt Shake

Homemade Granola

Emma's Favorite Fried Eggs

Basic Scrambled Eggs

Easy Scrambled Egg Additions

Southwest Scramble

Scrambled Eggs with Roasted Potatoes and Cheese

Spinach-Feta Scramble

Zucchini-Cheddar Scramble

Ham and Swiss Scramble

Quick French Toast

Michael and Donna's Magic Muffins

Cream Cheese and Scallions

Tofu Spread

Strawberry Butter

Banana–Peanut Butter Spread

Fresh Fruit with Yogurt-Nut Topping

Preparation time: 10 minutes

Fresh berries and grated apple topped with low-fat yogurt and chopped nuts make a complete breakfast. Vary the fruit according to the season.

1 apple, peeled and grated
1½ cups fresh berries (if using strawberries, cut in half)
½ cup plain or vanilla low-fat yogurt
1 tablespoon chopped walnuts or almonds

Divide the apples and berries among 4 bowls. Place 2 tablespoons of yogurt on top of each serving and sprinkle with the nuts.

YIELD: 4 servings
PER SERVING: 65 calories, 2 g protein, 2 g fat, 11 g carbohydrate, 21 mg sodium, 2 mg cholesterol

Breakfast Yogurt Shake

Preparation time: 5 minutes

Who says breakfast food has to be boring and repetitive? This quick drink, made in a blender or food processor, combines low-fat yogurt with fresh fruit and juice—but no sugar. You can substitute whatever type of fruit is in season. Other favorite combinations include peach-cantaloupe, raspberry-blueberry-orange, or plum-peach. This drink also makes a great snack or dessert.

½ **ripe banana, peeled**
¼ **cup strawberries, fresh or frozen**
2 tablespoons orange juice
½ **cup plain or vanilla low-fat yogurt**

Place the banana, strawberries, and orange juice in the container of a food processor or blender and puree. Add the yogurt and puree until smooth. Serve in tall glasses.

YIELD: about 1¼ cups, or 2 servings
PER SERVING: 75 calories, 3 g protein, 1 g fat, 14 g carbohydrate, 40 mg sodium, 3 mg cholesterol

Homemade Granola

Preparation time: 5 minutes
Cooking time: 20 to 25 minutes

If the idea of making your own granola makes you think "Forget it—I don't even have time to go grocery shopping," you haven't tried this simple recipe. Kids love to mix all the ingredients and help make their own breakfast cereal. Serve it with milk or yogurt and top with fresh fruit and berries and a sprinkling of shredded coconut. The granola will keep in an airtight jar for several weeks.

> **6½ cups rolled oats**
> **3 cups nuts and seeds (mix any combination of cashews, pecans,**
>   **almonds, walnuts, pumpkin seeds, sunflower seeds)**
> **¾ cup good-quality honey**
> **¾ cup vegetable oil**
> **1½ cups raisins**

Preheat the oven to 400 degrees. Thoroughly mix all the ingredients except the raisins in a large roasting pan. Bake for about 20 to 25 minutes, stirring the mixture every 5 minutes or so to prevent burning. (Beware: granola can burn quickly. If the phone rings during the last 5 minutes of baking, don't answer it!) The granola is done when it is a light golden brown throughout.

Remove from the oven and let cool. If you like your granola loose and separated, immediately break it up with a large metal spoon. If you prefer a chunkier, bricklike cereal, let it sit a few minutes longer and then break it into clusters. Stir in the raisins and store in an airtight jar.

YIELD: about 10 cups
PER ½ CUP SERVING: 348 calories, 7 g protein, 19 g fat, 41 g carbohydrate, 4 mg sodium,
    0 mg cholesterol

Emma's Favorite Fried Eggs

Preparation time: 5 minutes
Cooking time: 5 minutes

My five-year-old daughter, Emma, devised this recipe for a fried egg sprinkled with grated cheese and drizzled with olive oil. It's quite delicious.

½ teaspoon butter
1 large egg
1 tablespoon grated Cheddar cheese or cheese of choice
Salt and freshly ground black pepper
Drizzle olive oil
1 slice toast

Melt the butter in a small skillet over moderate heat. When it's bubbling, crack the egg in. Sprinkle on the cheese, salt, pepper, and olive oil and cook 1 minute. Flip and let cook another minute. Using a spatula, place the cooked egg on the toast.

YIELD: 1 serving
PER SERVING: 207 calories, 10 g protein, 12 g fat, 13 g carbohydrate, 261 mg sodium, 225 mg cholesterol

Basic Scrambled Eggs

Preparation time: 5 minutes
Cooking time: 5 minutes

Consider this recipe a base on which to experiment. There are four variations that follow, but just about any herb, spice, fruit, or vegetable can be worked into scrambled eggs. This is a classic first dish for kids learning to cook.

4 large eggs
1 tablespoon milk or water
Pinch salt and freshly ground black pepper
1 tablespoon butter, margarine, or cooking oil

In a small bowl, vigorously whisk together the eggs, milk, salt, and pepper. Heat the butter in a medium skillet over moderately high heat until sizzling. Beat the eggs into the skillet with a fork, and cook, whisking constantly, until they are as firm as you like them. Remove from the heat and serve immediately.

YIELD: 2 to 4 servings
PER SERVING: 102 calories, 6 g protein, 8 g fat, 18 g carbohydrate, 127 mg sodium, 221 mg cholesterol

Easy Scrambled Egg Additions

Add any of the following when you add the eggs to the skillet:

- 1 tablespoon cream cheese, cut into small cubes, with 1 teaspoon chopped chives or scallions
- ½ cup chopped cooked pasta
- ½ cup chopped ripe tomatoes with 1 tablespoon chopped fresh basil
- 1 teaspoon sesame seeds
- ¼ cup thinly sliced smoked fish and a handful of chopped fresh chives
- 1 chopped roasted red pepper (see recipe, page 442) and a handful of chopped fresh parsley

- 1 to 2 tablespoons pesto sauce (see recipes, pages 438–41).
- ¼ cup cooked asparagus cut into bite-size pieces, along with 2 tablespoons chopped ham
- Top scrambled eggs with a few tablespoons of Salsa Dipping Sauce (see recipe, page 445) or a pesto (see recipes, pages 438–41).

Southwest Scramble

Preparation time: 5 minutes
Cooking time: 12 to 14 minutes

These colorful eggs are best when served with warm tortillas or English muffins and hot pepper sauce or the Salsa Dipping Sauce on page 445.

1 tablespoon butter or oil
¼ cup chopped scallion or onion
½ cup chopped green or red bell pepper or a combination
¼ cup chopped ripe tomato
¼ cup thinly sliced avocado (optional)
Ingredients for Basic Scrambled Eggs (page 22)
½ cup sour cream

In a medium skillet, heat the butter over moderate heat. Add the scallion and sauté for about 5 minutes, or until soft. Add the bell pepper and tomato and sauté another 3 minutes. Stir in the avocado if desired. Raise the heat to medium-high and add the egg mixture along with 2 tablespoons of the sour cream. Whisk with a fork until the eggs are set. Top with a dollop of sour cream and serve with hot pepper sauce or salsa on the side.

YIELD: 2 to 4 servings
PER SERVING: 196 calories, 8 g protein, 17 g fat, 35 g carbohydrate, 173 mg sodium, 241 mg cholesterol

Scrambled Eggs with Roasted Potatoes and Cheese

Preparation time: 5 minutes
Cooking time: 8 to 10 minutes

A quick meal in one—scrambled eggs mixed with sautéed scallions or shallots, roasted potato cubes, and grated cheese. Serve with bagels or toast. This is a great way to use up leftover roasted potatoes.

1 teaspoon olive oil or butter
2 scallions or 1 shallot, thinly sliced
1 roast potato, cubed
2 large eggs
⅓ cup finely chopped fresh parsley
Salt and freshly ground black pepper
3 to 4 tablespoons grated cheese, Cheddar or other favorite

In a medium skillet, heat the oil over moderate heat. Add the scallions or shallot and sauté for 2 minutes. Add the potato cubes and sauté another minute.

In a bowl, whisk together the eggs, parsley, salt, and pepper. Add the eggs to the skillet with the scallions and potatoes, and scramble with a fork to keep the eggs moving around. Just before the eggs come together, sprinkle in the cheese. Serve hot.

YIELD: 2 servings
PER SERVING: 181 calories, 10 g protein, 11 g fat, 9 g carbohydrate, 148 mg sodium, 226 mg cholesterol

Spinach-Feta Scramble

Preparation time: 5 minutes
Cooking time: 15 minutes

A classic combination—spinach and feta—mixed with scrambled eggs. Serve with warm pita bread or toast.

> **2 cups fresh spinach leaves**
> **1 tablespoon olive oil or butter**
> **Ingredients for Basic Scrambled Eggs (page 22)**
> **⅓ cup crumbled feta cheese**

Wash the spinach well and place it in a medium saucepan with ⅓ cup water. Bring to boil, cover, and steam about 5 minutes, or until soft and tender. Drain thoroughly, dry on paper towels, and chop finely.

Heat the oil in a medium skillet over moderate heat. Add the spinach and cook 1 minute. Raise the heat to moderately high, add the egg mixture and the feta, and whisk with a fork until set. Remove from the heat and serve.

YIELD: 2 to 4 servings
PER SERVING: 168 calories, 9 g protein, 14 g fat, 2 g carbohydrate, 274 mg sodium, 231 mg cholesterol

Zucchini-Cheddar Scramble

Preparation time: 8 minutes
Cooking time: 15 minutes

You can substitute any favorite vegetable or cheese.

1 tablespoon butter or oil
½ cup diced zucchini
Ingredients for Basic Scrambled Eggs (page 22)
⅓ cup grated Cheddar cheese
2 tablespoons chopped fresh parsley or chives (optional)

Heat the butter in a skillet over moderate heat. Add the zucchini and sauté for 7 minutes, or until soft and golden brown. Raise the heat to moderately high and add the egg mixture and cheese. Whisk with a fork until set. Remove from the heat, sprinkle with the parsley, and serve.

YIELD: 2 to 4 servings

PER SERVING: 168 calories, 9 g protein, 14 g fat, 1 g carbohydrate, 215 mg sodium, 238 mg cholesterol

Ham and Swiss Scramble

Preparation time: 8 minutes
Cooking time: 10 to 12 minutes

A favorite combination that goes well with a wide variety of herbs—tarragon, basil, chives, sage, parsley, or your favorite.

> **1 tablespoon butter**
> **⅓ cup diced cooked ham**
> **1 tablespoon fresh herbs or 1 teaspoon dried**
> **Ingredients for Basic Scrambled Eggs (page 22)**
> **¼ cup grated Swiss cheese**

In a medium skillet, heat the butter over moderate heat. Add the ham and herbs and sauté for 2 minutes. Raise the heat to moderately high and add the egg mixture and cheese. Cook, whisking with a fork, until the eggs are set. Remove from the heat and serve.

YIELD: 2 to 4 servings
PER SERVING: 171 calories, 11 g protein, 13 g fat, 1 g carbohydrate, 314 mg sodium, 241 mg cholesterol

Quick French Toast

Preparation time: 5 minutes
Cooking time: 5 minutes

This is a classic that is loved from one generation to another. Use whatever type of bread you have on hand—white, wheat, raisin, challah, or oatmeal.

1 large egg
½ cup low-fat milk
Pinch ground cinnamon
Pinch ground nutmeg
⅛ teaspoon vanilla extract (optional)
2 slices bread
1 tablespoon butter or margarine
Maple syrup

In a bowl, whisk together the egg, milk, cinnamon, nutmeg, and vanilla if using. Add the bread and let soak on both sides.

Heat the butter in medium skillet over moderate heat. Add the batter-drenched bread and cook about 2 minutes. Flip the bread and cook another 2 to 3 minutes, or until golden brown. Serve with maple syrup.

YIELD: 1 serving
PER SERVING: 362 calories, 14 g protein, 20 g fat, 31 g carbohydrate, 510 mg sodium, 249 mg cholesterol

Michael and Donna's Magic Muffins

Preparation time: 10 to 15 minutes
Cooking time: 20 to 25 minutes

A homemade muffin recipe may seem misplaced in the Quick Weekday Breakfasts chapter. But consider this: these muffins can be put together in less than 15 minutes, and they finish baking in another 20 to 25 minutes. Mix the batter, put them in the oven, hop in the shower, get dressed, and breakfast is ready. Serve with fresh fruit, butter (or a fruit butter; see recipes, pages 33 and 454), and hot chocolate, coffee, or tea.

1½ cups all-purpose or whole-wheat flour
1 cup quick-cooking oats
2 teaspoons baking powder
Pinch salt
1 cup low-fat milk
1 large egg, lightly beaten
¼ cup vegetable oil
½ cup honey
2 tablespoons maple syrup (optional)
4 carrots, shredded
1½ ounces raisins

Preheat the oven to 375 degrees. Lightly grease a 12-cup muffin pan.

In a large bowl, mix the flour, oats, baking powder, and salt. In a separate bowl, whisk together the milk, egg, oil, honey, and maple syrup if using. Add the wet ingredients to the dry ingredients and gently stir together. Gently fold in the carrots and raisins. Divide the batter among the prepared muffin cups and bake for about 20 to 25 minutes, or until golden brown and puffed.

YIELD: 12 muffins
PER SERVING: 210 calories, 4 g protein, 7 g fat, 35 g carbohydrate, 129 mg sodium, 19 mg cholesterol

Cream Cheese and Scallions

Preparation time: about 5 minutes

Specialty food shops and delicatessens offer a wide variety of flavored cream cheese combinations. Making your own flavored cream cheese, however, is quite simple—as well as a lot less expensive. This is a basic recipe to which you can add any variety of flavors and textures, such as chopped fresh or dried herbs, chopped nuts, chopped dried fruits like dates, apricots, and pineapple, grated vegetables, raisins and cinnamon, or chopped smoked salmon or fish. Spread on toasted bagels, French bread, English muffins, or toast.

> **1 cup soft low-fat cream cheese**
> **1 cup finely chopped scallions**
> **1 tablespoon chopped fresh chives (optional)**
> **Freshly ground black pepper**

In a bowl, mix all the ingredients. Serve at room temperature.

YIELD: about 1 cup, or 16 servings
PER SERVING: 37 calories, 2 g protein, 3 g fat, 1 g carbohydrate, 76 mg sodium, 8 mg cholesterol

Tofu Spread

Preparation time: about 5 minutes

Here is a nondairy spread, similar to a garlicky cream cheese, that wakes up a toasted bagel, toast, or French bread. This is an ideal spread for anyone on a dairy-free diet; it has all the creaminess of sour cream or cream cheese without the lactose. You can also serve this as a dip with raw vegetables and pita bread.

1 package (19 ounces) silken or soft tofu
1 to 2 cloves garlic
2 tablespoons chopped fresh parsley
1 teaspoon chopped fresh thyme or ½ teaspoon dried
1 tablespoon chopped fresh basil or 1 teaspoon dried
1 tablespoon chopped fresh chives or 1 scallion, chopped
Salt and freshly ground black pepper

Place all the ingredients in the container of a food processor or blender and puree until smooth and creamy. Taste for seasoning, adding more garlic, herbs, salt, and pepper if needed.

YIELD: about 2 cups, or 32 servings
PER SERVING: 11 calories, 1 g protein, 0.4 g fat, 1 g carbohydrate, 11 mg sodium, 0 mg cholesterol

Strawberry Butter

Preparation time: 10 minutes
Cooking time: 3 minutes

Spread a touch of this sweet, fruity butter on pancakes, waffles, pound cake, French toast, tea sandwiches, or muffins. For fun, you can let it chill for several hours (or freeze it) and then cut it into shapes using cookie cutters or a butter mold.

¼ **pound fresh or frozen strawberries or any type of berry, stemmed**
3 **tablespoons maple syrup**
1 **stick (½ cup) butter, softened**
⅛ **teaspoon vanilla extract (optional)**
¼ **cup finely chopped nuts, such as almonds, walnuts, or pecans (optional)**

Mash the berries with a fork or potato masher. Place in a small saucepan and mix with the syrup. Bring to a boil and simmer for 3 minutes. Remove from the heat and cool.

Using a fork, combine the berry mixture with the softened butter. If using, gently mix in the vanilla and nuts. Place in a piece of plastic wrap and shape into a log or fat cigar shape. You can slice off ½-inch discs and serve right away. Alternately, freeze the butter for about an hour or until firm, then roll it out with a rolling pin to cut into shapes.

YIELD: 1 cup, or 16 serving
PER SERVING: 63 calories, 0.10 g protein, 6 g fat, 3 g carbohydrate, 59 mg sodium, 16 mg cholesterol

Banana-Peanut Butter Spread

Preparation time: 5 minutes

Two favorite flavors are mixed in this simple spread. Serve on toast or English muffins for a fast, nutritious breakfast treat. You can also use this as a breakfast dip for apple slices or biscuits. Add raisins and chopped almonds for an even richer taste and texture.

½ ripe banana, peeled
3 tablespoons peanut butter
Pinch ground cinnamon
Drizzle honey or maple syrup

Mash the banana in a bowl. Mix in the remaining ingredients.

YIELD: 1 serving

PER SERVING: 360 calories, 14 g protein, 25 g fat, 27 g carbohydrate, 228 mg sodium, 0 mg cholesterol

Chapter Three

Weekend Breakfasts

❧

Breakfast, especially a weekend breakfast, can be truly curative for the soul. The whole family sitting around in their pajamas, the funnies spread across the table, the afternoon stretching out ahead with infinite possibilities—what better way to savor each other's company and bask in that delicious sensation of laziness that's all too rare nowadays.

These recipes are for those Saturday and Sunday mornings when there is time to whip up a batch of blueberry and ricotta pancakes or French toast flavored with orange, cinnamon, and maple syrup. Try a fabulous frittata (a cross between an omelette and a soufflé) with an addicting accompaniment of maple-grilled bacon, home fries, and to top it all off, a moist sour cream coffee cake. Check the "Drinks" chapter for other ideas.

Apple, Raisin, and Cinnamon Pancakes

Cinnamon Sugar

Blueberry and Ricotta Pancakes

Raspberry-Almond Pancakes

Orange, Maple, and Cinnamon French Toast

Cheese Blintzes

Eggs in the Hole

Vegetable and Cheese Frittata

Chicken Hash

Down-Home Home Fries

Sautéed Baked-Potato Slices

Apple, Raisin, and Cinnamon Pancakes

Preparation time: 15 minutes
Sitting time: 1 to 4 hours
Cooking time: about 15 to 20 minutes

Serve these sweet cakes for breakfast, brunch, or dessert. They go particularly well with hot cider served in mugs with a cinnamon stick "straw."

PANCAKE BATTER:
   1½ cups all-purpose flour
   ¼ cup sugar
   2 teaspoons baking powder
   ¾ teaspoon salt
   ½ teaspoon ground allspice
   ½ teaspoon ground cinnamon
   About 1¼ cups low-fat milk
   2 large eggs
   3 tablespoons butter, melted
   ¼ teaspoon vanilla extract

APPLE AND RAISIN FILLING:
   2 tablespoons butter
   4 large tart apples, peeled, cored, and cut into very thin slices
   3 tablespoons sugar
   ¾ teaspoon ground cinnamon
   ½ cup raisins

   Melted butter
   Cinnamon sugar (recipe follows)
   Maple syrup

To make the batter, in a large bowl, sift the flour, sugar, baking powder, salt, allspice, and cinnamon together. In another bowl, lightly whisk together 1 cup of the milk, the eggs, the melted butter, and vanilla. Add the egg mixture to the dry ingredients and mix until just blended. Cover and chill 1 to 4 hours.

To make the apple and raisin filling, melt 2 tablespoons of the butter in large heavy skillet over moderate heat. Add the apples, sugar, and cinnamon and cook until the apples begin to soften, stirring occasionally, 3 to 5 minutes. Mix in the raisins. Let cool.

Stir the pancake batter. If needed, thin the batter to a pouring consistency with the remaining ¼ cup milk.

Heat a griddle or large heavy skillet over moderately high heat and brush lightly with melted butter. Ladle the batter onto the griddle using a ½-cup measure. Top each pancake with 2 tablespoons of the sautéed apple mixture. Cook until bubbles appear, about 3 minutes. Turn and cook until the bottom is golden brown, about 2 to 3 minutes. Transfer to a heated platter. Repeat with the remaining batter, brushing the griddle with additional melted butter if needed.

Top the pancakes with the remaining apple mixture and sprinkle with cinnamon sugar. Serve immediately with butter and maple syrup.

YIELD: four 6-inch pancakes
PER SERVING: 611 calories, 11 g protein, 21 g fat, 99 g carbohydrate, 895 mg sodium, 153 mg cholesterol

Cinnamon Sugar

Preparation time: 2 minutes

Keep cinnamon sugar in a shaker or small bowl to sprinkle on hot cereal, toast, muffins, French toast, or pancakes.

¼ **cup sugar**
½ **teaspoon ground cinnamon**

Mix the sugar and cinnamon in a bowl.

YIELD: ¼ cup, or 12 servings
PER SERVING: 16 calories, 0 g protein, 0 g fat, 4 g carbohydrate, 0.1 mg sodium, 0 mg cholesterol

Blueberry and Ricotta Pancakes

Preparation time: 20 minutes
Cooking time: about 12 minutes

Light, creamy, and exceptionally fluffy, these pancakes should be assembled and cooked immediately; if the batter sits around, the pancakes won't rise. Try frozen or canned blueberries if fresh aren't available. If using frozen berries, thaw first; if using canned, drain well.

BLUEBERRY SYRUP:

  2 cups fresh, frozen, or canned blueberries

  ½ cup sugar

  ½ cup water

  1 teaspoon lemon juice

  ⅛ teaspoon vanilla extract

PANCAKE BATTER:

  4 large eggs, separated

  1 cup ricotta cheese

  ⅓ cup sour cream, regular or low-fat

  ⅔ cup all-purpose flour

  ½ teaspoon salt

  2 teaspoons baking powder

  ¼ cup low-fat milk

  2 cups fresh, frozen, or canned blueberries

Melted butter

To make the syrup, put all the ingredients into a medium saucepan and bring to a boil. Reduce the heat and let simmer, uncovered, for about 8 minutes, or until the mixture becomes slightly syrupy and the blueberries are soft but still intact. Set aside.

To make the pancakes, in a large mixing bowl, whisk the egg yolks, ricotta cheese, and sour cream until smooth. Sift the flour, salt, and baking powder over this mixture and stir until smooth. Whisk in the milk and gently fold in the blueberries.

In a medium bowl, whip the egg whites until stiff but not dry. Gently fold the beaten whites into the batter.

Heat a griddle or large skillet over high heat, then brush it lightly with melted butter. When the griddle is hot (a drop of water or a bit of batter will sizzle), ladle out the batter to form several 3-inch pancakes. Cook for 1½ to 2 minutes, then gently flip the pancakes over. Cook another 1 to 1½ minutes on the other side, until golden brown. Serve with the warm blueberry syrup.

YIELD: 4 to 6 servings

PER SERVING: 413 calories, 14 g protein, 17 g fat, 52 g carbohydrate, 521 mg sodium, 206 mg cholesterol

Raspberry-Almond Pancakes

Preparation time: 30 minutes
Cooking time: 10 minutes

Serve these hearty pancakes with maple syrup and a bowl of fresh berries.

⅓ **cup sliced almonds**
⅔ **cup whole-wheat flour**
1 **teaspoon baking powder**
½ **teaspoon salt**
2 **tablespoons coarsely chopped almonds**
½ **cup milk**
1 **large egg yolk**
2 **tablespoons melted butter, plus extra for griddle**
2 **tablespoons maple syrup or honey**
2 **large egg whites**
Pinch cream of tartar
1 **cup fresh whole raspberries**

Grind the sliced almonds in a food processor or coffee grinder. In a bowl, sift together the flour, baking powder, and salt. Mix in the ground almonds and the 2 tablespoons chopped almonds.

In a separate bowl, whisk together the milk, egg yolk, melted butter, and maple syrup or honey. Add the sifted dry ingredients to the milk mixture and stir gently until just moistened.

In a large bowl, beat the egg whites with the cream of tartar until stiff but not dry. Gently fold one-fourth of the egg whites into the batter, then fold in the remaining whites. Very gently fold in the raspberries and let the mixture stand for 10 minutes.

Heat a griddle or large skillet over moderately high heat; brush lightly with melted butter. Ladle 2 tablespoons of batter onto the griddle for each pancake. Cook until bubbles begin to appear on the surface, about 2 minutes. Flip and cook on the other side for 1 to 2 minutes more, or until golden brown. Transfer to a heated platter and repeat with the remaining batter.

YIELD: 4 servings
PER SERVING: 331 calories, 9 g protein, 21 g fat, 31 g carbohydrate, 560 mg sodium, 88 mg cholesterol

Orange, Maple, and Cinnamon French Toast

Preparation time: 20 minutes
Cooking time: 3 minutes

There's nothing like real maple syrup to instill a love of breakfast food in your children. This recipe calls for a double dose—some goes in the batter, the rest goes on the toast. Be sure to warm the syrup so it doesn't chill the toast.

6 large eggs
2 tablespoons low-fat milk
2 tablespoons maple syrup
1 tablespoon orange juice, fresh or from concentrate
¼ teaspoon ground cinnamon
¼ teaspoon ground nutmeg
Dash vanilla extract
½ teaspoon grated orange zest
8 thick slices or 12 thin slices bread
Butter
1 cup pure maple syrup
6 tablespoons confectioners' sugar mixed with ½ teaspoon ground cinnamon

In a medium bowl, whisk the eggs with the milk, maple syrup, orange juice, cinnamon, nutmeg, vanilla, and orange zest. Soak the bread in the liquid, one piece at a time, for about 1 minute on each side.

In a medium skillet, heat ½ tablespoon of butter over moderate heat. Add the bread and cook for about 1½ minutes, or until golden brown. Flip and cook the other side for about 30 seconds, or until golden brown. Add more butter to the pan as needed.

In a small saucepan, heat 1 cup of maple syrup over low heat. Serve the French toast with the warm syrup and a dusting of confectioners' sugar and cinnamon.

YIELD: 4 to 6 servings
PER SERVING: 458 calories, 12 g protein, 10 g fat, 81 g carbohydrate, 353 mg sodium, 263 mg cholesterol

Cheese Blintzes

Preparation time: 1 hour 20 minutes (including time for batter to sit)
Cooking time: 20 minutes

Blintzes are thin crepes wrapped around a sweet farmer's cheese or cottage cheese filling. Traditionally they're fried, but baking cuts down on both time and calories without skimping on taste. Serve blintzes for a Sunday breakfast or a special dessert, accompanied by a pitcher of maple syrup and, if desired, a bowl of yogurt or sour cream.

CREPES:

> 3 large eggs
> 1 cup low-fat milk
> 2 tablespoons melted margarine, butter, or cooking oil
> Pinch salt
> ⅔ cup all-purpose flour
> Oil for skillet

FILLING:

> 2 cups cottage cheese, well drained, or farmer's cheese
> 1 large egg
> 3 tablespoons sugar
> 1 tablespoon melted margarine or butter
> 1½ teaspoon lemon juice
> ½ teaspoon vanilla extract
> ¼ teaspoon ground cinnamon
> Pinch salt

OPTIONAL TOPPINGS:

> Maple syrup
> Sour cream or plain or vanilla low-fat yogurt

To make the crepes, in a medium bowl, beat the eggs, milk, margarine, and salt. Sift the flour on top and slowly mix until the batter is smooth and thin. Cover and refrigerate for 1 hour.

To make the filling, in a medium bowl, thoroughly mix the cottage cheese with the remaining filling ingredients. Cover and refrigerate until ready to use.

Heat a 6-inch skillet or crepe pan over moderately high heat. Add a small amount of oil to coat the bottom of the pan and heat until a drop of water splatters. Pour about ¼ cup of crepe batter into the hot pan, quickly tilting the pan to spread the batter. Cook about 1 minute, or until the edges begin to brown. Using a spatula, flip the crepe and cook about 30 seconds more. Repeat with the remaining batter, using additional oil if needed. Stack the finished crepes on a plate.

Preheat the oven to 350 degrees. Lightly butter a 9-by-13-inch baking dish. Place each crepe on a work surface and spoon about 1½ tablespoons of filling onto the center. Fold the two opposite sides of the crepe inward, then fold over the two remaining sides to form a rectangle. Place the blintzes, seam side down, in the baking dish. (The recipe can be made ahead of time up to this point and refrigerated for several hours.)

Bake for 15 minutes and serve immediately, topped with maple syrup or sour cream if desired.

YIELD: about 16 blintzes

PER SERVING: 333 calories, 20 g protein, 16 g fat, 27 g carbohydrate, 576 mg sodium, 178 mg cholesterol

Eggs in the Hole

Preparation time: 5 minutes
Cooking time: about 8 minutes

There is a wonderful scene in the 1987 film Moonstruck *in which Olympia Dukakis cooks eggs according to an old Italian tradition. A small hole is cut in the center of a thick slice of good bread and then an egg is fried in the center. This dish is delicious on its own, or you can make it even more enticing by topping it with thin slices of smoked salmon or a touch of sour cream, avocado, and salsa.*

2 thick slices good bread
1 to 2 teaspoons butter
2 large eggs
Salt and freshly ground black pepper

Cut a small 2-inch circle out of the middle of each slice of bread and discard. In a medium skillet, heat half the butter over moderate heat. Add the bread slices and let cook 1 minute. Crack an egg into the center of each hole, sprinkle with salt and pepper, and let cook about 2 to 3 minutes, until just set and the bread is beginning to turn golden brown. Gently flip each toast and egg with a spatula and cook another 1 to 2 minutes, depending on how you like your eggs.

YIELD: 2 servings
PER SERVING: 228 calories, 9 g protein, 15 g fat, 15 g carbohydrate, 316 mg sodium, 236 mg cholesterol

Vegetable and Cheese Frittata

Preparation time: 20 minutes
Cooking time: 28 minutes

A frittata is an open-faced omelette that is baked in the oven. It's very dramatic because it puffs up like a soufflé, but it couldn't be easier to prepare. Use any combination of cooked vegetables you have on hand, and serve the frittata hot, warm, or at room temperature.

2 tablespoons olive oil or butter

1 small onion, thinly sliced

2½ cups bite-size pieces of cooked vegetables, such as broccoli, zucchini, carrots, or leafy greens (kale, Swiss chard)

8 large eggs

1 tablespoon chopped fresh herbs (tarragon, basil, parsley, thyme, or dill) or 1 teaspoon dried, crumbled

Salt and freshly ground black pepper

¾ cup freshly grated Parmesan, Cheddar, or Muenster cheese or a combination of cheeses

Preheat the oven to 425 degrees. On the stove, heat the oil or butter over moderate heat in a large, ovenproof skillet or shallow casserole. Add the onion and sauté for about 8 minutes, or until soft but not brown. Remove from the heat. Arrange the cooked vegetables over the onions.

In a medium bowl, lightly whisk the eggs with the herbs and salt and pepper to taste. Pour the eggs over the vegetables and sprinkle with the cheese. Bake until golden and puffy, about 20 minutes. The frittata is done when a toothpick inserted into the center comes out clean.

YIELD: 4 servings

PER SERVING: 364 calories, 23 g protein, 22 g fat, 18 g carbohydrate, 507 mg sodium, 439 mg cholesterol

Chicken Hash

Preparation time: 10 minutes
Cooking time: 30 minutes

Try making this old-fashioned hash with leftover turkey, roast beef, corned beef, or ham instead of chicken. Serve on toast topped with a poached egg.

2½ tablespoons vegetable or olive oil
1 medium onion, finely chopped
1 cup peeled and cubed cooked potatoes
2 cups cubed or thinly shredded cooked chicken or other meat
1 tablespoon chopped fresh sage, thyme, or basil or 1 teaspoon dried
Salt and freshly ground black pepper

In a medium skillet, heat the oil over moderate heat. Add the onion and sauté until soft and golden, about 5 minutes. Gently stir in the potatoes and heat about 2 minutes. Reduce the heat to low and stir in the chicken, herbs, salt, and pepper. Press down the mixture with a spatula to form a large pancake. Cook about 10 minutes, or until golden and crusty on the bottom. Gently flip the hash and brown for another 10 minutes.

YIELD: 2 to 3 servings
PER SERVING: 345 calories, 29 g protein, 18 g fat, 15 g carbohydrate, 85 mg sodium, 83 mg cholesterol

Down-Home Home Fries

Preparation time: 10 minutes
Cooking time: 15 minutes

There are dozens of variations on this recipe—sauté a chopped clove of garlic with the onion, sprinkle on some fresh or dried herbs, or add bits of cooked bacon or cubed ham to the finished potatoes.

2 tablespoons vegetable or olive oil
1 large red onion, coarsely chopped
1 clove garlic, finely chopped (optional)
4 baked or boiled potatoes, cut into cubes
Salt and freshly ground black pepper

In a large skillet or griddle, heat the vegetable oil over moderate heat. Add the onion and sauté about 5 minutes, until softened and beginning to turn golden brown.

Add the garlic and potatoes and sauté another 10 minutes, gently turning the potatoes every few minutes. The potatoes should get a crispy, golden-brown crust. Season to taste with salt and pepper.

YIELD: 4 to 6 servings
PER SERVING: 200 calories, 4 g protein, 6 g fat, 35 g carbohydrate, 15 mg sodium, 0 mg cholesterol

Sautéed Baked-Potato Slices

Preparation time: 5 minutes
Cooking time: 5 minutes

Top these with a little shredded cheese and salsa or add a dollop of sour cream, salmon caviar, and chopped chives.

2 tablespoons butter
2 teaspoons olive oil or vegetable oil
2 cups thinly sliced baked or boiled potatoes, unpeeled
Salt and freshly ground black pepper

Heat the butter and the oil in a medium skillet over moderately high heat. Add the potato slices and sauté for about 2 minutes on each side, or until golden brown. Season with salt and pepper to taste; serve hot.

YIELD: 4 servings
PER SERVING: 156 calories, 2 g protein, 8 g fat, 20 g carbohydrate, 65 mg sodium, 16 mg cholesterol

Bacon Broiled with Maple Syrup

Preparation time: 5 minutes
Cooking time: 3 to 4 minutes

Under the heat of the broiler, maple syrup forms a sweet, sticky glaze on strips of bacon. You may want to double the recipe because kids really flip for this dish.

8 strips bacon
¼ cup maple syrup

Preheat the broiler. Place the bacon on a rack in a broiler pan (so the fat can drip through) and broil for about 2 minutes (depending on the thickness of the bacon), being careful not to let the bacon burn or catch on fire. Flip the bacon, drizzle with the maple syrup, and broil an additional minute or two.

YIELD: 2 to 4 servings
PER SERVING: 122 calories, 4 g protein, 6 g fat, 13 g carbohydrate, 204 mg sodium, 11 mg cholesterol

Fried Tomatoes

Preparation time: 5 minutes
Cooking time: about 10 minutes

Everyone knows about Fried Green Tomatoes, *the popular book, movie, and dish. In this recipe, however, ripe red summer tomatoes are sliced, lightly coated with seasoned flour, and sautéed in a hot pan. This is a favorite breakfast treat, served with fried eggs, home-fried potatoes, toast, and hot pepper sauce. It also goes well with savory dishes.*

> **About ⅓ cup all-purpose flour**
> **Salt and freshly ground black pepper**
> **1 tablespoon chopped fresh thyme (optional)**
> **2 large ripe tomatoes, thickly or thinly sliced**
> **About 1 tablespoon olive oil, butter, or vegetable oil**

Mix the flour, salt, pepper, and thyme on a large plate. Dredge the tomato slices in the flour, coating both sides.

In a large skillet, heat the oil over moderately high heat. Fry the tomatoes in the hot oil about 4 minutes on each side, or until golden brown and soft. Serve hot.

YIELD: 4 servings
PER SERVING: 91 calories, 2 g protein, 4 g fat, 13 g carbohydrate, 10 mg sodium, 0 mg cholesterol

Strawberry Muffins

Preparation time: 20 minutes
Cooking time: 25 minutes

Be sure to let these muffins cool before removing them from the pan or they will fall apart.

FRUIT MIXTURE:

1½ cups chopped fresh strawberries

1 tablespoon sugar

½ teaspoon vanilla extract

1⅛ teaspoon ground ginger

⅛ teaspoon ground cinnamon

BATTER:

2 cups flour (all-purpose, whole-wheat, or a mixture)

½ cup sugar

½ teaspoon salt

1 tablespoon baking powder

½ teaspoon baking soda

1 large egg, beaten

5 tablespoons melted butter

1 cup buttermilk

½ teaspoon vanilla extract

½ teaspoon ground ginger

¼ teaspoon ground cinnamon

TOPPING:

2 tablespoons sugar

¼ teaspoon ground cinnamon

⅛ teaspoon ground ginger

Preheat the oven to 350 degrees. Grease a 12-cup muffin pan. In a small bowl, combine the ingredients for the fruit mixture; let sit for 10 minutes.

To make the batter, in a large bowl, mix the flour, sugar, salt, baking powder, and baking soda. Add the egg, butter, buttermilk, vanilla, ginger, and cinnamon. Stir until smooth. Gently stir in the fruit mixture.

In a small bowl, combine the topping ingredients. Spoon the batter into the prepared muffin cups and sprinkle with the topping. Bake for 20 to 25 minutes, or until a toothpick inserted in the center of a muffin comes out clean. Let cool before removing the muffins from the pan. They will firm up as they cool.

YIELD: 12 muffins
PER SERVING: 145 calories, 3 g protein, 7 g fat, 18 g carbohydrate, 308 mg sodium, 38 mg cholesterol

Cranberry Muffins

Preparation time: 15 minutes
Cooking time: 30 minutes

If you like a sweeter muffin to offset the tartness of the cranberries, use the larger amount of sugar. Serve these muffins warm with the cranberry butter on page 454.

4 tablespoons butter, plus extra for greasing muffin pan
¾ to 1 cup sugar
2 large eggs
½ cup whole or low-fat milk
½ cup sour cream
2 cups all-purpose flour
2 teaspoons baking powder
Pinch salt
1½ cups cranberries, coarsely chopped
2 tablespoons grated orange zest

Preheat oven to 400 degrees. Lightly grease a 12-cup muffin pan. Cream the butter and sugar together, then add the eggs and beat until smooth.

In a small bowl, combine the milk and sour cream. Sift together the flour, baking powder, and salt and add to the butter-sugar mixture alternately with the milk–sour cream mixture. Gently stir in the cranberries and orange zest. Spoon the batter into the muffin cups, filling each about two-thirds full. Bake 20 to 30 minutes, or until a toothpick inserted into the center of a muffin comes out clean.

YIELD: 12 muffins
PER SERVING: 225 calories, 4 g protein, 7 g fat, 35 g carbohydrate, 147 mg sodium, 53 mg cholesterol

Sour Cream Coffee Cake

Preparation time: 25 minutes
Cooking time: 45 to 55 minutes

The ultimate in A.M. dining—or at any time of day, for that matter.

BATTER:

¾ cup butter or margarine, at room temperature, plus extra for
  greasing cake pan
1 cup sugar
2 large eggs
1 teaspoon vanilla extract
1 cup regular or low-fat sour cream
2 cups all-purpose flour
½ teaspoon ground cinnamon
½ teaspoon ground nutmeg
1 teaspoon baking powder
1 teaspoon baking soda
½ teaspoon salt

NUT TOPPING:

4 tablespoons butter or margarine, melted
1 cup brown sugar
1½ teaspoons ground cinnamon
½ cup coarsely chopped walnuts
⅓ cup coarsely chopped pecans

Confectioners' sugar (optional)

Preheat the oven to 375 degrees. Lightly grease and flour a 10-inch tube pan.

To make the batter, in a large bowl, cream the butter and sugar until light and fluffy. Add the eggs and vanilla and beat until fully incorporated. Stir in the sour cream. In a separate bowl, sift together the flour, cinnamon, nutmeg, baking powder, baking soda, and salt. Add to the butter mixture and blend just until smooth.

In a small bowl, combine all of the ingredients for the nut topping. Spoon half of the batter into the prepared pan. Sprinkle with half of the nut topping and cover with the remaining batter. Sprinkle with the rest of the topping.

Bake the coffee cake in the middle of the oven for about 45 to 55 minutes, or until a toothpick inserted in the center comes out clean. Cool in the pan on a wire rack. Use a thin spatula or a flat-edged knife to loosen the cake from the pan and invert onto a serving plate. Sprinkle with confectioners' sugar if desired before serving.

YIELD: 10 to 12 servings

PER SERVING: 490 calories, 5 g protein, 27 g fat, 58 g carbohydrate, 420 mg sodium, 95 mg cholesterol

———————— ❧ ————————

Eating Out with the Kids:
The Pleasures and Pitfalls

It's Friday night, and you're exhausted from a long, hard week. Cooking dinner for the family is the last thing you feel like doing. What you would really like is to go to that fabulous Italian restaurant down the street, but every babysitter in town is booked. That leaves going out to dinner with the kids. Not a bad idea, since you haven't spent nearly enough time with them this week. But where can you go?

You want a place that's quiet and serves good food. The Golden Arches are definitely out, and so are any number of intimate dining spots you've been hoping to try. And so you begin the search for the perfect family restaurant—a place where both parents and adults can order food that they like, where you don't have to feel uptight even if your child misbehaves, and where the bill for dinner won't amount to a small fortune.

This isn't a fantasy. There are ways to take the whole family out to eat and make the experience successful and even relaxing. Try to be realistic about your expectations. Taking a young child to a fancy, romantic restaurant isn't fair to anyone, but that doesn't mean you have to settle for a fast-food or chain restaurant. Taking the family to such a restaurant may be convenient and cheap, but the food is generally mediocre and not particularly healthy, and the atmosphere is anything but relaxing.

The attitude toward children has changed dramatically in recent years in a wide range of American restaurants. "It used to be that one did not bring children to white tablecloth restaurants," explains John Mariani, author of *America Eats Out* (William Morrow). "But, these days, between the recession, two-career families, and people having kids at an older age and wanting to be with them more, a restaurant virtually has to cater to the family trade, or they could go out of business."

Mariani, the father of two sons, claims that restaurateurs who also are parents tend to have a more open attitude about children. He tells the story of Jasper White, owner of the now-defunct Jasper's, a popular Boston restaurant. "When Jasper first opened," Mariani says, "he was not very interested in having kids come to his restaurant. But when he had his first child, he said he would happily make baby food for a client. He brought in high chairs and booster seats. He wasn't trying to turn the place into a Denny's, but he felt that having children in his restaurant was a wonderful thing."

Of course, no one thinks having children in a restaurant is a "wonderful thing" if they are badly behaved. You can't expect a child who spends no more than five minutes at the dinner table at home to suddenly behave like a perfect little adult when she is taken out to dinner. If meals at your house consist of your child taking a few bites of food and then running into the living room to watch a video, then going out to a restaurant is bound to be a failure. For some families the first step to a successful restaurant experience is teaching their children to sit down at the dinner table at home.

Going to a restaurant provides a good opportunity to talk to your children about manners and etiquette. Let your child know what is and isn't acceptable behavior in a restaurant *before* you get there. But don't expect your children to go through sudden personality changes when you arrive at a restaurant. Chances are, they will still be fidgety, talk a bit too loudly, and bicker with their siblings. There's nothing wrong with this behavior, so long as you can keep it under control. Try to stay relaxed, and remember that restaurants that allow and even cater to children are well aware that kids behave differently than adults.

There are also a number of tricks you can use to make restaurant-going more relaxing. Many parents like to arrive with their child's favorite books, small toys, crayons, and coloring books. This equipment can be incredibly helpful, especially with younger kids, when the food takes a long time to arrive or your child finishes eating before you do. By asking for a table in the corner of the restaurant, not in the center, you'll have more of a sense of privacy. Ask for a booth or banquette table so that you'll have extra room to spread out your things. Taking your kids for a "walk" between courses can break up the waiting time and help release some of their energy.

Many restaurants now cater to kids by giving out crayons and activity pages to keep them entertained. (This practice, of course, has been popularized at fast-food restaurants that lure in young children with promises of toys and popular cartoon character figures.) At Tennessee Mountain, a barbecue restaurant in New York City, families are greeted with crayons, coloring pads, finger puppets, a puzzle, and a chef's hat with the restaurant's logo on it. "We felt that if we were going to attract families with children," manager Jesse Feldman explains, "it made sense to give them something more to do than bang soup spoons and saltshakers." Feldman says that the restaurant's business has definitely increased since they began giving out these activity kits. "The kids are so much more well behaved. Parents can really enjoy their dinner," Feldman reports.

Another way to involve your kids in the experience of eating out is to choose a restaurant that offers exciting foods. Ethnic restaurants—particularly Mexican, Chinese, Thai, Japanese, and Italian—tend to be very family oriented, and moderately priced. Not only can your family experience new foods that you wouldn't ordinarily cook at home, but they might just learn something new about a different culture.

Restaurants can also provide the backdrop for memories and family rituals. Think back to that Chinese restaurant your parents took you to on Sunday nights. Maybe you remember the hot-and-sour soup, but more likely what comes to mind is a picture of your father, more relaxed than usual, or the jokes you and your brothers used to make about the paper umbrellas that arrived in every drink. And you'll probably never forget the first fancy restaurant your parents took you to because it was there that you realized you were finally grown up.

There's something liberating about sitting down at a table in a good restaurant, being served delicious food, and not having to worry about cooking or doing the dishes. The sheer luxury of this experience can free a family to share stories and to talk in an intimate way that often doesn't happen at home.

———————— ❖ ————————

How to Eat Out and Make It a Success

• Choose a restaurant that looks casual and kid-friendly. You definitely don't want to go somewhere that is going to take hours before you get your food. John Mariani says there are certain clues you should look for: "Watch out for any place that has a tiny dining room and a lot of precious antiques. A brass plaque announcing the restaurant's name or 'Founded in 1769' is not a good sign. Lots of beautifully manicured flowers are not a good sign either."

• Colman Andrews, an editor of *Saveur* magazine and the father of two young daughters, says he often peeks inside a restaurant to see if there are other children eating. "If there aren't any kids," says Andrews, "and the room is really quiet or stuffy, I know it's a place to avoid." Andrews also says he often goes to a restaurant first with just his wife to see if it is an appropriate place to bring the kids.

• Try to eat dinner relatively early—6:00 or 6:30 P.M.—when restaurants tend to be less crowded and kids are not so tired.

• Talk to your kids before you go out to eat and explain what kind of restaurant you'll be visiting and what the rules and regulations are going to be—that is, how to dress, act, and so on.

• If you're really in doubt about whether a place will be appropriate for your child, call ahead and ask about the restaurant's policy toward children.

• Find out, too, if the restaurant provides booster seats and high chairs so that you don't have to bring your own.

- Try taking your child out for breakfast or lunch, when most kids are in a good mood and not sleepy. Many restaurants offer lunch menus that are similar to their dinner menus but at considerably lower prices.
- If your kids are picky eaters, choose a place that offers a children's menu.
- If you're taking a toddler or a younger child out to eat, bring along some of her smaller favorite toys. Washable pencils and markers and coloring books can provide a quiet activity while you wait for your food.
- Many restaurants now have open kitchens where you can watch the cooks at work. While you're waiting for your order to arrive, take the kids to see the action.
- As soon as you sit down, ask the waiter to bring drinks and some bread and butter so the kids don't get too hungry or cranky.
- Don't wait to have a serious or controversial family discussion in a restaurant. A public dining room is not the place to hash out highly emotional issues.
- If your child does get out of hand in a restaurant, take him out for a walk and discuss the ground rules. If all else fails, ask the waiter to wrap your food to go, and chalk the evening up as a learning experience.

Chapter Four

Quick Weekday Lunches

ℰ❧

Weekday lunches tend to be full of repetition. Here you'll find loads of new ideas for food to put in your child's and your own lunch bag—everything from innovative sandwich fillings and make-ahead quiches to quick pizzas and soups. These recipes will also appeal to parents who are at home with their children.

A word of warning: don't try out a new dish by packing it up in your child's lunchbox. This is not the time for experimentation; children want to eat foods that are familiar when they're at school. Be sure to try out a recipe at home and see how your child likes it before putting it in her lunch bag.

Zucchini Soup

Spinach-Lemon Soup

Cream of Potato and Leek Soup

Gazpacho

Deviled Eggs

Favorite Egg Salad

Egg Salad Variations

Tuna Sandwiches with Lemon and Dill

Healthy Tuna Pockets

Cream Cheese, Raisin, and Nut Sandwiches

Emma's Pistachio Bagel Faces

Pita Rolls with Veggie Cream Cheese Spread

Zucchini Soup

Preparation time: 5 minutes
Cooking time: about 12 to 15 minutes

If you prefer, use peeled, seeded, and chopped cucumbers instead of zucchini. Serve this soup hot or cold, with a garnish of yogurt or sour cream.

1 tablespoon vegetable or olive oil
½ cup chopped onion
2 cloves garlic, chopped
2 pounds zucchini, chopped
Salt and freshly ground black pepper
1 tablespoon chopped fresh thyme or 1 teaspoon dried
4 cups chicken broth or low-sodium chicken broth
¼ cup low-fat yogurt or sour cream

In a large pot, heat the oil over moderate heat. Add the onion and garlic and sauté for about 5 minutes; do not brown. Add the zucchini, salt, pepper, and thyme and sauté another minute. Add the broth and simmer until the zucchini is tender, about 6 to 10 minutes.

Puree the soup in a blender or food processor. Serve hot or chill for several hours and top with a garnish of yogurt or sour cream.

YIELD: 4 servings
PER SERVING: 109 calories, 7 g protein, 5 g fat, 11 g carbohydrate, 1,004 mg sodium, 1 mg cholesterol

Spinach-Lemon Soup

Preparation time: 5 minutes
Cooking time: 10 minutes

Popeye would heartily approve of this variation on the classic Greek egg-lemon soup.

4 cups chicken broth
10 ounces fresh spinach, washed
1 large egg yolk
Juice of 1 lemon
Salt and freshly ground black pepper
½ cup finely chopped fresh parsley or chives

Bring the broth to a boil in a large pot. Add the spinach and remove the pot from the heat. Puree the broth and spinach in a blender or a food processor.

Transfer the mixture back to the pot and place over moderate heat. Beat the egg yolk in a small bowl with the lemon juice, salt, and pepper. Add a few tablespoons of the hot soup to the bowl, mix well, and then slowly pour the yolk and broth back into the pot, stirring constantly. Taste for seasoning. Serve hot or cold, topping each serving with a generous pinch of parsley or chives.

YIELD: 4 servings
PER SERVING: 62 calories, 6 g protein, 3 g fat, 5 g carbohydrate, 1,047 mg sodium, 53 mg cholesterol

Cream of Potato and Leek Soup

Preparation time: 10 minutes
Cooking time: about 25 minutes

A surprisingly small amount of cream imparts a rich flavor. The soup can be served hot or cold.

1 tablespoon vegetable or olive oil
3 leeks, washed and diced
3 potatoes, peeled and diced
Salt and freshly ground black pepper to taste
4 cups low-sodium chicken broth
½ cup low-fat sour cream, heavy cream, or crème fraîche
⅓ cup chopped fresh parsley

In a large pot, heat the oil over moderate heat. Add the leeks and sauté until soft, about 3 to 4 minutes. Add the potatoes, salt, and pepper and cook another minute. Add the broth and bring to a boil. Reduce the heat and simmer about 15 minutes, until the potatoes are tender when pierced. Puree the soup in a blender or a food processor. Transfer the puree back to the pot and stir in the sour cream. Serve hot or chill the soup for several hours and garnish with the parsley.

YIELD: 4 to 6 servings
PER SERVING: 168 calories, 6 g protein, 7 g fat, 26 g carbohydrate, 135 mg sodium, 8 mg cholesterol

Gazpacho

Preparation time: 10 minutes
Chilling time: at least 1½ hours

Those who like a spicier version of this chilled vegetable soup can add a little Tabasco or Worcestershire sauce.

> **2 ripe tomatoes, diced (about 1 to 1½ pounds)**
> **5 tablespoons chopped onion (1 small onion)**
> **½ clove garlic, chopped**
> **1 large green bell pepper, diced**
> **2 stalks celery, chopped**
> **1 cup chopped cucumber**
> **2 teaspoons red wine vinegar, or to taste**
> **2 cups low-sodium tomato juice**
> **Salt and freshly ground black pepper**
> **¼ cup finely chopped parsley**

Place the tomatoes, onion, garlic, and half of each of the green pepper, celery, and cucumber in a food processor or blender. Add the vinegar and tomato juice and puree. Taste and season with salt and pepper.

Serve chilled, topped with the remaining chopped pepper, celery, and cucumber and the parsley.

YIELD: 4 to 6 servings
PER SERVING: 54 calories, 2 g protein, 1 g fat, 13 g carbohydrate, 39 mg sodium, 0 mg cholesterol

Deviled Eggs

Preparation time: 15 minutes
Cooking time: about 10 minutes

Deviled eggs, always a hit with kids, are dressed up here with a number of unusual fillings. Cook the eggs the night before and you can put this together in no time.

6 large eggs
2 tablespoons mayonnaise
½ teaspoon Worcestershire sauce
Salt and freshly ground black pepper
2 tablespoons finely chopped fresh parsley
¼ cup diced red bell pepper
¼ cup diced smoked ham
1 teaspoon curry powder
Sweet paprika

Place the eggs in a saucepan and cover with boiling water. Let simmer for about 10 to 12 minutes. Drain and place the eggs in a bowl of cold water to cool, or refrigerate overnight.

Peel the eggs and cut in half lengthwise. Remove the yolks and place in a small bowl. Using a fork or potato masher, combine the yolks with the mayonnaise, Worcestershire sauce, salt, pepper, and parsley. Divide the yolk mixture among 3 bowls, add one of the next 3 ingredients to each, and spoon the mixture back into the egg whites. Sprinkle with paprika and place on a serving platter.

YIELD: 6 to 12 servings
PER SERVING: 61 calories, 4 g protein, 5 g fat, 1 g carbohydrate, 89 mg sodium, 109 mg cholesterol

Favorite Egg Salad

Preparation time: 10 minutes
Cooking time: about 10 to 12 minutes

This classic is one of my daughter's favorite lunches, and every time we make it, we add something a little different to spice it up. Here is the basic recipe with several variations listed below.

8 large eggs
½ cup finely chopped celery
Salt and freshly ground black pepper
About ½ cup mayonnaise
1 tablespoon Dijon mustard

Bring a large saucepan of water to a boil over high heat. Reduce the temperature to moderate and carefully add the eggs. Let simmer for about 10 to 12 minutes. Drain and place the eggs in cold water. (The cold water makes it easier to peel the eggs.)

Peel the eggs and chop finely, with a potato masher or fork. Add the celery, salt, pepper, mayonnaise, and Dijon mustard. Add more mayonnaise if you like moister egg salad. Serve on toast or as a salad.

YIELD: 4 to 6 servings
PER SERVING: 287 calories, 10 g protein, 26 g fat, 2 g carbohydrate, 307 mg sodium, 353 mg cholesterol

Egg Salad Variations

- Add 1 tablespoon drained capers for a tart flavor.
- Add 1 to 2 tablespoons chopped gherkin pickles.
- Substitute chopped fresh fennel for the celery to add a crisp, licorice flavor.
- Add ¼ cup chopped green and/or black (pitted) olives.
- Add 2 tablespoons finely chopped or grated carrot.
- Add 2 tablespoons finely chopped scallions.
- Add 1½ tablespoons mango chutney and a pinch of curry powder.

- Puree a roasted red pepper in a blender or food processor and add to the mayonnaise.
- Add fresh or dried basil, thyme, sage, rosemary, or lovage.
- For adventurous eaters, top your egg salad sandwich with a few anchovy fillets.
- Make a spicy mixture by adding a few drops of your favorite hot chili sauce.

Tuna Sandwiches with Lemon and Dill

Preparation time: about 5 minutes

"You're not really going to put a recipe for tuna sandwiches in a cookbook," my eight-year-old said incredulously. "Everyone knows how to make that." Of course, she is right, but there are two little tricks that make this tuna something more than just plain tuna. Lemon juice adds a fresh flavor and thins out the mayonnaise nicely, and dill gives the sandwich a fresh garden flavor. Fresh dill is available in most supermarkets year round.

> 1 can (6 ounces) tuna packed in water, drained
> 1 stalk celery, finely chopped
> 1 to 1½ tablespoons finely chopped fresh dill
> About 3 tablespoons mayonnaise
> 1½ tablespoons lemon juice
> Freshly ground black pepper
> 8 slices lightly toasted sandwich bread

ACCOMPANIMENTS:
> Fresh lettuce leaves
> Thinly sliced ripe tomatoes
> Thinly sliced ripe avocado
> Bean sprouts
> Thinly sliced pitted black olives
> Thinly sliced pickles
> Thinly sliced green bell pepper

Place the drained tuna in a bowl and, using a fork, separate it into flakes. Add the celery and dill and mix well. Stir in the mayonnaise and lemon juice, adding more mayonnaise if the tuna isn't moist enough. Season with pepper and serve on lightly toasted bread with lettuce and whatever other accompaniments you like.

YIELD: 4 medium sandwiches
PER SERVING: 260 calories, 16 g protein, 10 g fat, 26 g carbohydrate, 473 mg sodium, 22 mg cholesterol

Healthy Tuna Pockets

Preparation time: 10 minutes

Chopped celery, bean sprouts, and lettuce, plus a touch of mayo or yogurt, make this tuna salad refreshingly light. Serve it on pita bread or toasted rye.

1 can (6 ounces) tuna packed in water, drained
¼ cup finely chopped celery
¼ cup finely chopped black or green pitted olives, drained
2 tablespoons lemon juice
2 tablespoons low-fat mayonnaise or plain low-fat yogurt
¼ cup shredded lettuce
¼ cup bean sprouts (optional)
1 large pita bread or 2 slices rye bread or other thinly sliced bread

In a small bowl, mix together all the ingredients except the lettuce, sprouts, and bread. Cut the pita bread crosswise in half and divide the mixture between the two halves, then top with the lettuce and sprouts.

YIELD: 2 servings
PER SERVING: 261 calories, 28 g protein, 6 g fat, 22 g carbohydrate, 719 mg sodium, 39 mg cholesterol

Cream Cheese, Raisin, and Nut Sandwiches

Preparation time: about 10 minutes

Here's a great variation on the standard cream cheese and jelly sandwich. These sandwiches are perfect for lunchboxes or a party or holiday buffet.

1½ **cups regular or low-fat cream cheese, at room temperature**
½ **cup finely chopped raisins**
½ **cup finely chopped walnuts or almonds**
Pinch ground cinnamon
½ **teaspoon vanilla extract**
12 thin slices black bread or raisin bread

In a medium bowl, mix the cream cheese, raisins, and nuts. Add the cinnamon and vanilla extract.

Spread 6 slices of the bread with the cream cheese mixture. Top with the remaining bread, then use a cookie cutter to cut 2 shapes out of each sandwich (or simply cut the sandwich into 2 or 4 small triangles).

YIELD: 6 servings
PER SERVING: 366 calories, 8 g protein, 27 g fat, 26 g carbohydrate, 348 mg sodium, 62 mg cholesterol

Emma's Pistachio Bagel Faces

Preparation time: 5 minutes

My children love to spread cream cheese on bagels and create "faces" using a variety of raw vegetables, nuts, and herbs. Emma, my younger daughter, created this bagel topping one afternoon. You can use any of the following to make your bagel face: fresh peas, chopped celery, red and green pepper strips, small florets of broccoli, chopped fresh herbs, nuts, honey, grated zucchini, and so on.

1 bagel, cut in half
2 to 3 tablespoons regular or low-fat cream cheese, at room temperature
1 to 2 teaspoons shelled pistachio nuts
1 tablespoon chopped fresh chives or parsley
1 tablespoon thinly sliced carrots

Toast the bagel halves until golden brown.

Place the cream cheese, nuts, chives, and carrots in small individual bowls. Invite your child to create his or her own bagel face. Emma's suggestion: use the pistachio nuts for eyes and cheeks, carrots for a smiley face, and chives or parsley for hair.

YIELD: 1 serving
PER SERVING: 346 calories, 11 g protein, 15 g fat, 41 g carbohydrate, 487 mg sodium, 39 mg cholesterol

Pita Rolls with Veggie Cream Cheese Spread

Preparation time: 10 minutes

This colorful vegetable-filled spread goes particularly well with whole-wheat pitas.

½ cup grated carrot
1 small radish, grated
1 scallion, finely chopped
½ cup low-fat cream cheese, softened
1 large pita bread, preferably whole-wheat
½ cup cucumber, sliced paper thin

In a small bowl, blend the carrot, radish, and scallion with the cream cheese. Cut the pita bread horizontally into 2 rounds and spread the filling over the inside surface of each. Arrange the cucumber slices on top, then roll each round into a cigar shape, slice in half, and serve.

YIELD: 1 to 2 servings
PER SERVING: 221 calories, 9 g protein, 10 g fat, 26 g carbohydrate, 514 mg sodium, 30 mg cholesterol

Quesadilla Pockets

Preparation time: about 5 minutes

You can serve these Mexican-style sandwiches cold or heat them in a microwave or toaster oven until the cheese melts.

1 large pita bread
½ cup refried beans
2 tablespoons mild salsa
½ cup grated Monterey Jack or Cheddar cheese
4 thin slices ripe avocado
2 tablespoons sour cream (optional)

Cut the pita bread crosswise in half, creating 2 half-moon pockets. In a small bowl, blend the beans and the salsa, then spread the mixture inside each of the pita halves. Tuck the cheese and avocado slices into the pocket, heat if desired, then spoon in the sour cream.

YIELD: 1 to 2 servings
PER SERVING: 594 calories, 28 g protein, 27 g fat, 61 g carbohydrate, 1,469 mg sodium, 60 mg cholesterol

Pita Club

Preparation time: 5 minutes

For the traditional club sandwich effect, cut the pita into quarters and stack.

  1 tablespoon mayonnaise
  ½ tablespoon catsup
  1 tablespoon pickle relish
  1 large pita bread, cut in half or quarters
  4 thin slices roast beef, turkey, ham, or a combination
  2 thin slices any cheese
  1 tomato, thinly sliced
  Lettuce leaves

In a small bowl, mix the mayonnaise, catsup, and relish. Spread half of the dressing inside each pita half, then fill each with half of the meat, cheese, tomato, and lettuce.

YIELD: 1 to 2 servings
PER SERVING: 269 calories, 15 g protein, 12 g fat, 25 g carbohydrate, 433 mg sodium, 41 mg cholesterol

Chicken Salad with Grapes

Preparation time: 10 minutes

Simple, light, and refreshing is how I would describe this salad. It can be served with toast, on a bed of lettuce, or surrounded by an assortment of thinly sliced raw vegetables. For variation, add a pinch of curry or cumin powder to the salad. It adds an exotic flavor and good color.

3½ cups cooked chicken
1 large stalk celery, thinly sliced
½ to ¾ cup mayonnaise
Juice of 1 lemon
Salt and freshly ground black pepper
Pinch ground cumin or curry powder (optional)
2 tablespoons finely chopped fresh parsley or chives (optional)
1¼ cups red or green grapes or a combination, cut in half
1 to 2 cups mixed greens

In a large bowl, toss the chicken and celery. Gently fold in about ½ cup of the mayonnaise and the lemon juice. Add the salt, pepper, cumin or curry powder if desired, and parsley. Add more mayonnaise if you like a moister salad. Gently fold in the grapes.

Place the salad on a bed of mixed greens or use to make sandwiches.

YIELD: 6 servings
PER SERVING: 338 calories, 24 g protein, 24 g fat, 5 g carbohydrate, 211 mg sodium, 86 mg cholesterol

Turkey-Pear Pockets

Preparation time: 5 minutes

For a similar blend of meat and sweet, substitute ham and apple for the turkey and pear.

1 large pita bread
1 tablespoon mayonnaise mixed with 1 tablespoon mustard, or 2
tablespoons of either one
4 thin slices turkey breast or smoked turkey breast
½ cup very thinly sliced ripe pear

Cut the pita in half crosswise and spread the mayonnaise mixture inside each pocket. Fill each pocket with half of the turkey and pear.

YIELD: 1 to 2 servings
PER SERVING: 202 calories, 12 g protein, 7 g fat, 23 g carbohydrate, 338 mg sodium, 24 mg cholesterol

Smoked Turkey Sandwiches with Apple and Chutney Butter

Preparation time: 10 minutes

This flavor combination also works with regular turkey, ham, roast beef, or even Cheddar cheese. Serve on your child's favorite bread. Substitute mayonnaise for butter if you like.

3 tablespoons butter, at room temperature
3 tablespoons mango chutney
1 teaspoon mustard (optional)
12 thin slices bread
12 thin slices smoked turkey
1 large apple, peeled, cored, and thinly sliced

In a small bowl, mix the butter, chutney, and mustard, if using. Spread this mixture on 6 slices of the bread. Place a slice of turkey on top of each piece of bread, then add a few slices of apple. Place another piece of bread on top, and cut in halves or quarters.

YIELD: 6 to 8 servings

PER SERVING: 227 calories, 14 g protein, 9 g fat, 26 g carbohydrate, 901 mg sodium, 45 mg cholesterol

Confetti Pasta Salad

Preparation time: 10 minutes
Cooking time: 8 to 12 minutes

There's enough salad here to serve a crowd or to last for several days. This is ideal to serve at a party.

1 pound elbow macaroni or small shaped dried pasta
2 carrots, diced
2 stalks celery, diced
1 small cucumber, peeled and diced
1 large red bell pepper, diced
About 1 cup mayonnaise, or ½ cup mayonnaise and ½ cup low-fat yogurt or sour cream
3 tablespoons olive or vegetable oil
1½ tablespoons lemon juice or vinegar
⅓ cup finely chopped fresh parsley (optional)
Salt and freshly ground black pepper

Bring a large pot of water to a boil, add the pasta, and cook until tender, about 8 to 12 minutes, depending on the type of pasta. Drain and rinse under cold running water. Drain again.

In a large bowl, mix the pasta with the carrots, celery, cucumber, and bell pepper. In a small bowl, blend the mayonnaise, oil, and lemon juice. Pour over the pasta, add the parsley and salt and pepper to taste, and toss. Cover and refrigerate until ready to serve.

YIELD: 12 servings
PER SERVING: 312 calories, 5 g protein, 19 g fat, 31 g carbohydrate, 118 mg sodium, 11 mg cholesterol

Chinese-Style Rice Salad

Preparation time: 15 minutes
Cooking time: 15 minutes

Whatever type of cooked rice you have on hand will taste great in this Asian salad, but brown rice gives it the best texture.

DRESSING:

2½ tablespoons peanut butter, chunky or smooth
1 teaspoon finely chopped fresh ginger
5 tablespoons vegetable or olive oil
3 tablespoons red wine vinegar
1½ tablespoons Asian sesame oil
Salt and freshly ground black pepper

SALAD:

5 cups cooked rice
2 scallions, thinly sliced
1 large carrot, chopped into small pieces
1 stalk celery, chopped into small pieces
1 cup thinly sliced water chestnuts, fresh or canned
1 cup red bell pepper, chopped into small pieces
½ cup chopped peanuts

To make the dressing, mix the peanut butter and ginger in a small bowl. Stir in the vegetable oil, vinegar, sesame oil, salt, and pepper and blend until smooth. Taste for seasoning and adjust as needed.

To make the salad, put the rice in a large mixing bowl, breaking up any clumps with the side of a spoon. Mix in the scallions, carrot, celery, water chestnuts, and bell pepper. Pour the dressing over the rice and gently mix until the entire salad is coated with the dressing. Mound the salad in the center of a serving bowl and scatter the chopped peanuts on top.

YIELD: 6 servings as a main course; 8 as a side dish
PER SERVING: 534 calories, 9 g protein, 24 g fat, 71 g carbohydrate, 111 mg sodium, 0 mg cholesterol

John's Tropical Banana, Grapefruit, and Avocado Salad

Preparation time: 10 minutes

My husband, John Rudolph, created this refreshing salad. It sounds like an unlikely combination, but it's sweet and juicy and appealing to both kids and adults.

1 grapefruit, cut in half
1 orange, cut in half
6 large leaves romaine lettuce
1 banana, peeled and sliced
1 ripe avocado, thinly sliced or cut into chunks
2 tablespoons red wine vinegar or balsamic vinegar
¼ cup light olive oil
Salt and freshly ground black pepper
4 slices toast

Using a small, sharp knife, remove the sections from the grapefruit and the orange, reserving the juices.

Place the lettuce leaves on a serving plate or in a bowl and top with the fruit and avocado.

In a small bowl, mix the vinegar, reserved citrus juices, oil, salt, and pepper. Spoon over the salad. Serve with toast.

YIELD: 4 servings
PER SERVING: 335 calories, 4 g protein, 23 g fat, 33 g carbohydrate, 142 mg sodium, 0.3 mg cholesterol

Sour Cream Vegetable Quiche

Preparation time: 15 minutes
Cooking time: 60 minutes

Bake this cheesy pie the night before and simply reheat it for 10 to 15 minutes in a warm oven before serving.

1 tablespoon olive or vegetable oil
2 small zucchini, thinly sliced
2 red bell peppers, thinly sliced
3 large eggs
1 cup low-fat sour cream
⅔ cup grated Cheddar, Muenster, or Monterey Jack cheese
1 tablespoon fresh thyme leaves or 1 teaspoon dried
Salt and freshly ground black pepper
9-inch pie shell, homemade or store-bought

Preheat the oven to 350 degrees. In a large skillet, heat the oil over moderate heat. Add the zucchini and bell pepper slices and sauté 3 to 4 minutes on each side, or until golden brown. Drain on paper towels.

In a mixing bowl, vigorously beat the eggs. Whisk in the sour cream, cheese, thyme, salt, and pepper. Line the bottom of the pastry shell with the zucchini and pepper slices. Pour the sour cream mixture on top and bake for an hour, or until the quiche has puffed up and is a light golden brown. Remove from the oven and let cool for at least 10 minutes before serving.

YIELD: 4 to 6 servings
PER SERVING: 383 calories, 12 g protein, 26 g fat, 27 g carbohydrate, 369 mg sodium, 159 mg cholesterol

Crispy Corn Fritters

Preparation time: 5 to 15 minutes
Cooking time: about 10 minutes

Serve with yogurt or a mild red cocktail sauce.

½ **cup all-purpose flour**
½ **teaspoon salt**
½ **teaspoon baking powder**
¼ **cup low-fat milk**
1 large egg, lightly beaten
2 cups fresh or frozen corn kernels
Vegetable oil

Preheat the oven to 200 degrees. In a large bowl, sift the flour, salt, and baking powder. Add the milk and whisk until smooth. Beat in the egg and gently mix in the corn.

In a large skillet, heat about ¼ inch of oil over moderately high heat. Drop 2 to 3 tablespoons of batter into the hot oil and fry about 3 minutes on each side, until golden brown. Drain on paper towels and keep warm in the oven.

YIELD: 12 fritters, or about 4 servings
PER SERVING: 78 calories, 2 g protein, 4 g fat, 9 g carbohydrate, 123 mg sodium, 18 mg cholesterol

Basic Pizza

Preparation time: 5 minutes
Cooking time: about 10 minutes

Be creative and adorn this standard tomato-sauce-and-cheese pizza with any toppings that your children like. The following three recipes give you some ideas, but you might also want to consider chopped olives, sun-dried tomatoes, grilled chicken strips, chopped ham or bacon, or sausage slices. Add the toppings after about 4 minutes of baking, just to warm them through.

2 English muffins or rounds of pita bread, split in half, or 1 small prepared pizza crust
½ **cup tomato sauce**
½ **cup grated mozzarella cheese**

Preheat the oven to 350 degrees. Place the muffins, pitas, or crust on a baking sheet. Spoon the tomato sauce equally over the bread and sprinkle the cheese on top. Bake for about 8 to 10 minutes, or until the cheese is golden brown and bubbling.

YIELD: 2 to 4 servings
PER SERVING: 116 calories, 5 g protein, 4 g fat, 16 g carbohydrate, 370 mg sodium, 11 mg cholesterol

Olive and Pepper Pizza

Preparation time: 5 minutes
Cooking time: about 15 minutes

The combination of black olives and red and green peppers makes a particularly colorful, zesty dish.

½ teaspoon olive oil
½ small green bell pepper, cut into strips
½ small red bell pepper, cut into strips
¼ cup thinly sliced pitted black olives
Salt and freshly ground black pepper
2 English muffins or rounds of pita bread, split in half, or 1 small prepared pizza crust
½ cup grated mozzarella cheese

In a small skillet, heat the oil over moderate heat. Add the peppers and sauté for about 5 minutes, or until soft but not limp. Remove from the heat and stir in the olives, salt, and pepper.

Preheat the oven to 350 degrees. Place the muffins, pitas, or crust on a baking sheet. Arrange the peppers and olives on the bread and top with the cheese. Bake about 10 minutes, or until the cheese is golden brown and bubbling.

YIELD: 2 to 4 servings
PER SERVING: 139 calories, 5 g protein, 6 g fat, 16 g carbohydrate, 259 mg sodium, 11 mg cholesterol

Spinach Pizza

Preparation time: 15 minutes
Cooking time: about 20 minutes

A white-sauce pizza is a nice break from the classic tomato-based pizzas that are so common. Even non-spinach-lovers will go for it.

½ **pound fresh spinach**
1 **teaspoon olive oil**
Pinch ground nutmeg
Salt and freshly ground black pepper
1 **teaspoon flour**
½ **cup low-fat milk**
¼ **cup plus 2 tablespoons grated mozzarella or Parmesan cheese**
2 **English muffins or rounds of pita bread, split in half, or 1 small prepared pizza crust**

Preheat the oven to 350 degrees. Wash the spinach and place it in a medium saucepan with some water still clinging to the leaves. Steam over high heat until the spinach begins to wilt, about 5 minutes. Drain and refresh under cold running water. With your hands, squeeze out all the excess water. Finely chop the spinach.

In a medium saucepan, heat the oil over moderate heat. Add the chopped spinach, nutmeg, salt, and pepper and sauté for about 30 seconds. Stir in the flour and let cook about 1 minute. Slowly add the milk, whisking to create a smooth sauce. Let the sauce simmer about 5 minutes, or until it begins to thicken. Sprinkle in ¼ cup of the cheese and stir until melted.

Place the muffins, pitas, or crust on a baking sheet. Spoon the spinach sauce over the bread and top with the remaining grated cheese. Bake about 10 minutes, or until the cheese is golden brown and bubbling.

YIELD: 2 to 4 servings
PER SERVING: 137 calories, 7 g protein, 5 g fat, 17 g carbohydrate, 232 mg sodium, 11 mg cholesterol

Three-Cheese Pizza

Preparation time: 5 minutes
Cooking time: about 10 minutes

Use the freshest, ripest tomatoes for this one. If tomatoes are not in season, substitute tomato sauce. The ham can be omitted to create a vegetarian pizza.

2 English muffins or rounds of pita bread, split in half, or 1 small prepared pizza crust
2 tablespoons grated Parmesan cheese
2 medium ripe tomatoes, thinly sliced, or ½ cup tomato sauce
2 tablespoons chopped cooked ham
3 tablespoons grated mozzarella cheese
1 tablespoon grated Cheddar or other mild cheese

Preheat the oven to 350 degrees. Place the muffins, pitas, or crust on a baking sheet. Sprinkle the Parmesan cheese on the bread and top with the tomato slices, overlapping them if necessary. Sprinkle the ham and then the mozzarella and Cheddar on top. Bake about 10 minutes, or until the cheese is golden brown and bubbling.

YIELD: 2 to 4 servings
PER SERVING: 121 calories, 6 g protein, 4 g fat, 16 g carbohydrate, 281 mg sodium, 11 mg cholesterol

Asparagus-Ham Sauce for Pasta

Preparation time: 5 minutes
Cooking time: about 13 minutes

This simple sauce is delicious tossed with pasta, but it also makes a good topping for polenta, couscous, or rice.

1½ teaspoons olive oil
½ cup cubed or chopped smoked ham
1 teaspoon fresh thyme or ½ teaspoon dried
½ cup chicken stock
1 tablespoon milk or cream
1 pound Basic Baked Asparagus (see recipe, page 213), cut into
   1-inch pieces
¼ cup chopped fresh parsley
½ pound macaroni, penne, or other small dried pasta, cooked

In a skillet, heat the oil over moderate heat. Add the ham and thyme and sauté for about 3 minutes. Add the stock and simmer for about 8 minutes. Add the milk or cream and cook another minute, or until slightly thickened. Add the chopped asparagus and parsley and heat through. Toss with the pasta.

YIELD: 4 servings
PER SERVING: 321 calories, 13 g protein, 9 g fat, 49 g carbohydrate, 386 mg sodium, 9 mg cholesterol

Pasta with Herb-Cheese Sauce

Preparation time: 5 minutes
Cooking time: 25 minutes

Topped with this speedy, simple sauce, leftover pasta tastes even better than it did the day before. Virtually any type of pasta will work.

2 tablespoons butter
1 tablespoon flour
1 cup milk
2 tablespoons chopped fresh basil or 1 tablespoon dried
⅓ cup chopped fresh parsley
½ cup grated Parmesan cheese
Salt and freshly ground black pepper
2 cups cooked pasta
1 cup leftover meatballs, sausage, ham, chicken, or seafood, cut into small pieces (optional)

Preheat the oven to 400 degrees. Melt 1 tablespoon of the butter in a medium saucepan over moderate heat. Add the flour and blend to create a roux (a thick paste). Gradually add the milk, whisking until smooth. Bring to a boil, then reduce the heat and simmer until slightly thickened. Add the basil and 2 tablespoons of the parsley. Slowly whisk in all but a few tablespoons of the grated cheese. Season to taste with salt and pepper.

Grease a 2-quart casserole with the remaining butter. Add the pasta and mix with the leftover meat if desired. Pour the sauce over the pasta and stir gently, making sure to coat all of the pasta as well as the bottom of the casserole. Top with the remaining cheese, cover, and bake for 10 minutes. Remove the lid and bake 5 more minutes to brown the cheese. Garnish with the remaining parsley.

YIELD: 2 to 4 servings
PER SERVING: 488 calories, 20 g protein, 23 g fat, 51 g carbohydrate, 555 mg sodium, 64 mg cholesterol

———————— ✦ ————————

Picky Eaters, Or What to Do When Your Kids Won't Eat Anything Except Hot Dogs and Peanut Butter

When I was pregnant with my first daughter, friends joked that she would be raised on a diet of sun-dried tomatoes and homemade pasta. Since food is so important to my husband and me, everyone assumed I would give birth to a miniature gourmet. So did I. And while other parents worried about their babies' sleeping habits and IQ's, I secretly panicked that my baby would grow up to eat only grilled cheese and hot dogs. But from the very start, my daughter loved to eat and was almost always open to new flavors and textures in food.

Then along came daughter number two. Friends warned that this child would be the picky eater. "You got lucky the first time," they told me. "You can't have two kids that eat everything." But by the age of three, as she begged for shrimp and lobster for her birthday dinner, I was sure that neither of my daughters was destined to become a picky eater.

I was wrong. Although I had an unusually easy time with both girls during their first few years, things did eventually change. Now my oldest daughter won't eat fish or seafood. If I left it up to her, she would eat hot dogs, chicken, potato chips, and cheese sticks at every meal. And my youngest daughter's current craze is for dairy foods—ice cream, yogurt, cheese, and sour cream. These days, when I serve dinner, I hear "gross" and "I hate that" a lot more frequently than I expected. The truth is that most children go through a period of picky eating. Some pass through this phase in several months, while others remain picky eaters throughout their lives.

Naturally, everyone wants to know why some children insist on eating very few foods, while others enjoy everything.

Even the experts have few clues. Gary Beauchamp, director of the Monnel Chemical Senses Center, an independent academic research institute in Philadelphia, has done extensive research studying babies and their culinary likes and dislikes. "Despite all the studies," Beauchamp admits,

"I don't have a clue as to why some babies are picky eaters and others aren't. One hypothesis is that picky eaters may have had less exposure to a variety of flavors in utero or early on."

In an admittedly unscientific survey, I interviewed dozens of parents and children from around the country about their eating habits. Most of the kids I talked with acknowledged that they beg for the same foods over and over again—usually ones that are not considered particularly healthy. From a kid's perspective, a limited repertoire of food doesn't pose a problem. "Hey, I only like ice cream and mozzarella cheese," one little girl told me. "What's the big deal?" Parents, however, have a different point of view.

Having a picky eater in the family can make mealtime very stressful. Many parents report nightly scenes that end in tears and frustration. I spoke with one mother who admitted that her son's picky eating habits make her "so crazy" that she starts thinking she "must be a bad mother to have made him this way."

For many parents food is equated with love and being a good provider. If a child rejects the food that's cooked for her night after night, does that mean she is really rejecting her mother? Eating and food can easily become a power play between parent and child, with parents generally on the losing side.

I know a woman whose three-year-old son, Lorne, loves peanut butter, ice cream, cereal, and milk. The catch is that these are the *only* foods Lorne will eat. His mother cooks a wide variety of foods for her family, but Lorne will have no part of it. And almost every night a fight ensues, as Mom and Dad try to "persuade" Lorne to taste new foods and Lorne refuses. Inevitably, Lorne winds up with an oversized bowl of Cheerios for dinner because his mother is scared that if she doesn't give it to him he'll starve to death.

The fear that children will starve or become ill if they don't eat properly is common among parents of picky eaters. But in most cases it's unfounded. According to Dr. Gail Simonds, a pediatrician in Portsmouth, New Hampshire, many of her patients are picky eaters, but they are generally "perfectly healthy kids." The problem, Simonds observes, is that "parents often get panicked that children aren't eating enough and they worry needlessly about the child's health." Her advice to parents: "Avoid making a big issue out of your child's diet. Trust that your child will eat when he is hungry and stop eating when he is full."

Nancy Samalin, director of the Manhattan-based Parent Guidance Workshops and author of *Love and Anger: The Parental Dilemma* (Penguin Books) says that "it's ridiculous to try and force a kid to taste certain foods. No one can force a baby to breast feed for longer than he wants to. Why try and force your child to eat when she isn't hungry? Kids know what they want to eat and how much they want to eat."

Some parents are their own worst enemies when it comes to dealing with their child's eating habits. I'll never forget the time we were invited to a friend's house for dinner. She served roast chicken and potatoes, creamed spinach, and salad. Her husband turned to their oldest son and said, "I know you hate spinach and chicken, but you *have* to try them." The child was indignant and was soon sent away from the table in a rage. The boy was backed up against the wall; even before he'd had a chance to taste his food, he was told he would hate it. It wasn't surprising that he fought back.

Imagine the scene a different way. Dinner is served and nothing is said to the boy; there is no emotional setup about what he likes and dislikes. The boy turns to his father and says, "But Dad, I hate chicken and spinach!" The father offers the boy extra potatoes and salad and says in a calm tone, "That's O.K. You may change your mind one day. When I was your age I didn't like spinach either. But now it's one of my favorite foods." In this scene the boy's preferences are acknowledged, but there is still a window of possibility left open. He is a lot like his dad. One day, his tastes will change and he might learn to like chicken and spinach. But for now no one is going to force it down his throat.

When my husband was growing up, the rule in his house was that *everyone* had to taste at least one bite of every food served at each meal. Once they had tasted the food, it was perfectly acceptable to reject it. Alice Waters, food advocate, cookbook author, and owner of the highly acclaimed restaurant Chez Panisse in Berkeley, California, has the same rule with her ten-year-old daughter. "Before Fanny can dismiss something, she has to know what it tastes like," explains Waters. "One bite is all I ask."

My husband and I have tried to follow this philosophy with our children as well, although the rule is not written in stone. I always ask my daughters to try a new food, but if I see that it makes them gag or get nervous, I don't force the issue. I don't believe you're going to encourage any child to open up to new foods by forcing her to taste it. I have found that our enthusiasm

("Wow, this is delicious") has often swayed my daughters to try a food that initially made them suspicious.

Parents are children's most important role models, and their attitude toward food is no exception. If Dad eats steak and potatoes for dinner every night, his kids quickly get the message that a limited diet is perfectly acceptable. You can't eat the same foods every day, or live on a diet of junk food, and expect your children to follow healthy eating patterns. It's like lighting up a cigarette and telling your kids they'd better not smoke.

A common misconception among parents is that their children will only eat "kid food." Alice Waters claims that this idea is "an easy cop-out sold to the American public. If you watch television commercials and eat in fast-food restaurants, you might think that the only food worth serving to kids is hamburgers, pizza, pasta, and hot dogs. But it's just not true."

If you want your children to be well-rounded eaters, you have to offer them a wide range of foods. I'm not suggesting that you cook squid and risotto for your family every Tuesday night, but if you don't expose your children to new foods, who will? They certainly aren't going to learn about healthy eating in the school cafeteria. What strikes me most when my daughter's friends eat dinner at our house is not that they are picky about the foods they eat, but that they have been exposed to only a limited number of foods. I've met many seven-year-olds from well-educated, caring families who have never seen—not to mention tasted—an avocado, an asparagus, or an artichoke.

You won't change your child's eating patterns overnight, but slow and subtle changes will happen with time. If your child only wants to eat hot dogs, cucumbers, and Cheddar cheese, try to include at least one of those foods at every meal. But don't stop introducing new foods. When a child sees you, a sibling, or a peer eating a wide range of new and different foods, you are sending important messages: There are lots of foods in the world. We enjoy all kinds of food; you might, too.

One of the most common complaints I hear from parents is that their kids won't eat fruit or vegetables. Alice Waters suggests that if you want to get a child to try fruits and vegetables, you have to "serve them in season when they are deliciously ripe." She suggests taking children to an orchard or pick-your-own farm. "No one can resist putting a few raspberries straight from the vine into their mouth," says Waters. She also encourages parents to let kids become involved in the process of preparing food. "Take your children out to a garden, a farmer's market, or a good produce shop and let them pick fresh peas. Have the kids help you shell them and, by all means, let them snack while they are shelling."

Snack time can also be a problem. For most kids snacks mean sugary treats, greasy chips, or soda. One mother I interviewed complained that her daughter comes home from school every day and eats chocolate chip cookies. "I have celery and carrots and cottage cheese in the house," she tells me, "but she never goes for those foods." Well, I asked my friend, would you?

Nancy Samalin claims that we expect our children to have more self-discipline than we do. "If I came home from work at three in the afternoon and there was a Sara Lee chocolate cake sitting on the counter, I would eat it," she admits. Samalin points out that parents do have a certain amount of control over what their kids eat. "When you go shopping," Samalin says, "avoid buying junk food. If you don't want your kids to eat certain foods, then don't have them in the house." (For more on shopping tips, see pages 11–15.)

Having healthy foods available for kids can make a difference. Place the foods you want your children to eat on a refrigerator or pantry shelf at kid's-eye level. (This is exactly what supermarkets do. They put the most sugary cereals and most chocolate-filled cookies right where kids will see them, so when you push your cart up and down the aisles, these foods catch your child's eye and he will ask for it or grab it.) Simple tricks like peeling carrots and cutting celery into child-size serving pieces or carving cucumber slices into a boat shape and filling them with a spoonful of fat-free cream cheese or cottage cheese makes it easy for kids to choose healthy snacks. Buy fat-free pretzels instead of oily potato chips. Have low-fat yogurt on hand to use as a dip for crackers or vegetables.

The advice most experts give parents is to stay calm and patient with your picky eater. I was visiting a friend recently when her ten-year-old daughter stormed into the kitchen and demanded, "What gross foods are we having for dinner tonight?" My friend, quite accustomed to her daughter's behavior, smiled and calmly said, "Chicken and rice." Her daughter scowled. "But don't worry," her mother continued. "It won't kill you. I haven't poisoned any of my children yet!" The girl lost her composure and began laughing. A tense moment was transformed into a joke. Dinner would go on. Everyone would get through it.

———————— ❧ ————————

Tips for Dealing with Your Picky Eater

- Whenever possible, go grocery shopping without the kids so you can control what food comes into the house. If you buy junk, they'll eat junk.
- Buy fruits and vegetables that are in season and deliciously ripe.
- Take a child to an orchard or a pick-your-own farm. When fruit and vegetables are ultra fresh, they become very enticing, even to the pickiest eaters. Encourage your children to pick the produce straight from the vine and taste fruit and vegetables at their peak.
- Grow a garden with your child or take her to a farmer's market or good produce shop and pick berries or green beans together.
- Another successful way to introduce vegetables and fruits to wary children is to combine them with other favorite foods: grate carrots into cream cheese and spread it on a toasted bagel, add fresh peas or zucchini to macaroni or pasta, or make a breakfast shake by blending bananas, apples, and pears with low-fat vanilla yogurt.
- Introduce fresh fruits on cereals, waffles, and pancakes and in muffins, pies, and snacks.
- Many pediatricians advise that if a child's diet is so restricted that he is missing a major food group, you might want to consider giving him a multivitamin. Check with your pediatrician or a nutritionist.
- Kids' tastes are constantly changing. Give your children a chance to go through periods when they don't like certain foods and love other ones. Colman Andrews, an editor at *Saveur* magazine, says he tries never to push his two young daughters into trying foods against their will. "I would rather that they see me enjoy eating something, and then, maybe, one day they'll say, 'Everyone else seems to like it; maybe I'll try it too.'"
- Remember that kids learn by watching you, not listening to you. Set a good example by eating a wide variety of healthy foods. If your children see you eating hamburgers and French fries every night, they get the message that being a picky eater is acceptable.

Chapter Five

Weekend Lunches

During the weekend, when most parents actually have time to be together with their children, lunch takes on a different focus. You can indulge in a leisurely meal: cook up a pot of soup, toss a mixed green or tomato salad, and heat up some apple cider with a cinnamon stick. The recipes found in this chapter take a bit longer to prepare but are still quite simple. Take the time to savor steamed shrimp dumplings, barbecued vegetable shish kebabs, a Greek spinach pie, or a hearty beef potpie.

French-Style Vegetable Soup

Granny's Turkey-Vegetable-Rice Soup

Cream of Asparagus Soup

Asparagus Salad with Feta

All-American Potato Salad

Baked Goat Cheese with Tomatoes

Baked Goat Cheese with Mushrooms

Gingered Fish Pâté

Steamed Shrimp Dumplings

Roasted Eggplant Spread

Corn, Tomato, and Olive Bruschetta

Ham and Cream Cheese Swirls

Light Macaroni and Cheese

Cheese Soufflé

French-Style Vegetable Soup

Preparation time: about 20 minutes
Cooking time: about 1 hour

If you don't believe that a good home-cooked meal can be made in a short time, this recipe might turn you from a skeptic into a believer. This homemade French-style vegetable soup (chock full of greens, potatoes, celery, and broccoli) can be made, from start to finish, in a little over an hour. If you like, a few tablespoons of pesto can be stirred in just before serving, which creates a rich, basil-infused broth that gives the soup added dimension.

View this soup as a master recipe, and use virtually any combination of vegetables you like. It's a great way to use up leftover bits and pieces. You can make it even heartier by adding pieces of smoked ham or turkey. Serve with very crusty bread (great for dunking into the soup), a big tossed salad, and apple cider.

1 tablespoon olive oil

3 leeks or onions, chopped

2 cloves garlic, finely chopped

6 carrots, chopped

4 stalks celery, chopped

2 large potatoes, peeled and cubed, or 4 new potatoes, unpeeled and cubed

2 zucchini, cubed

½ head broccoli, cut into florets

3 scallions

½ cup chopped fresh parsley

4 ripe tomatoes, cored and cubed, or 3 cups canned whole tomatoes, chopped

Salt and freshly ground black pepper

1 bay leaf

4 cups homemade or low-sodium canned chicken broth or water

1½ cups water

¼ cup dry white wine (optional)

1 cup fresh or canned corn kernels (optional)

1 can (19 ounces) white beans, drained (optional)

About ½ cup pesto (see recipe, page 438) (optional)
1 cup grated Parmesan cheese

In a large pot, heat the oil over moderate heat. Add the leeks and sauté about 4 minutes, until tender but not brown. Add the garlic, carrots, celery, and potatoes and sauté another 3 minutes. Add the zucchini, broccoli, scallions, and half of the parsley and stir well. Add the tomatoes, salt, pepper, bay leaf, broth, water, and wine and raise the heat to high. Bring to a boil, reduce the heat to moderately low, cover partially, and let simmer about 30 to 45 minutes, or until the potatoes and vegetables are tender.

Remove the bay leaf from the soup, and taste for seasoning. If the soup tastes weak, simmer vigorously for another 5 to 10 minutes. Add the corn and beans if using, and simmer another 2 minutes. Add 3 to 5 tablespoons of the pesto to the hot soup if desired (it only needs a gentle stirring; it will blend into the soup easily) and taste for seasoning. Sprinkle the soup with the remaining parsley just before serving. Serve the remaining pesto and the grated cheese on the side.

YIELD: 8 servings
PER SERVING: 202 calories, 10 g protein, 7 g fat, 30 g carbohydrate, 312 mg sodium, 8 mg cholesterol

Granny's Turkey-Vegetable-Rice Soup

Preparation time: about 20 minutes
Cooking time: about 25 minutes

This is the perfect way to make use of Thanksgiving leftovers. The turkey carcass is used to make a rich broth, and the soup is then filled with small chunks of carrots, celery, onions, and rice. You can add any other vegetables you have on hand (zucchini, brussels sprouts, peppers, etc.).

1 cup white rice
10 cups turkey broth (see recipe, page 435) or low-sodium canned
** chicken broth**
5 carrots, cut into small pieces
5 stalks celery, cut into small pieces
3 onions, cut into quarters
Salt and freshly ground black pepper
1 to 2 cups cooked turkey, cut into cubes or small strips
1 cup finely chopped fresh parsley (optional)

Place the rice in a medium saucepan and mix with 2 cups cold water and a pinch of salt. Bring to a boil over high heat, reduce the heat to low, cover, and simmer until the rice is cooked, about 10 minutes. Remove the rice from the heat and let it "dry out" to remove any excess moisture. (You don't want to add wet rice to the soup or it will turn mushy.)

In a large saucepan, heat the turkey broth. Add the carrots, celery, and onions and let simmer, partially covered, over moderately high heat for about 20 minutes. Season to taste with salt and pepper. Carefully stir in the turkey and about three-quarters of the rice, breaking up any clumps so each grain is separate, and heat for 5 minutes. The rice will soak up some of the soup, so don't add too much. Add the parsley and serve piping hot.

YIELD: 8 servings
PER SERVING: 213 calories, 15 g protein, 5 g fat, 33 g carbohydrate, 211 mg sodium, 20
  mg cholesterol

Cream of Asparagus Soup

Preparation time: 10 minutes
Cooking time: about 1 hour

This ideal spring soup can be served hot or cold.

1 tablespoon butter
1½ teaspoons vegetable or olive oil
1 large onion, thinly sliced
3½ cups chicken broth
1½ pounds asparagus
Salt and freshly ground black pepper
½ cup milk or heavy cream (optional)

In a soup pot, heat the butter and oil over moderately low heat. Add the onion and sauté about 15 minutes without browning. Add the broth and bring to a boil. Trim off the tips of the asparagus and reserve. Discard the tough bottoms of the stalks. Cut the remaining asparagus into 1-inch pieces and add to the broth. Cover, reduce the heat, and simmer for about 30 minutes, or until the asparagus are tender.

Puree the soup in a blender or food processor until smooth and creamy. Strain the mixture back into the pot and add the reserved asparagus tips, salt and pepper to taste, and the milk or cream if desired. Simmer until the tips are just tender, about 8 minutes.

YIELD: 4 servings
PER SERVING: 99 calories, 6 g protein, 6 g fat, 8 g carbohydrate, 896 mg sodium, 8 mg cholesterol

Asparagus Salad with Feta

Preparation time: 10 minutes
Marinating time: 30 to 60 minutes
Cooking time: about 10 to 15 minutes

Serve this light, refreshing salad with a warm loaf of crusty French or Italian bread.

1 pound asparagus, tough ends trimmed
3 tablespoons red wine vinegar
6 tablespoons olive oil
Salt and freshly ground black pepper
¼ cup capers or finely chopped sour pickles
2 tablespoons chopped scallions
½ cup crumbled feta cheese

Bake the asparagus as described on page 213 (Basic Baked Asparagus) or steam until tender but not limp. Place on a medium serving plate and let cool.

In a small bowl, whisk together the vinegar and oil. Add salt and pepper to taste, the capers or pickles, and the scallions. Pour the dressing over the cooled asparagus and let marinate for 30 minutes to an hour. Top with the feta cheese just before serving.

YIELD: 4 servings
PER SERVING: 261 calories, 4 g protein, 24 g fat, 9 g carbohydrate, 301 mg sodium, 15 mg
   cholesterol

All-American Potato Salad

Preparation time: 10 minutes
Cooking time: 10 to 20 minutes
Cooling time: 1 hour or more

A standard item at most barbecues and summer cookouts, this potato salad is moist and creamy. There's enough here to feed a crowd.

20 medium new potatoes or 10 large baking potatoes, peeled
6 stalks celery, finely chopped
3 scallions, finely chopped
¼ cup finely chopped fresh parsley (optional)
1 tablespoon Dijon mustard
About 1 cup mayonnaise
¼ cup low-fat milk
Salt and freshly ground black pepper

Place the potatoes in a large pot, cover with boiling water, and let cook for about 10 to 20 minutes, depending on their size, or until tender throughout. Drain the potatoes and let cool.

Place the potatoes in a large wooden bowl and coarsely chop. Stir in the celery, scallions, and parsley. Gently stir in the mustard, mayonnaise, and milk. Season with salt and pepper to taste. Cover and refrigerate for at least 1 hour before serving.

YIELD: 12 to 14 servings
PER SERVING: 255 calories, 4 g protein, 14 g fat, 30 g carbohydrate, 155 mg sodium, 10 mg cholesterol

Baked Goat Cheese with Tomatoes

Preparation time: 10 minutes
Cooking time: 20 minutes

Even picky eaters love this melted cheese dish. Don't tell them it's goat cheese, because it tastes like a rich cream cheese. Serve with a good crusty bread.

1 small log plain goat cheese (*chèvre*), about 4 ounces
1 ripe tomato, cored and chopped
2 scallions, chopped
1 tablespoon olive oil
½ cup chopped walnuts
Salt and freshly ground black pepper

Preheat the oven to 350 degrees. Place the cheese in a medium casserole and surround with the tomato and scallions. Drizzle half the oil over the tomato and scallions. Top the cheese with the walnuts and drizzle the remaining oil on top. Season with salt and pepper and bake for about 20 minutes, or until the cheese is beginning to ooze and melt around the sides.

YIELD: 4 servings
PER SERVING: 235 calories, 9 g protein, 21 g fat, 5 g carbohydrate, 151 mg sodium, 22 mg cholesterol

Baked Goat Cheese with Mushrooms

Preparation time: 10 minutes
Cooking time: 15 to 20 minutes

This is an extraordinarily simple dish that offers a range of complex flavors. Wild mushrooms are now available in many supermarkets and gourmet food shops; by all means seek them out because their earthy flavor adds great dimension to this dish. Serve with thinly sliced toasted French or Italian-style bread.

- **1 tablespoon olive oil**
- **3 large porcini, shiitake, or other wild mushrooms or ½ cup button mushrooms, thinly sliced**
- **2 cloves garlic, chopped**
- **Salt and freshly ground black pepper**
- **⅓ cup finely minced fresh parsley**
- **1 small log plain goat cheese (*chèvre*), about 4 ounces**
- **1 tablespoon fresh rosemary or 1 teaspoon dried**

Preheat the oven to 350 degrees. In a small casserole or shallow ovenproof skillet, heat half of the olive oil over moderate heat. Add the mushrooms and garlic and sauté about 5 minutes, or until just soft. Season with salt and pepper and stir in the parsley. Remove from the heat.

Place the goat cheese in the center of the casserole, pushing the mushrooms to the sides. Sprinkle with the rosemary and the remaining olive oil and roast for 15 to 20 minutes, or until the cheese is soft and oozing.

YIELD: 4 servings
PER SERVING: 137 calories, 6 g protein, 12 g fat, 2 g carbohydrate, 149 mg sodium, 22 mg cholesterol

Gingered Fish Pâté

Preparation time: 10 minutes
Cooking time: 8 to 12 minutes

Don't be put off by the thought of making pâté; this is a quick and simple recipe. Serve on buttered toast points or crackers along with a bowl of soup or salad. Or serve with pickles, lettuce, and assorted crackers and toast.

1 tablespoon olive oil
½ pound bluefish (or any other full-flavored fish, such as salmon, snapper, or mackerel), bones and skin removed
Freshly ground black pepper
3 ounces soft cream cheese
2 tablespoons fresh lemon juice
2 tablespoons chopped fresh ginger
Dash hot pepper sauce
4 scallions, chopped
1 lemon, cut into paper-thin slices

Preheat the broiler. Grease an ovenproof skillet with the oil, add the fish, sprinkle with pepper, and broil for 8 to 12 minutes, or until cooked. Let cool. Place the cooked fish, cream cheese, lemon juice, ginger, and hot pepper sauce in a food processor and blend until smooth. (This can also be done in a blender in 2 batches.) Add the chopped scallions and process for just a second or two. Taste for seasoning.

Place the pâté in ramekins, a serving bowl, or a mold and garnish with lemon slices. The pâté will keep, covered and refrigerated, for up to 4 days.

YIELD: 4 to 8 servings
PER SERVING: 126 calories, 9 g protein, 9 g fat, 4 g carbohydrate, 68 mg sodium, 38 mg cholesterol

Steamed Shrimp Dumplings

Preparation time: 45 minutes
Cooking time: 10 to 15 minutes

A few tablespoons of ground pork add a rich flavor to the filling, but the dumplings are just as good made exclusively with shrimp. Serve as an appetizer, as a snack, or because kids love them so much, as a main meal. Wonton skins are available in many supermarkets or in Asian food markets.

DIPPING SAUCE:

1 cup light soy sauce
⅓ cup finely chopped scallions
1½ tablespoons finely chopped fresh ginger
1 teaspoon dark sesame oil

DUMPLINGS:

2 tablespoons ground pork (optional)
¼ pound medium shrimp, shelled, deveined, and finely chopped
1 tablespoon light soy sauce
1½ teaspoons dry sherry
1½ tablespoons finely chopped scallions
1 teaspoon finely chopped fresh ginger
1 teaspoon dark sesame oil
30 wonton skins, thawed if frozen
Iceberg lettuce leaves

To make the dipping sauce, mix all the ingredients for the sauce in a small bowl. Cover and refrigerate until ready to serve.

To make the dumplings, place the pork, shrimp, soy sauce, sherry, scallions, ginger, and sesame oil in a small bowl and mix together well. Lay each wonton skin on a clean, dry work surface and place a heaping teaspoon of the shrimp mixture in the center. Fold the wonton skin over the filling to form a half moon. Use your fingers to press the dumpling tightly closed. (If necessary, seal the dumpling by moistening the edges with a touch of water.)

Line a plate or a Chinese steamer tray with lettuce leaves. Arrange the dumplings on top. In a large pot or wok, bring 2 inches of water to a boil and lower the plate or tray of dumplings into the pot. (If using a plate, place a wire steamer in the pot to elevate the plate of dumplings above the water.) Cover and steam for 5 to 7 minutes. Serve immediately with the dipping sauce.

YIELD: about 25 dumplings

PER SERVING: 33 calories, 2 g protein, 0.49 g fat, 5 g carbohydrate, 416 mg sodium, 6 mg cholesterol

Roasted Eggplant Spread

Preparation time: 10 minutes
Cooking time: 45 minutes to 1 hour

This is my version of the popular Middle Eastern dip baba ganoush. *Eggplant is roasted, which adds a subtle smoky flavor, and then pureed with garlic, lemon, tahini, and olive oil. Serve with warm pita bread or raw vegetables, or as a sandwich spread.*

1 large eggplant
1 to 2 cloves garlic
Juice of 1 large lemon
3 tablespoons olive oil
2 tablespoons tahini (ground sesame paste)
Salt and freshly ground black pepper
Dash hot pepper sauce (optional)

Preheat the oven to 400 degrees. Trim the stem end off the eggplant and wrap tightly in aluminum foil. Roast for 45 minutes to an hour, or until very tender. Let cool slightly and, using your fingers, peel the skin off.

Place the eggplant, garlic, lemon juice, and olive oil in a food processor and puree until smooth. Add the tahini, salt and pepper to taste, and a dash of pepper sauce if desired. Puree until smooth.

YIELD: 4 to 6 servings
PER SERVING: 140 calories, 2 g protein, 11 g fat, 9 g carbohydrate, 12 mg sodium, 0 mg
   cholesterol

Corn, Tomato, and Olive Bruschetta

Preparation time: about 30 minutes
Cooking time: about 5 minutes

This is the perfect dish for August, when farm stands are brimming with bushels of fresh corn and ripe, juicy tomatoes. Thin slices of French or Italian bread are grilled with a touch of olive oil and then topped with a simple, fresh-tasting corn, tomato, and olive mixture. Serve it as an hors d'oeuvre, as a lunch dish (call it an open-faced sandwich), or as an accompaniment to roast chicken.

3 tablespoons olive oil
12 thin slices French or Italian bread
1 clove garlic, peeled and left whole
4 ears fresh corn or 2 cups frozen or canned corn
2 ripe tomatoes, cored and finely chopped
½ cup pitted black olives
1 tablespoon chopped scallions or chives
Salt and freshly ground black pepper

Preheat the broiler. Place 2 tablespoons of the oil in a small bowl and use a pastry brush or the back of a spoon to lightly coat one side of the bread slices. Toast for about 2 minutes, or until golden brown. Turn the bread slices over, brush again with oil, and toast until golden brown, about 1 to 2 minutes. Remove the toast and rub one side (the one that looks the most appealing) of each slice with the garlic so that it gets just the essence. (This recipe can be prepared to this point up to 2 hours ahead of time.)

With a sharp knife, cut the kernels off the ears of corn. In a medium bowl, mix the corn with the tomatoes, olives, scallions, and salt and pepper to taste. Stir in the remaining tablespoon of olive oil. Taste for seasoning.

Place the toast on a large platter and carefully spoon the topping onto each piece. Place any remaining topping in the center of the plate.

YIELD: 4 to 6 servings
PER SERVING: 204 calories, 5 g protein, 10 g fat, 27 g carbohydrate, 283 mg sodium, 0 mg cholesterol

Ham and Cream Cheese Swirls

Preparation time: 25 minutes
Chilling time: 1 to 4 hours

If you want to serve something a little out of the ordinary, these nutty swirls will appeal to both children and adults. The pinwheel-shaped sandwiches must be chilled for at least an hour before serving, so plan accordingly.

9 ounces low-fat cream cheese, softened
2 tablespoons finely chopped fresh chives
1 tablespoon fresh lemon juice
⅓ cup very finely chopped walnuts or almonds
Salt and freshly ground black pepper
1 loaf unsliced white or whole-wheat bread
About ½ pound very thinly sliced ham

In a small bowl, mash the cream cheese until it's soft and spreadable. Stir in the chives, lemon juice, nuts, salt, and pepper.

Cut the crust from the top, bottom, and sides of the bread loaf. Slice the loaf lengthwise into 8 rectangular pieces about ½ inch thick. Using a rolling pin, roll out each slice of bread until it's about ¼ inch thick.

Spread about 2 to 3 tablespoons of the cream cheese mixture on each slice of bread. Press a slice of ham on the mixture. Roll the bread up into a fat cigar shape, beginning at a short end, and seal the edge by pressing it into the roll. Wrap each roll tightly in a piece of plastic wrap and refrigerate for 1 to 4 hours.

Remove the rolls from the plastic wrap and slice them crosswise into miniature pinwheel-shaped sandwiches about 1½ inches thick.

YIELD: 10 to 12 servings
PER SERVING: 222 calories, 10 g protein, 10 g fat, 23 g carbohydrate, 603 mg sodium, 23 mg cholesterol

Light Macaroni and Cheese

Preparation time: 20 minutes
Cooking time: 30 minutes

Regular macaroni and cheese is full of fat and calories. But don't even think about banishing such a favorite from the family table—try this reduced-fat version instead. The kids won't even notice the difference.

2 tablespoons olive or vegetable oil
½ pound dried macaroni
1 tablespoon flour
1 cup low-sodium chicken broth
Salt and freshly ground black pepper
1 teaspoon dry mustard (optional)
1 cup grated reduced-fat Cheddar cheese
¼ cup Parmesan cheese
2 tablespoons bread crumbs

Preheat the oven to 350 degrees. Lightly grease a 2-quart casserole or a 9-by-13-inch baking pan with 1 tablespoon of the oil.

Cook the macaroni in a large pot of boiling water until just tender. Drain thoroughly and place in the casserole.

In a small saucepan, heat the remaining tablespoon of oil over moderate heat. Add the flour and cook for 1 minute. Slowly add the broth, whisking continuously. Reduce the heat and let cook about 3 to 5 minutes, or until thickened. Whisk in the salt, pepper, and mustard if desired. Remove from the heat and whisk in the grated Cheddar cheese.

Stir the cheese sauce into the macaroni, coating thoroughly. Mix the Parmesan cheese with the bread crumbs and sprinkle over the macaroni. Bake, covered, for about 20 minutes. Remove the cover and bake an additional 10 minutes, or until the topping is golden brown and the casserole is bubbling.

YIELD: 4 to 6 servings
PER SERVING: 326 calories, 15 g protein, 12 g fat, 38 g carbohydrate, 384 mg sodium, 19 mg cholesterol

Cheese Soufflé

Preparation time: 25 minutes
Cooking time: 25 to 30 minutes

Forget all the warnings you've heard about making soufflés (you have to time them just right; you can't breathe or the thing will collapse; you must have the perfect soufflé dish). This one couldn't be simpler, and it can be made in any type of skillet or shallow casserole.

3 tablespoons margarine or butter
1 cup plus 2 tablespoons grated reduced-fat Cheddar, Muenster, or mozzarella cheese
2½ tablespoons flour
1½ cups low-fat milk
Salt and freshly ground black pepper
6 large egg whites

Preheat the oven to 400 degrees. Grease a 12-inch ovenproof skillet or a shallow casserole with ½ tablespoon of the margarine or butter. Sprinkle 1 tablespoon of the cheese on top. In a medium saucepan, melt the remaining 2½ tablespoons of margarine or butter over moderate heat. Add the flour, stir, and let cook for about 1 minute, until the mixture turns golden brown. Slowly add the milk and bring the sauce to a boil, whisking to keep it smooth. Season with salt and pepper, reduce the heat, and let cook about 5 minutes, until thickened. Remove from the heat and let cool.

In a medium bowl, beat the egg whites with an electric mixer or egg beater until soft peaks form. (Do not overbeat or the soufflé will be dry.) Using a rubber spatula, gently fold a quarter of the whipped egg whites into the cooled sauce. Fold in all but 1 tablespoon of the cheese, then add the remaining egg whites. Spoon the mixture into the skillet, sprinkle the remaining tablespoon of cheese on top, and place on the middle shelf of the oven. Immediately reduce the heat to 350 degrees and bake for about 25 minutes, or until the soufflé is puffed up and golden brown. If it looks wobbly, bake an additional 5 minutes.

YIELD: 4 to 6 servings
PER SERVING: 207 calories, 14 g protein, 12 g fat, 8 g carbohydrate, 363 mg sodium, 21 mg cholesterol

SOME THOUGHTS ABOUT . . .
Cheese and Health

If children were left to choose their own lunch or supper every night, imagine what the menus would consist of: pizza, cheeseburgers, macaroni and cheese, and tacos topped with—what else?—cheese. Whether chopped, grated, cubed, or melted, cheese is one of the few nutrient-packed foods that most American kids will devour in a flash.

Not only is cheese loaded with vitamin A, protein, and riboflavin, but it is also just about the best source of calcium around, especially for children who don't like milk. And cheese can transform even the pickiest eater into a more adventurous culinary spirit. Don't expect a child to chow down on ripe, smelly Camembert, but see how eagerly she'll sample a new vegetable if it's topped with a Cheddar cheese sauce or grated mozzarella.

Alas, there is a caveat: cheese is extremely high in fat. Make that saturated fat. One ounce of Cheddar, for instance, contains 9 grams of the cholesterol-boosting substance, which means that a colossal 74 percent of its 114 calories are from fat. Indeed, just two slices of American cheese contain almost as much fat as a McDonald's Quarter Pounder. With numbers like these, it's easy to see how kids can take in as much fat from this one simple ingredient as they're supposed to have in an entire day.

So what's a parent to do? Phil Kibak, a health and science editor for the American Heart Association, has one word of advice: moderation. "When serving it as a snack, for instance, try grating it or slicing it thinly with a cheese slicer rather than cutting it into sizable chunks." And always offer cheese along with some other food like fruit, bread, or crackers so that children begin to view it as a condiment rather than as the main attraction.

Also, Kibak suggests that parents consider switching to the reduced-fat or light cheeses currently available in most supermarkets. These lighter varieties may taste a bit "thinner" than regular cheese, but the flavor difference is negligible when they're used in cooking. Be aware, though, that they're still not exactly low in fat. An ounce of Cabot's Light (a popular low-fat Cheddar), for example, contains about 5 grams of fat, compared to the 9 in regular Cheddar, but that means that 64 percent of its calories still come from fat.

SOME THOUGHTS ABOUT . . .

Skimming the Fat: A User's Guide to Cheese

The numbers given below provide a general idea of the grams of fat per ounce. Most of these cheeses are also available in entirely fat-free versions.

- *American cheese:* A processed cheese that has a semisoft texture and an extremely mild flavor (9 grams fat; reduced-fat versions, about 2 grams).
- *Cheddar:* Firm in texture, Cheddar comes in orange, white, and yellow varieties and ranges from mild to extra sharp in flavor (9 grams fat; reduced-fat Cheddar, about 5 grams).
- *Cottage cheese:* This curded white cheese ranks particularly low on the scale for fat (½ cup creamed, 5 grams; ½ cup dry curd, 5 grams). There are also low-fat and no-fat varieties available.
- *Cream cheese:* A soft, smooth cheese that's a favorite spread for bagels and bread (10 grams fat; light cream cheese, about 5 grams).
- *Feta:* Known for its salty flavor, this Greek cheese is made from sheep's or cow's milk (6 grams fat).
- *Mozzarella:* The classic pizza cheese. It's especially good grated and melted (6 grams fat; skim-milk mozzarella, about 4 grams).
- *Muenster:* A semisoft mild cheese, usually found with a light orange edible rind (9 grams fat; reduced-fat Muenster, about 7 grams).
- *Parmesan:* Authentic Parmesan cheese is made in Italy and sold exclusively under the name Parmigiano Reggiano. It's a hard, granular cheese with a sweet taste (7 grams fat).
- *Ricotta:* Soft, moist, and ideal for baking, this white Italian cheese is unusually high in fat (½ cup whole-milk ricotta, 16 grams fat; part-skim-milk ricotta, about 10 grams).
- *Soy cheese:* Made from soy milk or tofu, this product looks like cheese, but unfortunately its texture and taste are closer to rubber. It's useful, though, for people who are allergic to dairy products and is lower in fat than cheese made from milk (about 5 grams).
- *Swiss:* This firm-textured cheese has a mild, nutty flavor (8 grams fat; reduced-fat Swiss cheese, about 6 grams).

Spanakopita

Preparation time: 45 minutes
Cooking time: 45 minutes

The prep time for this Greek spinach pie is a bit hefty, but it can be made a day ahead and then baked just before serving.

2 pounds fresh spinach, stemmed, or 2 frozen 10-ounce packages, thawed
About ¼ cup plus 1 tablespoon olive oil
1 large onion, chopped
¼ teaspoon ground nutmeg
Salt and freshly ground black pepper
1 cup crumbled feta cheese
1 cup small-curd low-fat cottage cheese, drained
1 pound phyllo pastry dough

If using fresh spinach, rinse well, leaving some water clinging to the leaves, and place in a large pot, pushing down to fit all the spinach in. Steam over high heat for about 3 to 5 minutes, or until wilted. Drain and refresh under cold running water. With your hands, squeeze out all the excess water. Finely chop the spinach. If using frozen spinach, place in a large skillet and toss over low heat until the water has evaporated. Finely chop and set aside.

In a large skillet, heat 1 tablespoon of the olive oil over moderate heat. Add the chopped onion and sauté about 5 minutes, until translucent.

Add the spinach, nutmeg, and salt and pepper to taste. Sauté 3 minutes, remove from the heat, and pour off any liquid. Using a fork, stir the feta and cottage cheese into the spinach mixture and thoroughly combine.

Preheat the oven to 350 degrees. Lightly grease a 9-by-13-inch baking pan with olive oil. Place a sheet of phyllo dough on the bottom of the pan and fold the edges up along the sides. Brush lightly with the olive oil. Repeat, adding oil between each sheet, until you have a stack of 8 layers.

Spread half of the spinach filling over the dough. Add another 8 sheets of pastry, brushing oil on each layer. Spread the remaining filling on top. Trim the excess dough that hangs over the sides of the pan with a small sharp knife.

To make the pastry cover, place a sheet of phyllo on top of the dish with half of it hanging over. Brush with oil and then fold over the second half, as if you were closing a book. Brush with oil and repeat with three more sheets of dough. Brush the top layer with oil. (If making ahead of time, cover and refrigerate at this point. Bake for the same amount of time as you would if the dish were at room temperature.)

Bake for about 45 minutes, or until lightly browned and crispy. Cut into squares and serve hot, warm, or at room temperature.

YIELD: 8 servings

PER SERVING: 346 calories, 14 g protein, 13 g fat, 44 g carbohydrate, 608 mg sodium, 16 mg cholesterol

Cheese and Herb Pancakes

Preparation time: 10 minutes
Cooking time: about 10 minutes

These are like tiny grilled cheese sandwiches in the form of a pancake. They make an ideal lunch served plain or topped with melted butter, sour cream, or plain low-fat yogurt.

¾ **cup all-purpose flour**
1¼ **teaspoons baking powder**
½ **teaspoon salt**
½ **cup low-fat milk, at room temperature**
3 **tablespoons butter, melted, plus extra for griddle**
1 **large egg**
1 **tablespoon minced fresh basil or 1 teaspoon dried**
½ **teaspoon minced fresh thyme or ¼ teaspoon dried**
1½ **teaspoons minced fresh rosemary or ½ teaspoon dried**
1½ **teaspoons minced fresh sage or ½ teaspoon dried**
½ **cup grated Gruyère cheese (about 2 ounces)**
½ **cup grated Parmesan cheese (about 2 ounces)**

Sift the flour, baking powder, and salt into a large bowl. Add the milk, 3 tablespoons melted butter, the egg, and herbs and mix until smooth. Fold in the cheeses.

Heat a heavy skillet or griddle over moderate heat. Brush lightly with melted butter. Ladle a heaping tablespoon of batter onto the hot griddle and cook until the bottom is golden brown, about 2 minutes. Flip and cook until the other side is golden brown, about 1 minute. Transfer to a heated platter and repeat with the remaining batter, brushing the griddle occasionally with melted butter.

YIELD: twelve 2-inch pancakes
PER SERVING: 114 calories, 5 g protein, 7 g fat, 7 g carbohydrate, 292 mg sodium, 38 mg
   cholesterol

Vegetable Bread Pudding

Preparation time: 20 minutes
Cooking time: 30 minutes

This is one of the best ways to use up dried-up, leftover bread. In this savory version of a bread pudding, the bread is topped with vegetables and a cheese custard. The final result is a pudding that is a cross between a pizza, a soufflé, and a cheese-filled stuffing. You can use any type of leftover bread you have around.

1 tablespoon butter
4 slices stale bread, cut in half, crusts removed and reserved
4 thick strips bacon (optional)
1 teaspoon olive oil
1 small onion, finely chopped
3 tablespoons snipped fresh chives
¼ cup dry white wine
1½ cups raw vegetables (broccoli, zucchini, beans, or bell peppers,
    cut into bite-size pieces)
3 tablespoons chopped fresh parsley
Salt and freshly ground black pepper
1½ cups grated cheese, any variety
2 large eggs
1¼ cups milk

Preheat the oven to 375 degrees. Butter a shallow baking pan or a large shallow casserole. Line the bottom of the pan with the bread, using the crusts to fill in any spaces not covered. Fry the bacon, if using, in a medium skillet until crisp. Drain on paper towels and discard all but 1 teaspoon of the fat.

In the same skillet, heat the teaspoon of fat and the olive oil over moderate heat. (If you're skipping the bacon, use 2 teaspoons of olive oil.) Add the onion and half of the chives and sauté for 5 minutes, or until soft but not brown. Raise the heat to high and add the wine and vegetables, stirring well. Let simmer for about 5 minutes, or until the wine has almost completely evaporated and the vegetables are soft. Remove from the heat.

Crumble the bacon and add it to the vegetable mixture along with the parsley. Season with salt and pepper.

Spoon the vegetable mixture over the bread and top with the cheese. Whisk the eggs with the milk, the remaining chives, and salt and pepper; pour the mixture over the vegetables. Cover the dish with foil and bake for 15 minutes. Then remove the foil and bake an additional 10 to 15 minutes, or until the cheese is bubbling and the custard is set. Serve hot, warm, or at room temperature.

YIELD: 2 to 4 servings

PER SERVING: 530 calories, 26 g protein, 34 g fat, 28 g carbohydrate, 675 mg sodium, 226 mg cholesterol

Vegetable Shish Kebab

Preparation time: 30 minutes
Cooking time: 10 minutes

The list of recommended vegetables is just for starters; round it out with whatever is in season.

3 tablespoons olive oil
1 tablespoon finely chopped fresh basil or 1 teaspoon dried
12 small pearl onions, peeled
1 green bell pepper, cored, seeded, and cut into small cubes
1 red bell pepper, cored, seeded, and cut into small cubes
1 medium zucchini or summer squash, cut into small cubes
12 small mushrooms
Salt
1 cup plain low-fat yogurt (optional)

In a small bowl, mix the olive oil and basil and let sit at room temperature for at least 30 minutes or cover and refrigerate overnight.

Preheat the broiler or prepare a charcoal fire in an outdoor grill. Bring a large saucepan of water to a boil. Add the onions and let cook for 2 minutes. Drain and rinse under cold water.

Arrange the onions, peppers, zucchini, and mushrooms on skewers. Brush with the flavored oil and sprinkle with salt. Grill or broil the vegetables for 8 to 10 minutes, or until tender but not falling apart. Serve with plain yogurt for dipping if desired.

YIELD: 6 servings
PER SERVING: 88 calories, 1 g protein, 7 g fat, 5 g carbohydrate, 4 mg sodium, 0 mg cholesterol

Grilled Ratatouille

Preparation time: 40 minutes
Cooking time: 30 minutes

Grilling eggplant mellows its flavor, making it more palatable for kids. Serve this vegetable mixture hot, cold, or at room temperature. You can also chop the ratatouille and serve it cold on crackers of grilled French bread as an appetizer, hors d'oeuvre, or luncheon dish.

1 medium eggplant, peeled and cut into ½-inch-thick slices
Salt
1 medium zucchini, thinly sliced
1 large onion, thinly sliced
Olive oil
2 large ripe tomatoes, cored and cut into small cubes
¼ cup chopped fresh basil or 1 tablespoon dried (optional)
2 cloves garlic, chopped
Freshly ground black pepper

Place the eggplant in a colander and sprinkle generously with salt. Set over a large plate for about 30 minutes. (The salt will leach out the bitter juices.) Rinse with cold water and dry thoroughly.

Preheat the broiler or prepare a charcoal fire in an outdoor grill. Place the eggplant, zucchini, and onion on skewers and brush with olive oil. Broil or grill for 3 minutes on each side, or until just tender. Remove the vegetables from the skewers and place on a large piece of foil. If using the broiler, turn it off and preheat the oven to 450 degrees. Add the tomatoes, basil, garlic, salt, and pepper to the vegetables and seal the foil tightly.

Place the vegetable packet in the oven for 10 to 15 minutes or place it back on the grill for another 10 minutes, until the vegetables are tender. Transfer the ratatouille to a bowl, taste for seasoning, and serve.

YIELD: 4 to 6 servings
PER SERVING: 109 calories, 3 g protein, 6 g fat, 14 g carbohydrate, 231 mg sodium, 0 mg
    cholesterol

Stuffed Acorn Squash

Preparation time: 15 minutes
Cooking time: 1 hour

Here is a simple, meatless main course that kids will love. Serve couscous or rice on the side to soak up the savory juices.

2 acorn squash, cut in half, seeds removed
1½ cups coarsely chopped ripe tomatoes
3 scallions, thinly sliced
Salt and freshly ground black pepper
1 teaspoon chopped fresh sage or ½ teaspoon dried
1 cup diced Cheddar cheese
1 tablespoon butter, cut into 4 pieces

Preheat the oven to 400 degrees. Place the squash halves in a roasting pan, cut side up, and add about an inch of water to the bottom of the pan.

Combine the chopped tomatoes and scallions and spoon the mixture into the cavities of the 4 squash halves. Season liberally with salt and pepper and add a bit of sage to each half. Add 1 tablespoon of water to the cavity of each squash half and top the tomato mixture with the cheese and then the butter.

Bake for 1 hour, or until the squash is tender when it's pierced with a fork. If the filling looks like it's beginning to dry out, add another teaspoon or two of water to each squash half.

YIELD: 4 servings
PER SERVING: 256 calories, 11 g protein, 15 g fat, 22 g carbohydrate, 262 mg sodium, 45 mg cholesterol

Winter Vegetable Puree

Preparation time: 30 minutes
Cooking time: 15 minutes

Turnips add a pleasant touch of tartness to this sophisticated comfort food.

1 pound sweet potatoes, peeled and chopped
½ pound carrots, peeled and chopped
½ pound turnips or rutabagas, peeled and chopped
3 tablespoons butter
¼ cup heavy cream (optional)
Pinch ground nutmeg
Salt and freshly ground black pepper

Bring a large pot of salted water to a boil. Add the chopped vegetables and simmer about 15 minutes, or until tender. Drain and set aside. Mash with a potato masher or blend in a food processor until almost pureed.

Preheat the oven to 250 degrees. Melt the butter in a medium casserole. Add the mashed vegetables, cream if desired, nutmeg, and salt and pepper to taste, and beat until fluffy. Cover and keep warm in the oven until serving. (The recipe can be made up to a day ahead of time and reheated just before serving.)

YIELD: 8 servings
PER SERVING: 98 calories, 1 g protein, 4 g fat, 14 g carbohydrate, 74 mg sodium, 12 mg cholesterol

Ginger Beets

Preparation time: 20 minutes
Cooking time: 1 to 1½ hour

It's a mystery why beets have such a bad reputation with kids; they're beautiful to look at and sweet enough to pass for dessert. This recipe is bound to win over your children.

10 medium beets
6 tablespoons butter, at room temperature
2 tablespoons grated fresh ginger
Salt and freshly ground black pepper

Preheat the oven to 400 degrees. Cut off the beet greens and scrub the beets. Wrap them in aluminum foil and bake about 45 minutes to 1½ hours, depending on the size and freshness, or until tender when tested with a sharp knife.

Meanwhile, in a small saucepan, mix the butter with the ginger, salt, and pepper. Simmer the flavored butter for 2 to 3 minutes.

Remove the beets from the oven and let cool slightly. Use a small, sharp knife to peel off the outer layer of skin and cut the beets into quarters. (The recipe can be made up to this point 2 days ahead of time.) Before serving, simply toss the cooked beets with the ginger butter in a sauté pan until hot.

YIELD: 8 servings
PER SERVING: 122 calories, 2 g protein, 9 g fat, 10 g carbohydrate, 161 mg sodium, 23 mg
   cholesterol

Turkey Tonnato

Preparation time: 30 minutes
Cooling time: 4 to 24 hours

No need to tell the kids that the tonnato sauce contains anchovies or capers; all they'll recognize is the familiar flavor of tuna. This dish is served cold, so it should be made several hours ahead of time. Serve it as a salad or main course.

7-ounce can tuna, drained
1 cup olive oil
6 anchovy fillets
3 tablespoons capers
Juice of 1 large lemon
Freshly ground black pepper
½ cup mayonnaise mixed with 1 tablespoon lemon juice
12 to 14 thin slices cooked turkey

GARNISHES:

Bottled pimientos
Small gherkin pickles
Lemon wedges
Anchovies and capers (optional)

Place the tuna, olive oil, anchovies, capers, and lemon juice in a blender or processor and puree until smooth and creamy. Stir in the pepper and mayonnaise, and taste for seasoning.

Spread a third of the sauce on the bottom of a serving plate and arrange half of the turkey slices on top in a single layer. Cover the meat with another third of the sauce, and place another layer of turkey on top. Spread the remaining sauce over all. Cover and refrigerate for at least 4 hours, preferably overnight. Garnish with pimientos, pickles, lemon wedges, anchovies, and capers if desired.

YIELD: 6 servings
PER SERVING: 601 calories, 33 g protein, 52 g fat, 1 g carbohydrate, 505 mg sodium, 88 mg cholesterol

The Very Best
Beef Potpie

Preparation time: 1 hour
Cooking time: 1 hour

The perfect warmer-upper on a cold, wintery day, this potpie is one of the richest recipes in this book, but one taste will convince you that every calorie is worth it.

There are several steps involved in the preparation. To save time, make the pastry ahead of time and use leftover cooked beef and vegetables. Although you can use any cut of beef you have on hand, pot roast, beef stew, or braised beef makes the tenderest beef in this pie. Try it with chicken or turkey too.

PASTRY:

2½ cups sifted all-purpose flour

½ teaspoon salt

8 tablespoons (1 stick) cold butter, cut into small pieces

5 tablespoons lard or vegetable shortening, cut into small pieces

3 to 5 tablespoons ice-cold water

FILLING:

20 pearl onions, peeled

1½ cups thickly sliced carrots (about 3 to 4 carrots)

1½ cups thickly sliced celery (about 3 stalks)

3 tablespoons butter

3 tablespoons flour

3 tablespoons chopped fresh parsley

1 teaspoon dried tarragon, thyme, rosemary, or a combination

2½ cups beef or chicken broth

½ cup heavy cream, whole milk, or low-fat milk

1 cup thickly sliced mushrooms

2 cups cooked beef cut into chunks (about 1 pound)

Salt and freshly ground black pepper

GLAZE:

1 large egg yolk
1 teaspoon water

To make the pastry, sift the flour and salt into a large bowl. Add the butter and shortening and, using 2 knives or a pastry cutter, work the mixture until the dough resembles bread crumbs. Add just enough water to hold the dough together, and form it into a ball. Wrap in aluminum foil and refrigerate for at least 30 minutes.

To make the filling, bring a pot of water to a boil. Add the onions and simmer for 1 minute, then add the carrots and celery and simmer for 4 to 5 minutes, or until all the vegetables are almost tender. Drain.

In a large saucepan, melt the butter over moderate heat. Add the flour and cook for 1 minute, stirring constantly. Add the parsley and dried herbs, then gradually add the stock, whisking to create a smooth sauce. Bring to a boil, reduce the heat, and add the cream. Simmer for 10 minutes, stirring occasionally, or until thickened. Stir in the cooked vegetables, mushrooms, beef, and salt and pepper to taste.

Preheat the oven to 425 degrees. Remove the dough from the refrigerator and divide it in half. Roll out one half and use it to line the bottom and sides of a 2-quart baking dish or casserole, fluting the edges. Using a fork, prick the dough in several places. Bake until golden brown, about 10 minutes. Remove from the oven and reduce the temperature to 400 degrees.

Pour the filling into the pie crust. Roll out the remaining dough and place it on top of the pie. Seal the edge over the rim of the dish. Make the glaze by beating the egg yolk and water, then brush it on top of the pastry. Using a sharp knife, cut a few steam vents. (The potpie can be made up to this point and refrigerated, covered, overnight.) Bake for 30 minutes, or until the pastry is golden brown.

YIELD: 6 servings
PER SERVING: 713 calories, 24 g protein, 45 g fat, 52 g carbohydrate, 1,163 mg sodium, 177 mg cholesterol

Tamale Pie

Preparation time: 25 minutes
Cooking time: 30 minutes

This Mexican-inspired casserole combines tortilla chips, cheese, corn, chicken, and bell peppers with a cornmeal topping. Serve with an avocado or cucumber salad.

> **2 cups fresh, frozen, or canned corn**
> **1½ cups diced green and/or red bell peppers**
> **¼ cup finely chopped fresh parsley**
> **Salt and freshly ground black pepper**
> **About 8 cups tortilla chips**
> **3½ cups cubed cooked chicken or turkey or a combination**
> **3 cups chopped ripe tomatoes**
> **2½ cups grated mild Cheddar or Monterey Jack cheese**
> **½ cup cornmeal**

ACCOMPANIMENTS:
> **2 cups low-fat sour cream**
> **Tabasco or hot pepper sauce**
> **1 cup chopped or sliced black olives**
> **1 cup finely chopped fresh cilantro (optional)**

Preheat the oven to 350 degrees. If you're using fresh or frozen corn, steam over simmering water for 1 to 2 minutes, or until cooked but still firm. If you're using canned corn, drain.

In a bowl, mix the corn, bell peppers, and parsley and season to taste with salt and pepper.

Line a large casserole or baking dish with half of the tortilla chips, overlapping them to completely cover the bottom. Top with all of the turkey and/or chicken, then half of the tomatoes and half of the cheese. Layer the remaining tortilla chips, the corn mixture, and the rest of the tomatoes on top. Sprinkle with the cornmeal and the remaining half of the cheese.

Cover the casserole and bake for 25 minutes. Remove the cover and place the dish under the broiler for about 3 to 5 minutes, or until the cheese is bubbling and the cornmeal crust turns golden brown. Cut and serve like lasagna, making sure each serving goes down to the bottom of the casserole. Serve the accompaniments in separate bowls.

YIELD: 4 to 6 servings

PER SERVING: 1,327 calories, 69 g protein, 70 g fat, 114 g carbohydrate, 1,472 mg sodium, 223 mg cholesterol

Grilled Marinated Pork Tenderloin

Preparation time: about 5 minutes
Marinating time: 1 to 48 hours
Cooking time: about 55 to 60 minutes

If you let the pork marinate for 24 to 48 hours before grilling, you'll have meat that is thoroughly tender and flavorful. However, if it marinates for only an hour, you'll still have deliciously tender meat. Serve with a bowl of orange sections and a watercress salad. This recipe makes enough for plenty of leftovers and cold sandwiches the next day.

2 pork tenderloins, about ¾ pound each
1 cup orange juice, preferably fresh-squeezed
3 tablespoons low-sodium soy sauce
2 tablespoons Chinese rice wine, dry sherry, or white wine
1 tablespoon maple syrup or honey
2 cloves garlic, chopped
1 tablespoon hoisin sauce (optional)
2 oranges, peeled and cut into thin slices

Place the pork tenderloins in a large bowl. Add the remaining ingredients except the orange slices and toss well to thoroughly coat the meat. Cover and refrigerate for 24 to 48 hours.

Preheat the oven to 400 degrees. Roast the meat for about 45 to 55 minutes, or until the internal temperature is 150 degrees. Let sit for 5 minutes before cutting into thin slices. Serve with the orange slices on the side.

YIELD: 8 servings with leftovers
PER SERVING: 160 calories, 18 g protein, 5 g fat, 10 g carbohydrate, 268 mg sodium, 56 mg cholesterol

Marinated Butterfly of Lamb with Cucumber-Mint Yogurt Sauce

Preparation time: 15 minutes
Marinating time: 24 to 48 hours
Cooking time: 20 to 24 minutes

There is something so tender and buttery about butterfly of lamb that children who ordinarily don't like lamb chops or roast lamb love this dish. It's even more delicious when served with the minty yogurt-cucumber sauce.

A butterfly of lamb is nothing more than a leg of lamb that has been boned and then opened up and spread out, making the cut of meat resemble a butterfly with its wings spread out. Ask your butcher to butterfly half a leg of lamb for this recipe (they generally run about 2 to 3 pounds), or double the ingredients and use an entire leg of lamb (about 6 pounds).

2 to 3 pounds butterflied leg of lamb

MARINADE:

¼ cup red wine
¼ cup olive oil
¼ cup soy sauce
¼ cup chopped fresh mint leaves or 2 tablespoons dried, crumbled
1½ tablespoon prepared mustard

SAUCE:

1 cup plain low-fat yogurt
1 cup grated cucumber
¼ cup chopped fresh mint leaves

Rinse the lamb and pat dry with paper towels.

In a large bowl, mix the ingredients for the marinade. Add the leg of lamb and turn several times to coat. Cover and let marinate, refrigerated, for 24 to 48 hours.

To make the sauce, mix the yogurt, grated cucumber, and mint leaves in a small bowl and refrigerate. (Do not make the sauce more than a few hours before serving.)

Prepare a charcoal fire in an outdoor grill. Remove the lamb from the marinade, pat dry, and place over red-hot coals. Cook for about 8 to 10 minutes on each side, depending on how rare or well done you like your lamb.

If you like, boil down the marinade in a small saucepan for 10 to 15 minutes and serve over the meat.

YIELD: 6 servings

PER SERVING: 316 calories, 35 g protein, 17 g fat, 4 g carbohydrate, 655 mg sodium, 103 mg cholesterol

Barbecued Sausages

Preparation time: 10 minutes
Cooking time: 1 hour and 15 to 20 minutes

Use any kind of pork or chicken sausages with this recipe. The trick is to bake them slowly so that the sauce thickens.

6 sweet sausages
1 cup catsup
3 tablespoons frozen orange juice concentrate
2 tablespoons honey or maple syrup
1 tablespoon Worcestershire sauce or soy sauce
1 teaspoon chopped fresh garlic (optional)

Preheat the oven to 300 degrees. Place the sausages in a shallow baking dish.

In a small bowl, mix the catsup, orange juice concentrate, honey or syrup, Worcestershire or soy sauce, and chopped garlic if using. Pour the mixture over the sausages and bake for 1 hour. Raise the heat to 350 degrees and bake another 10 to 15 minutes. The sauce should be quite thick, and the sausages should look glazed and brown.

Remove from the oven, cool for a few minutes, and serve on a plate or insert a skewer into each sausage.

YIELD: 3 to 6 servings
PER SERVING: 348 calories, 18 g protein, 21 g fat, 22 g carbohydrate, 1,267 mg sodium, 65 mg cholesterol

Chapter Six

Quick Weekday Dinners

🍂

This chapter, the largest in the book, truly addresses the needs of exhausted, overworked parents. There are dozens of recipes here that are realistic for parents who arrive home late and are greeted by tired, hungry children who want dinner *now!* These dishes all require only a minimum of effort, but they are also creative, interesting, and healthy. You'll find ideas for dinners ranging from a quick vegetarian lasagna or stir-fried broccoli with hoisin sauce to London broil burritos or a roast chicken and vegetable dish that takes about an hour to cook—from start to finish.

Chinese Noodle Soup

Leek and Potato Soup with Cheese

Squash Soup with Apples

Corn Chowder

Fish Chowder

Springtime Pasta

Linguine with Garlic, Herb, and Sun-Dried Tomato Sauce

Spaghetti and Meatballs

Macaroni and Cheese

Broccoli-Stuffed Shells

Zucchini, Pea, and Walnut Sauce

Tomato-Olive Pasta Sauce

Basic Orzo

Roasted Leeks with Parmesan Cheese

Creamed Spinach

Stir-fried Broccoli with Hoisin Sauce

Honey-Kissed Greens

Other Ideas for Quick Dinners

🔊 Family Dining: The Importance of Eating Together

Chinese Noodle Soup

Preparation time: 15 minutes
Cooking time: 10 minutes

Make this soup with Chinese noodles, tofu, and vegetables. Add leftover cooked chicken or turkey if you like.

8 cups homemade or canned chicken or turkey broth (see recipe page 435)

1 pound soft tofu, cut into strips

1 medium zucchini, cut into strips

1 cup thin strips of cooked chicken, turkey, pork, or beef (optional)

1 pound fresh Chinese egg noodles, or 1 pound dried Asian wheat noodles

¼ pound fresh bean sprouts

3 tablespoons finely chopped fresh cilantro (optional)

3 scallions, thinly sliced

GARNISHES:

Soy sauce

Sesame oil

Chinese chili paste (optional)

In a large saucepan, bring the stock to a rapid simmer over moderate heat. At the same time, bring a saucepan of lightly salted water to a boil. Also pour 1 inch of water into another pot fitted with a steamer tray and bring to a boil.

Place the tofu and zucchini on the steamer tray and steam for about 3 minutes. If you're using leftover meat, add it to the vegetables. Set aside and keep warm.

When the pot of water comes to a boil, add the noodles and cook for about 3 to 5 minutes or according to package directions. Drain the noodles and divide among 4 large bowls.

Pour the hot broth over the noodles and add the vegetables, tofu, and meat if using. Sprinkle the fresh bean sprouts, cilantro, and green onions on top. Serve piping hot and let everyone add their own touch of soy sauce, sesame oil, and chili paste if desired.

YIELD: 4 to 6 servings

PER SERVING: 466 calories, 24 g protein, 10 g fat, 69 g carbohydrate, 2,332 mg sodium, 83 mg cholesterol

Leek and Potato Soup with Cheese

Preparation time: 20 minutes
Cooking time: 45 minutes

This soothing, hearty soup appeals to adults and children alike.

1 tablespoon vegetable or olive oil
1 clove garlic, minced
4 leeks, washed and thinly sliced
4 large potatoes, peeled and cut into thin slices or small cubes
4 cups low-sodium chicken broth
1 cup water
Salt and freshly ground black pepper
1½ tablespoons chopped fresh thyme or 1 teaspoon dried
½ cup grated reduced-fat Cheddar or Swiss cheese
¼ cup chopped fresh parsley or chives

In a large pot, heat the oil over moderate heat. Add the garlic and leeks and sauté for about 5 minutes, just until soft. Add the potatoes and sauté another minute. Add the chicken broth, water, salt and pepper to taste, and thyme. Simmer about 45 minutes, or until the potatoes are tender.

At this stage, if you prefer a thicker, creamier soup, puree all the ingredients in a food processor or blender and pour back into the soup pot. Over low heat, *slowly* add the grated cheese, stirring until melted. Sprinkle the chopped parsley or chives over each bowl before serving.

YIELD: 6 servings
PER SERVING: 177 calories, 7 g protein, 5 g fat, 27 g carbohydrate, 508 mg sodium, 7 mg cholesterol

Squash Soup with Apples

Preparation time: 10 minutes
Cooking time: about 20 minutes

The creamy texture in this low-fat soup comes from pureed vegetables. The tart flavor of the apples complements the natural sweetness of the squash.

1 tablespoon vegetable or olive oil
1 onion, chopped
¼ teaspoon grated nutmeg
1 tart apple, peeled, seeded, and chopped
2 cups fresh squash, peeled and cut into small pieces, or 2 cups
    Pumpkin Puree (see page 474)
2 cups chicken broth
½ cup fresh apple cider
Salt and freshly ground black pepper

GARNISHES:
    1 tart apple, peeled, seeded, and very finely chopped
    ¼ cup chopped fresh parsley

In a large pot, heat the oil over moderate heat. Add the onion and sauté for about 5 minutes, or until softened but not brown. Add the nutmeg and apple and sauté for another 2 minutes. Add the squash and stir well.

Slowly stir in the chicken broth, cider, and salt and pepper to taste. Simmer for 10 minutes, or until the apples and squash are tender. Puree in a blender or food processor and season to taste. If the soup is too thick, thin it with more chicken broth or cider. Serve hot, garnished with a sprinkling of apple and parsley.

YIELD: 6 servings
PER SERVING: 90 calories, 2 g protein, 3 g fat, 15 g carbohydrate, 333 mg sodium, 0 mg cholesterol

Corn Chowder

Preparation time: 10 minutes
Cooking time: about 35 minutes

An ideal soup for a cool summer night.

> 1½ tablespoons vegetable oil
> 1 medium onion, diced
> 3 potatoes, peeled and cubed
> 1 bay leaf
> Salt and freshly ground black pepper
> 3 cups milk, heated
> 4 cups fresh or frozen corn kernels
> 2 tablespoons flour
> Sweet Hungarian paprika

Heat the oil in a large pot. Add the onion and sauté for 5 minutes, until softened but not brown. Add the potatoes, 2 cups water, the bay leaf, and salt and pepper to taste. Bring to a boil, then reduce the heat and let simmer, uncovered, for about 25 minutes, or until the potatoes are just tender.

Add the warm milk and corn and stir well. Place the flour in a small bowl. Take 3 tablespoons of the hot chowder and whisk into the flour to form a paste. Slowly add the flour mixture to the pot, stirring to create a smooth soup. Let simmer 3 to 5 minutes, until thickened. Season and serve with a sprinkling of paprika.

YIELD: 6 servings
PER SERVING: 252 calories, 9 g protein, 9 g fat, 39 g carbohydrate, 79 mg sodium, 17 mg cholesterol

Fish Chowder

Preparation time: 15 minutes
Cooking time: about 45 minutes

A thick chowder that is hearty enough to be served as a main course. Accompany with bis-cuits, crackers, or a thick, crusty bread and a big tossed salad. You can use any combina-tion of fish and shellfish you have on hand.

If you prepare the fish stock ahead of time (or buy pre-made stock), the chowder can be put together in under an hour.

3 strips bacon or 1 teaspoon vegetable oil

2 leeks, washed and finely chopped, white part only

1 onion, finely chopped

1½ tablespoons flour

10 cups fish stock (see recipe, page 437) or clam juice

6 potatoes, peeled and cut into small chunks

1 bay leaf

4 sea scallops, quartered, or 8 bay scallops left whole

1 pound haddock or other firm-fleshed fish, such as cod or hake

½ pound swordfish, cut into small chunks

1 to 1½ pounds small shrimp, peeled and left whole

**8 littleneck or cherrystone clams, shucked (juices reserved) and
    chopped**

About 3½ cups milk or 3 cups milk plus ½ cup heavy cream

Salt and freshly ground black pepper

Paprika

3 tablespoons butter, cut into small cubes (optional)

In a large stockpot, cook the bacon over moderate heat until crispy. Remove the ba-con and drain on paper towels. Discard all but 1 teaspoon of the bacon fat and place the pot over moderate heat. (If you are not using bacon, heat the vegetable oil over moderate heat.) Add the leeks and onion and sauté for about 5 minutes, or until tender and golden brown. Sprinkle in the flour and stir well to coat the leeks and onions; cook 1 minute. Add the fish stock and bring the mixture to a boil. Reduce the heat and add the potatoes. Let simmer, partially covered, about 10 minutes, or until the potatoes are almost tender. Add the bay leaf, scallops, haddock, swordfish, shrimp, clams, and reserved clam juice and let simmer about 5 minutes.

Meanwhile heat the milk (and cream if using) in a saucepan until warm. Add the hot milk to the chowder and let cook, without boiling, until the fish and shellfish are cooked and the potatoes are tender, about 5 to 10 minutes. Remove the bay leaf and crumble in the reserved bacon. Taste for seasoning and add salt and pepper. If the soup tastes very strong, you may want to add another ½ cup warm milk. Serve hot, topped with paprika and a pat of butter if desired.

YIELD: 10 servings

PER SERVING: 300 calories, 32 g protein, 5 g fat, 30 g carbohydrate, 467 mg sodium, 124 mg cholesterol

Springtime Pasta

Preparation time: 10 minutes
Cooking time: about 12 minutes

You can use other combinations of vegetables in this sauce, but leeks and asparagus go particularly well together.

1 tablespoon plus 1 teaspoon olive oil
1 cup thinly sliced leeks
1½ tablespoons chopped fresh garlic
1 teaspoon dried thyme or 1 tablespoon chopped fresh thyme
1 cup cooked asparagus, cut on the diagonal into 2-inch pieces
½ cup chopped sun-dried tomatoes
⅛ cup pine nuts or walnuts
Salt and freshly ground black pepper
¾ pound dried linguine
About ¾ cup grated Parmesan cheese

Bring a large pot of salted water to boil for the pasta.

Meanwhile, in a large skillet, heat 1 teaspoon of the oil over moderate heat. Add the leeks and half the garlic and sauté about 5 minutes, until softened. Add the thyme, asparagus, sun-dried tomatoes, pine nuts, salt, pepper, and remaining garlic and stir well. Sauté another 3 minutes and keep warm over low heat.

Boil the pasta for about 10 minutes, or until *al dente*, drain and place in a bowl or serving platter and toss with the remaining tablespoon of oil and salt and pepper to taste. Spoon the sauce on top and serve with the cheese on the side.

YIELD: 2 to 4 servings
PER SERVING: 735 calories, 31 g protein, 23 g fat, 107 g carbohydrate, 797 mg sodium, 16 mg cholesterol

Linguine with Garlic, Herb, and Sun-Dried Tomato Sauce

Preparation time: 10 minutes
Cooking time: 10 to 12 minutes

This is one of those recipes that proves how much easier life can be if you have a well-stocked pantry. The sauce can be put together in about 10 minutes while the pasta is cooking. Kids love the chewy texture of the sun-dried tomatoes.

Salt
½ pound dried linguine
¼ cup olive oil
2 cloves garlic, finely chopped
1 tablespoon chopped fresh basil or thyme or 1 teaspoon dried
¼ cup chopped sun-dried tomatoes
Freshly ground black pepper
½ cup chopped fresh parsley (optional)
½ cup grated Parmesan cheese

Bring a large pot of water to a boil. Add salt and the linguine and cook until tender, about 10 to 12 minutes.

Meanwhile, in a small saucepan, heat the oil over moderate heat. Add the garlic and basil and sauté about 10 seconds. Add the dried tomatoes and sauté, stirring to coat them with the oil, for about 3 minutes. Add salt and pepper.

Drain the pasta, place in a large bowl, and toss with the warm sauce. Add the parsley if using and sprinkle on half of the cheese; serve the remaining cheese on the side.

YIELD: 2 servings as a main course; 4 as a side dish
PER SERVING: 790 calories, 25 g protein, 35 g fat, 94 g carbohydrate, 782 mg sodium, 16 mg cholesterol

Spaghetti and Meatballs

Preparation time: 15 minutes
Cooking time: 50 minutes

Kids and cooks alike will appreciate this one: a big pot of pasta and meatballs that can be on the table in less than an hour.

1½ pounds lean ground beef
2 tablespoons chopped fresh thyme or 2 teaspoons dried
Salt and freshly ground black pepper
1 large egg, beaten
¼ cup bread crumbs
1 tablespoon grated Parmesan cheese, plus extra for serving
½ cup finely chopped fresh parsley
2 teaspoons vegetable or olive oil
4 cups homemade or canned tomato sauce
1 bay leaf
1 pound dried linguine or spaghetti
1 tablespoon olive oil

In a large bowl, combine the ground beef, thyme, salt, pepper, egg, bread crumbs, cheese, and parsley. Using your hands, form the meat mixture into half-dollar-size meatballs.

In a large skillet, heat the oil over moderate heat. Add some of the meatballs (be careful not to crowd) and sauté for about 2 minutes on each side, or until golden brown. Remove the meatballs with a slotted spoon to drain the excess oil and set on a plate. Sauté the remaining meatballs.

Wipe the grease from the pan with a paper towel and return the cooked meatballs to the skillet. Pour the tomato sauce on top and add the bay leaf. Let the sauce simmer, partially covered, over low heat for about 30 minutes. (If you make the sauce ahead of time, simmer for about 15 minutes, then simmer again over low heat for another 15 minutes just before you're ready to use.)

Meanwhile, bring a large pot of lightly salted water to a boil. Cook the pasta according to package directions. Drain and place in a large serving bowl or platter. Toss with the olive oil and top with the meatballs and sauce. Before serving, sprinkle with additional Parmesan cheese.

YIELD: 4 to 6 servings

PER SERVING: 750 calories, 40 g protein, 27 g fat, 87 g carbohydrate, 1,653 mg sodium, 126 mg cholesterol

Macaroni and Cheese

Preparation time: about 20 minutes
Cooking time: about 15 to 20 minutes

I was going to call this the world's best macaroni and cheese, but modesty got hold of me. This classic is loved by all ages.

- **1 tablespoon butter**
- **1 tablespoon flour**
- **1 cup low-fat or whole milk**
- **Salt and freshly ground black pepper**
- **½ cup plus 2 tablespoons grated cheese or combination of cheeses (Parmesan, mozzarella, Cheddar)**
- **½ pound dried macaroni**
- **1 teaspoon olive oil or butter**
- **1½ tablespoons seasoned bread crumbs**

Preheat the oven to 350 degrees. In a medium saucepan, melt the butter over moderate heat. Add the flour and stir to create a paste. Let cook about 1 minute, or until golden brown. Slowly add the milk, a bit at a time, whisking until you have a smooth sauce. Let cook about 5 minutes, until thick enough to coat the back of a spoon. Add salt and pepper to taste. Slowly add the ½ cup of grated cheese and keep warm over very low heat.

Meanwhile, bring a large pot of lightly salted water to a boil. Add the macaroni and cook about 8 minutes, or until just tender. (Do not overcook or the pasta will start to fall apart.) Drain the pasta.

Grease a medium ovenproof skillet or casserole with the teaspoon of oil or butter. Add the drained macaroni and toss gently with the sauce, stirring well to coat all the pasta. Sprinkle the top with the bread crumbs and the remaining 2 tablespoons of cheese. Bake for 15 to 20 minutes, or until hot and bubbling.

YIELD: 4 servings

PER SERVING: 346 calories, 15 g protein, 9 g fat, 49 g carbohydrate, 565 mg sodium, 20 mg cholesterol

Broccoli-Stuffed Shells

Preparation time: 35 minutes
Cooking time: 30 minutes

Here is a great, if sneaky, way to get your kids to eat this allegedly cancer-preventing vegetable. The pureed broccoli also adds a fresh taste to the rich cheese filling.

1 tablespoon olive oil
3 cups low-sodium tomato sauce
20 large pasta shells (often called shells for stuffing)
1 large head broccoli, cut into small pieces
1 cup reduced-fat ricotta cheese
2 tablespoons chopped fresh basil or 1 teaspoon dried
½ cup grated low-fat mozzarella cheese
Salt and freshly ground black pepper

Preheat the oven to 350 degrees. Lightly grease a 9-by-13-inch baking pan with the olive oil. Coat the bottom of the pan with about ¼ cup of the tomato sauce.

In a large pot of salted water, boil the pasta shells according to the package directions until almost tender. Drain off the water, then add cold water to the pot. Let the shells sit in the water until you're ready to stuff them.

For the stuffing, steam the broccoli until tender, about 5 to 8 minutes. Plunge it into cold water and then drain. Place the cooked broccoli in a food processor along with the ricotta, basil, and salt and pepper to taste. Puree until smooth.

Remove each shell from the pot, gently drain off any water, and spoon in a generous portion of the filling. Place the stuffed shells in the baking pan and pour the remaining tomato sauce over them. Sprinkle with the grated mozzarella and bake, uncovered, for 30 minutes.

YIELD: 4 to 6 servings
PER SERVING: 338 calories, 19 g protein, 7 g fat, 52 g carbohydrate, 198 mg sodium, 11 mg cholesterol

Zucchini, Pea, and Walnut Sauce

Preparation time: 5 minutes
Cooking time: about 12 to 15 minutes

The combination of tender zucchini and peas with the crunch of chopped walnuts creates a very different pasta sauce. This sauce works best with a shaped pasta such as penne. The recipe makes enough sauce for ½ pound pasta.

1 teaspoon olive oil
1 cup cubed zucchini
½ cup fresh or frozen (but not thawed) peas
¼ cup chopped walnuts or pine nuts
Salt and freshly ground black pepper
3 tablespoons heavy cream

In a medium skillet, heat the oil over moderately high heat. Add the zucchini and sauté for 5 minutes, or until golden brown. Add the peas and sauté 2 minutes, then add the walnuts, salt, and pepper and stir. Raise the heat to high and add the cream; simmer about 3 minutes, or until thickened.

YIELD: 1 to 2 servings
PER SERVING: 468 calories, 11 g protein, 40 g fat, 22 g carbohydrate, 28 mg sodium, 61 mg cholesterol

Tomato-Olive Pasta Sauce

Preparation time: 5 minutes
Cooking time: 10 to 15 minutes

Make this quick, simple sauce to go over pasta—linguine, penne, and wagon wheels work particularly well—and top with grated Parmesan cheese. Or spoon it over broiled chicken breasts or fish fillets. The recipe makes enough sauce for ½ pound pasta.

> 1 tablespoon olive oil
> 2 cloves garlic, chopped
> 2 tablespoons chopped fresh parsley
> 1½ tablespoons chopped fresh basil or 1 teaspoon dried
> 3 tablespoons finely chopped pitted black olives or 2 tablespoons olive
>   puree or tapenade
> Salt and freshly ground black pepper
> 1½ cups homemade or canned tomato sauce

In a medium saucepan, heat the oil over moderate heat. Add the garlic and sauté 2 minutes, being careful not to let it burn. Add the parsley, basil, olives, salt, and pepper and sauté another minute. Add the tomato sauce, stir thoroughly, and let simmer about 5 to 10 minutes.

YIELD: 2 to 4 servings
PER SERVING: 91 calories, 2 g protein, 6 g fat, 10 g carbohydrate, 813 mg sodium, 0 mg
    cholesterol

Basic Orzo

Preparation time: 5 minutes
Cooking time: about 8 minutes

Orzo, a rice-shaped pasta, is the ultimate comfort food—slightly chewy with a soothing, creamy texture. Because orzo so closely resembles rice, it has great appeal to kids of all ages. In this simple presentation, it's simmered until tender and then tossed with a touch of olive oil, rosemary, and grated Parmesan cheese. This makes a terrific side dish for just about anything, but it also can be served on its own.

1 cup orzo
1 tablespoon good-quality olive oil or butter
Salt and freshly ground black pepper
1 tablespoon finely chopped fresh rosemary or 1 teaspoon dried (optional)
½ cup grated Parmesan cheese

Bring a large pot of lightly salted water to a boil. Add the orzo and let simmer about 8 minutes, or until just tender but with a slight resistance to the bite. Drain.

Meanwhile mix the oil, salt, pepper, and rosemary in a medium bowl. Add the drained orzo and toss well. Sprinkle with the cheese, toss, and serve.

YIELD: 4 servings as a side dish; 2 as a main dish
PER SERVING: 261 calories, 11 g protein, 7 g fat, 38 g carbohydrate, 190 mg sodium, 8 mg cholesterol

Labor Pizza

Preparation time: 20 to 25 minutes
Cooking time: 15 minutes

I was lucky enough to be invited to a home birth a few summers ago. Things were moving along at a good, steady pace, but it was getting late. The midwife was hungry, so I went into action and created this pizza, using prepared pizza dough from the supermarket and gathering everything I could find in my friend's refrigerator. This recipe is in honor of Linden Indigo Towle, who was born just an hour after the pizza was consumed.

1½ cups grated Parmesan, Romano, or mozzarella cheese or a combination of cheeses
1 prepared pizza dough
1 tablespoon chopped fresh thyme or 1 teaspoon dried
Salt and freshly ground black pepper
10 ounces fresh spinach, stemmed
1 tablespoon plus 1 teaspoon olive oil
2 cloves garlic, chopped
1 large red bell pepper, cut into thin slices
1 tablespoon chopped fresh parsley
1 tablespoon butter
1 cup chopped walnuts
¾ cup homemade or canned tomato sauce

Preheat the oven to 400 degrees. Sprinkle ½ cup of the cheese on the pizza dough and sprinkle with the thyme, salt, and pepper.

Wash the spinach leaves well and place in a saucepan or skillet with the water still clinging to the leaves. Steam for about 4 minutes, or until wilted, and rinse under cold water. Drain and refresh under cold running water. With your hands, squeeze out all the excess water. Finely chop the spinach. Heat 1 tablespoon of the oil in a medium skillet, add the garlic, and sauté for about 30 seconds; add the spinach and salt and pepper. Place in a small bowl and set aside.

Heat the remaining teaspoon of oil in the skillet over moderate heat and add the pepper slices. Sauté for about 5 minutes, or until softened. Add the parsley and salt and pepper to taste. Place in a small bowl and set aside.

Heat the butter in the skillet over moderate heat. Add the walnuts and salt and pepper and cook about 3 minutes.

Place the spinach on the pizza shell and spoon the tomato sauce on top. Add the pepper strips and then the walnuts. Sprinkle on the remaining cheese and bake for 15 minutes, or until the cheese is golden brown and bubbling.

YIELD: 4 servings

PER SERVING: 734 calories, 22 g protein, 43 g fat, 63 g carbohydrate, 1,129 mg sodium, 31 mg cholesterol

---

SOME THOUGHTS ABOUT . . .
Quiche: The Revival of a Classic

Quiche, the classic French pie made with cheese, eggs, cream, and bacon, has fallen out of favor since its heyday in the 1970s. Partly that's because new food fads have taken over, but it is also because quiche is so rich and fatty. With today's low-fat dairy alternatives, however, this one-dish pie can make a healthy dinner choice. It's wholesome, delicious, and amazingly simple to prepare.

When made with a store-bought pie crust, in fact, most quiches take no more than 15 minutes to assemble. Just sauté the vegetables, beat the eggs, and pour everything into the crust. Quiche is *the* ideal meal for a busy workday: put it together in the morning; store it, unbaked, in the refrigerator; and cook it in time for dinner. It's also delicious served at room temperature.

Sister Sister Quiche

Preparation time: 15 minutes
Cooking time: 45 minutes

My daughters, Maya and Emma, created this creamy, fresh-tasting pie made with spinach, ham, and ricotta cheese. It's a great way to use up Easter ham (see recipe, page 270), or it can be made without any meat.

  10 ounces fresh spinach, stemmed
  2 large eggs
  1 cup diced cooked smoked ham
  2 cups low-fat ricotta cheese
  1 cup grated cheese (Cheddar, Monterey Jack, Parmesan, or other)
  Salt and freshly ground black pepper
  Pinch ground nutmeg
  1 prepared 9-inch pie crust

Wash the spinach and place in a large pot with the water still clinging to the leaves. Cook over high heat, stirring frequently, until soft and wilted, about 5 minutes. Drain and refresh under cold running water. With your hands, squeeze out all the excess water. Finely chop the spinach and set aside.

Meanwhile, in a large bowl, beat the eggs. Add the ham, ricotta, and grated cheese. Add just a pinch of salt (particularly if you are using salty ham) and a generous grinding of pepper. Add the nutmeg and the chopped cooked spinach.

Preheat the oven to 400 degrees. Spoon the mixture into the pie shell and bake for about 45 minutes, or until puffed and golden brown and a toothpick inserted in the middle comes out clean.

YIELD: 4 servings
PER SERVING: 616 calories, 37 g protein, 39 g fat, 30 g carbohydrate, 1,243 mg sodium, 194 mg cholesterol

Broccoli-Tomato-Cheddar Quiche

Preparation time: about 10 minutes
Cooking time: 50 to 60 minutes

If tomatoes are out of season, simply omit or replace with sun-dried tomatoes.

1½ **cups low-fat sour cream**
2 **large eggs, beaten**
1 **cup grated Cheddar cheese**
1 **tablespoon chopped fresh thyme or 1 teaspoon dried**
Salt and freshly ground black pepper
2 **cups bite-size pieces cooked broccoli**
1 **prepared 9-inch pie crust**
1 **cup thinly sliced cherry tomatoes or 1 large ripe tomato, thinly**
   sliced, or ½ cup chopped sun-dried tomatoes

If using sun-dried tomatoes, soak them in hot water for 5 minutes, drain, and dry thoroughly before chopping.

Preheat the oven to 350 degrees. In a large bowl, mix the sour cream, eggs, cheese, thyme, salt, and pepper. Gently stir in the broccoli.

Line the bottom of the crust with the tomatoes. Pour the broccoli mixture on top and bake for 50 to 60 minutes, or until a toothpick inserted in the center comes out clean.

YIELD: 4 to 6 servings
PER SERVING: 410 calories, 15 g protein, 27 g fat, 31 g carbohydrate, 443 mg sodium, 133 mg cholesterol

Zucchini-Pepper-Ricotta Quiche

Preparation time: about 10 minutes
Cooking time: 45 to 60 minutes

A fresh-tasting, creamy pie with the bright colors of summer.

1½ teaspoons vegetable oil
2 onions, thinly sliced
1 zucchini, cubed
1 green, red, or yellow bell pepper, cubed
2 large eggs, beaten
1 cup low-fat ricotta cheese
½ cup grated Parmesan cheese
½ cup grated mozzarella cheese
Salt and freshly ground black pepper
1 prepared 9-inch pie crust

Preheat the oven to 350 degrees. Heat the oil in a medium skillet over moderate heat. Add the onions and sauté for 5 minutes, stirring frequently to prevent burning. Add the zucchini and bell pepper and sauté another 3 minutes. Remove from the heat.

In a bowl, mix the eggs, cheeses, salt, and pepper. Stir in the vegetables and pour the mixture into the pie shell. Bake for 45 to 60 minutes, or until a toothpick inserted in the center comes out clean.

YIELD: 4 to 6 servings
PER SERVING: 367 calories, 18 g protein, 24 g fat, 23 g carbohydrate, 495 mg sodium, 108 mg cholesterol

Cheese and Red Pepper Frittata

Preparation time: about 20 minutes
Cooking time: 10 to 15 minutes

A cross between an omelette and a soufflé, this frittata can be made with any cheese or vegetable combination you like. Serve with baked potatoes or home fries and toast for a simple, quick dinner.

1½ teaspoons olive oil
1 onion, thinly sliced
8 to 10 thin strips red bell pepper, raw or roasted (see recipe, page 442)
1 tablespoon chopped fresh basil or 1 teaspoon dried
1½ teaspoons chopped fresh thyme or ½ teaspoon dried
5 large eggs
Salt and freshly ground black pepper
1 cup crumbled soft goat cheese or grated hard cheese

Preheat the oven to 400 degrees. In a medium ovenproof skillet or shallow casserole, heat the oil over moderate heat. Add the onion slices and sauté, stirring frequently, for about 8 minutes, or until golden brown. Add the pepper strips; if they are raw, sauté about 3 minutes; if they are roasted, sauté for only 1 minute. Add half the basil and thyme, remove the vegetables to a plate, and set aside.

Meanwhile, in a bowl whisk the eggs with the salt, pepper, and remaining basil and thyme.

Place the skillet or casserole over moderately high heat. Add the eggs and top with the sautéed vegetables. Sprinkle with the cheese and let cook 1 minute. Remove from the heat and place on the middle shelf of the preheated oven. Bake for about 10 to 15 minutes, or until puffed up and golden brown. Serve immediately.

YIELD: 4 servings
PER SERVING: 221 calories, 15 g protein, 15 g fat, 6 g carbohydrate, 205 mg sodium, 281 mg cholesterol

Basic Quesadillas

Preparation time: 5 minutes
Cooking time: about 3 to 4 minutes

A quesadilla is a corn or flour tortilla with melted cheese and a variety of other toppings. This is the basic recipe to which you can add any number of the toppings listed below. A quesadilla is great for a quick dinner, snack, or lunch, depending on how simple or fancy you make it. It's also an ideal dish to serve to kids or adults at a party.

2 corn or flour tortillas
**About ⅓ cup grated sharp Cheddar, Monterey Jack, or any hard
    cheese**

OPTIONAL TOPPINGS:
> **Sour cream**
> **Chopped pitted black olives**
> **Finely chopped fresh cilantro**
> **Salsa—hot, medium, or mild**
> **Chopped tomatoes**
> **Chopped cucumbers**
> **Finely chopped scallions**
> **Finely chopped ripe avocado**
> **Cooked black beans**
> **Caramelized onions**
> **Sautéed mushrooms and olives**
> **Grilled shrimp**
> **Cooked sausage slices**

Place a large skillet over moderate heat. If the skillet is large enough, cook both tortillas at the same time; if it is small, cook the tortillas one at a time. Add the tortillas and heat about 10 seconds. Flip the tortillas over and sprinkle each with half of the grated cheese. Heat, spinning the tortillas around every few seconds to prevent burning or sticking, until the cheese is completely melted, about 3 minutes. Add the toppings of your choice. You can either fold the tortillas in half or place one tortilla on top of the other and cut into quarters.

YIELD: 1 to 2 servings

PER SERVING: 131 calories, 6 g protein, 7 g fat, 12 g carbohydrate, 156 mg sodium, 20 mg cholesterol

Granny's Summer Rice Dish

Preparation time: 15 minutes
Cooking time: about 45 minutes

Here is a one-dish dinner that is ideal for a summer's night—and gives you a great way to use up summer's bounty. You can use any fresh vegetables you have on hand. Unlike a traditional risotto, which needs to be stirred constantly, this dish cooks virtually on its own. You can omit the sausage to make it a vegetarian dish.

1 tablespoon olive oil
2 cloves garlic, chopped
2 onions, chopped
½ pound linguica or Italian sausage, thinly sliced
1 green bell pepper, cut into thin strips
1 large zucchini, cut into thin strips
2 ripe tomatoes, cored and chopped
Salt and freshly ground black pepper
About ¼ teaspoon curry powder
1½ cups basmati or good-quality white rice
1 cup chicken broth
About ½ cup grated Parmesan cheese

In a large shallow casserole, heat the oil over moderate heat. Add the garlic and sauté for about 30 seconds, then add the onions and cook about 2 minutes. Add the sausage, bell pepper, zucchini, and tomatoes and cook, stirring, for 5 minutes. Add salt, pepper, and curry powder to taste. Add the rice, stirring constantly, and cook for 1 minute. Add the broth and let simmer, stirring occasionally, for about 20 minutes, or until the broth has been absorbed and the rice is tender. If the rice does not taste cooked, add ½ to 1 cup water and cook until the water is absorbed and the rice is tender. Taste for seasoning. Just before the rice is cooked, stir in ¼ cup of the cheese. Serve hot with the remaining cheese on the side.

YIELD: 4 servings
PER SERVING: 573 calories, 23 g protein, 26 g fat, 68 g carbohydrate, 892 mg sodium, 51 mg cholesterol

SOME THOUGHTS ABOUT . . .
A Primer on Rice

When our younger daughter was a preschooler, we took her to a Chinese restaurant for the first time. "Yuck! This food is weird," she protested loudly when the waiter brought our platters to the table. Then three little bowls of white rice arrived, shaped into perfect domes. "Ooh," she cried with delight, "I like that." Just about all kids do. Rice is one of the most neutral, soothing, appealing foods imaginable. It's also nutritious, packed with complex carbohydrates and minerals. According to the U.S. Rice Council, more than 40,000 varieties are grown worldwide. Fortunately, parents doing the grocery shopping only have to choose among a few of them.

• *White rice*: By far the most popular type sold in this country, white rice is processed by removing the grain's outer husk and the first few layers (the bran). The rice is then enriched with iron, niacin, and thiamine. Three varieties are available: long-grain cooks up dry and fluffy; medium-grain is shorter, moister, and more tender; short-grain is a wetter rice that holds together well, making it ideal for dishes like sushi. The advantages of all three types of white rice are their speedy cooking time (about 20 minutes) and their neutral taste and color. There's almost nothing white rice doesn't go with. (Partially cooked white rice, known as instant or quick rice, cooks in less than 5 minutes.)

• *Brown rice*: The least-processed form of rice, brown rice has all of its layers of bran intact; only the outer husk has been removed. As a result, it contains slightly more protein, calcium, and vitamin E and substantially more phosphorus and potassium than white rice. It also has a chewy texture and nutty flavor that are particularly appealing. The one drawback is that brown rice takes longer to cook, about 45 minutes. (A partially cooked quick version takes 15 minutes to prepare.)

• *Arborio rice*: A short, stubby grain grown in northern Italy, arborio has a creamy texture that makes it the rice of choice for risotto, a classic Italian dish.

• *Basmati rice*: A long-grain rice from Pakistan and India, basmati has a distinctive aromatic flavor and a dry, fluffy texture. It's often used in curry dishes.

Fried Rice with Chicken and Peanuts

Preparation time: 10 minutes
Cooking time: 10 minutes

The secret to making this classic Chinese dish is starting with room-temperature rice and sautéing it over very high heat in a well-seasoned wok or frying pan.

1 tablespoon safflower oil

1 tablespoon minced fresh ginger

3 scallions, finely chopped

½ cup chopped celery

1 cup thinly sliced cooked chicken, turkey, duck, pork, or beef

½ cup unsalted peanuts

2½ cups cooked white or brown rice, at room temperature

2 large eggs

1 teaspoon dark sesame oil, plus extra for serving

Soy sauce

In a wok or a large skillet, heat the safflower oil over high heat. Add half of the ginger and half of the scallions, and sauté for a few seconds. Add the celery and cook for 2 minutes, stirring. Mix in the chicken and the remaining ginger and scallions and stir-fry for another minute or two.

Add the peanuts and rice to the wok, being sure to break up any clumps, and stir-fry for 3 minutes, tossing constantly so that they don't burn or stick. In a small bowl, beat the eggs with 1 teaspoon of the sesame oil. Add the egg mixture to the wok and stir-fry for 2 to 3 minutes more, until the eggs are thoroughly cooked and blended into the rice. Serve with soy sauce and additional sesame oil on the side.

YIELD: 2 servings as a main course; 4 as a side dish

PER SERVING: 564 calories, 28 g protein, 25 g fat, 55 g carbohydrate, 107 mg sodium, 183 mg cholesterol

London Broil Burritos

Preparation time: 20 to 30 minutes
Cooking time: 20 to 30 minutes

London broil may be pricier than hamburger, but it's one of the leanest and tastiest cuts around. Rolled up with beans and garnishes, it makes a meal-size burrito.

1½ pounds London broil
1 clove garlic, finely chopped
Salt and freshly ground black pepper
1 tablespoon vegetable oil
1 onion, very thinly sliced
1½ cups refried beans
About 8 large flour or corn tortillas

GARNISHES:

1 cup salsa
1 cup shredded lettuce
1 cup grated Cheddar cheese
1 cup sour cream
1 ripe avocado, peeled, pitted, and thinly sliced
⅓ cup finely chopped fresh cilantro (optional)

Preheat the broiler. Place the meat on a broiler pan and rub the garlic, salt, and pepper on both sides. Let sit for 15 minutes before cooking.

Meanwhile, heat the oil in a medium skillet over moderate heat. Add the onion and sauté for 5 minutes. Add the beans and stir until heated through.

Place the meat under the preheated broiler. Broil for 6 to 7 minutes on each side for rare; about 8 to 10 minutes for medium to well-done. Let stand for 5 minutes before slicing thinly on the diagonal.

Meanwhile, in a large skillet over moderate heat, warm the tortillas about 1 minute on each side. Place the warm tortillas in a basket lined with a clean tea towel and cover them.

Place the sliced meat along with any juices on a serving platter. Surround the platter with small bowls filled with the garnishes. Let everyone assemble their own burritos.

YIELD: 4 to 8 servings

PER SERVING: 467 calories, 28 g protein, 21 g fat, 40 g carbohydrate, 757 mg sodium, 65 mg cholesterol

Stir-fried Steak Strips with Red Peppers and Cashews

Preparation time: about 10 minutes
Marinating time: 30 minutes to 24 hours
Cooking time: about 15 to 20 minutes

If you marinate the steak in the morning, you can put this dish together in very little time. Put on a pot of rice and dinner will be ready in under 30 minutes. Hoisin sauce is available at Asian markets and specialty food stores.

1 pound boneless steak, such as strip steak (also called Delmonico or New York cut)
3 tablespoons low-sodium soy sauce
1½ tablespoons mirin (Japanese rice wine), dry white wine, or sherry
1 tablespoon balsamic or red wine vinegar
2 tablespoons finely chopped fresh ginger or 2 teaspoons ground
1 tablespoon vegetable oil
2 cloves garlic, finely chopped
1 large red bell pepper, cut into thin strips
6 scallions, cut into 2-inch pieces
1 cup cashews, preferably unsalted
1½ tablespoons hoisin sauce
¼ cup water

Cut the steak into thin slices, trimming any excess fat. Place the meat in a bowl and cover with the soy sauce, mirin, vinegar, and 1 tablespoon of the ginger. Toss to make sure the meat is covered on both sides. Cover and let marinate for at least 30 minutes or refrigerate for up to 24 hours.

Remove the steak from the marinade, reserving the marinade.

In a wok or a large skillet, heat half the oil over high heat. Add half of the garlic, half of the remaining ginger, and all the steak strips. Cook, stirring constantly, for about 5 minutes. Remove the meat with a slotted spoon and set aside.

Put the remaining oil into the wok. Add the bell pepper, scallions, and remaining garlic and ginger and cook, stirring frequently, for about 4 minutes. Return the steak strips to the wok and cook another 2 to 3 minutes, or until the meat is cooked through and the vegetables are tender. Add the cashews during the last minute of cooking. Remove the mixture to a serving platter.

Add the hoisin sauce to the hot wok and stir in the reserved marinade and the water, stirring well to create a smooth sauce. Let simmer for about 3 minutes, or until thickened. Spoon the sauce over the meat and vegetables and serve immediately.

YIELD: 4 servings
PER SERVING: 334 calories, 28 g protein, 16 g fat, 16 g carbohydrate, 642 mg sodium, 69 mg cholesterol

Grilled Steaks Provençal Style

Preparation time: 10 minutes
Marinating time: 1 to 24 hours
Cooking time: 8 to 12 minutes

If you let the meat marinate for about an hour, it will be especially flavorful. New York steaks (also called strip or Delmonico) are particularly good with this recipe, but you can substitute your favorite cut. Serve with baked potatoes or pasta and a sliced tomato salad.

4 steaks, about 1½ inches thick (about 12 ounces each)
1 tablespoon olive oil
2 cloves garlic, finely chopped
2 teaspoons finely chopped fresh rosemary or 1 teaspoon dried
2 teaspoons finely chopped fresh basil or 1 teaspoon dried
2 teaspoons finely chopped fresh thyme or 1 teaspoon dried
Salt and freshly ground black pepper

Place the beef in a shallow dish and rub with the oil, garlic, and herbs. Cover and let marinate for 1 hour or refrigerate overnight.

Preheat the broiler or prepare a charcoal fire in an outdoor grill. Cook the steaks about 4 minutes on each side for rare; 6 minutes on each side for medium-well. Season with salt and pepper.

YIELD: 8 servings
PER SERVING: 313 calories, 32 g protein, 19 g fat, 0 g carbohydrate, 72 mg sodium, 103 mg cholesterol

Sautéed Steak with Caramelized Shallots in a Red Wine and Cream Sauce

Preparation time: 5 minutes
Marinating time: at least 5 minutes
Cooking time: about 25 minutes

A delicious way to prepare just about any cut of steak, this dish takes only about 30 minutes to prepare. Serve with baked white or sweet potatoes—or try the Roast Potatoes with Caramelized Pears on page 295—and green beans or spinach.

1 to 1½ pounds boneless steak, such as strip steak (also called Delmonico or New York cut), about 1 inch thick
3 teaspoons olive oil
1 teaspoon dried thyme
1 teaspoon dried rosemary
1 large or 2 small shallots, chopped
1 small onion, chopped
Salt and freshly ground black pepper
3 tablespoons red wine
2 tablespoons heavy cream

Place the meat on a plate and rub ½ teaspoon olive oil on each side. Rub the thyme and rosemary into the meat and let marinate until ready to cook—at least 5 minutes or up to an hour.

In a medium skillet, heat 1 teaspoon oil over moderately low heat. Add the shallots, onion, salt, and pepper and sauté about 8 minutes, stirring frequently to prevent browning. You want the shallots and onion to cook slowly and caramelize. Remove the shallots and onion and set aside.

In the same skillet over moderately high heat, sauté the steak in the remaining teaspoon of oil for about 5 minutes on each side for medium-rare. Remove the meat and set aside. Remove any excess grease from the pan and place over high heat. Add the wine and let simmer about 20 seconds. Add the cream and caramelized shallots and onion and let simmer about 3 minutes, or until thickened. Thinly slice the steak and spoon the sauce on top.

YIELD: 2 to 4 servings

PER SERVING: 350 calories, 41 g protein, 17 g fat, 5 g carbohydrate, 116 mg sodium, 129 mg cholesterol

Ma Po Dofu
(Spicy Sichuan-Style Tofu)

Preparation time: about 10 minutes
Cooking time: about 15 minutes

Ma Po Dofu is a traditional Chinese dish that combines ground meat and tofu in a ginger-spiced broth. The dish takes minutes to put together and can be seasoned to suit a variety of tastes. The first time you serve it, add the smaller amount of optional ingredients; if it goes over well, increase the amounts for a spicier version. Serve with steamed white or brown rice and top with chopped scallions. This is a very soothing one-dish dinner that even people who claim to hate tofu enjoy.

1 teaspoon vegetable or peanut oil
2 cloves garlic, finely chopped
1½ tablespoons chopped fresh ginger
6 scallions, very finely chopped
1 teaspoon to 1 tablespoon chopped fermented Chinese black beans
   (optional)
½ to 1 teaspoon Chinese chili paste (optional)
1 pound low-fat ground beef or turkey
2 tablespoons soy sauce
2 cups low-fat chicken broth or water
1 pound firm tofu, cut into small cubes
1 tablespoon cornstarch
2 to 3 tablespoons finely chopped fresh cilantro (optional)
4 cups steamed white or brown rice

In a wok or a large skillet, heat the oil over high heat. Add half of the garlic and ginger and a handful of scallions and stir-fry for about 30 seconds, stirring constantly to prevent burning. Add the black beans and chili paste if desired and then the meat. Stir frequently for about 5 minutes, or until the meat is almost cooked through. Add the soy sauce and chicken broth and bring to a boil. Gently slip the tofu into the wok along with the remaining garlic and ginger and another handful of scallions. Cover and let simmer about 3 minutes.

In a small cup or bowl, stir the cornstarch with a few tablespoons of hot broth from the wok. Slowly add the paste into the wok and let simmer about 2 minutes, or until the sauce is slightly thickened. Stir in 1 tablespoon of the cilantro if desired. Taste for seasoning. If you want a spicy stew, add more chili paste to taste.

Serve over steamed rice and sprinkle each bowl with the remaining scallions and cilantro.

YIELD: 4 servings

PER SERVING: 765 calories, 45 g protein, 36 g fat, 68 g carbohydrate, 1,105 mg sodium, 80 mg cholesterol

Stuffed Peppers

Preparation time: about 40 minutes
Cooking time: 30 to 45 minutes

A combination of ground turkey, rice, raisins, almonds, and cinnamon is stuffed into green or red bell peppers and then baked with a simple tomato sauce. You can choose to omit the ground turkey and make this a hearty vegetarian dish. This is one of those recipes that can be made completely ahead of time and reheated before serving.

1½ tablespoons olive oil
1 large onion, coarsely chopped
2 cloves garlic, chopped
1½ teaspoons ground cinnamon
1½ teaspoons dried thyme
½ pound ground turkey or beef
1 cup slivered almonds
½ cup raisins
2 cups cooked rice
1 cup homemade or canned tomato sauce
Salt and freshly ground black pepper
Dash hot pepper sauce (optional)
4 very large green or red bell peppers or 6 small to medium

Heat 1 tablespoon of the oil in a large skillet over moderate heat. Add the onion and garlic and sauté 5 minutes, or until soft but not brown. Add 1 teaspoon of the cinnamon and 1 teaspoon of the thyme and stir well. Add the ground turkey and cook, stirring frequently, about 10 minutes, or until the meat shows no sign of pinkness. Add the almonds and raisins and cook another minute. Remove from the heat and stir in the cooked rice, making sure to break up any clumps. Add ½ cup of the tomato sauce, the remaining ½ teaspoon of cinnamon and ½ teaspoon of thyme, and salt and pepper to taste. Add a few shakes of hot pepper sauce if desired.

Slice the tops off the peppers and remove the seeds and core. Place the peppers on a flat surface; if any of them don't sit flat, cut a thin slice off the bottom (making sure not to open up the bottom of the pepper).

Spread the remaining ½ tablespoon of oil on the bottom of a large casserole or a large ovenproof skillet. Using a spoon, press the stuffing into the peppers, pressing down to stuff as much filling into each pepper as possible. Place the peppers in the casserole or skillet and pour the remaining ½ cup tomato sauce on top. Cover. (The dish can be made to this point up to 24 hours ahead of time.)

Preheat the oven to 400 degrees. Bake the peppers for about 30 to 45 minutes, or until they are soft and the filling is hot throughout. Spoon the sauce over the peppers once or twice during the baking time.

YIELD: 4 to 6 servings
PER SERVING: 590 calories, 23 g protein, 28 g fat, 69 g carbohydrate, 435 mg sodium, 41 mg cholesterol

Meat Loaf

Preparation time: 15 minutes
Cooking time: 1 hour

Although meat loaf is usually made with ground beef, you can also make this recipe using half ground turkey or veal and half beef.

1 tablespoon butter or vegetable oil
1 cup finely chopped onion
1 large egg
Salt and freshly ground black pepper
½ teaspoon dried thyme or 1 teaspoon chopped fresh thyme
1 pound ground meat (see note above)
⅓ cup bread crumbs or rolled oats
¼ cup chopped nuts (optional)
1½ cups tomato sauce
1 bay leaf

Preheat the oven to 350 degrees. In a medium skillet, melt the butter over moderate heat. Add the onion and sauté until soft.

In a large bowl, mix the egg with the onion, salt, pepper, and thyme. Add the ground meat and stir well. Fold in the bread crumbs, nuts, and ½ cup of the tomato sauce. Form the mixture into a loaf and place it in a roasting pan. Cover with the rest of the tomato sauce and the bay leaf. Bake for 1 hour, basting occasionally.

YIELD: 4 to 6 servings
PER SERVING: 227 calories, 19 g protein, 11 g fat, 14 g carbohydrate, 627 mg sodium, 115 mg cholesterol

Salsa Burgers

Preparation time: 5 minutes
Cooking time: 6 to 10 minutes

Serve with warm tortillas and top with salsa, sour cream, and slices of ripe avocado.

1 pound ground chuck
¼ cup mild salsa
2 tablespoons sour cream or plain yogurt
½ teaspoon ground cumin (optional)

In a bowl, mix all the ingredients thoroughly. Form into 6 burgers and grill, broil, or sauté until cooked, about 3 to 5 minutes on each side for medium-rare.

YIELD: 6 small burgers
PER SERVING: 159 calories, 13 g protein, 11 g fat, 1 g carbohydrate, 104 mg sodium, 49 mg cholesterol

Greek-Style Lamb Burgers

Preparation time: about 5 minutes
Cooking time: about 12 minutes

Accompany with mint jelly, chutney, or catsup.

1 pound ground lamb
⅓ cup pine nuts or chopped almonds
¼ cup chopped fresh parsley
2 tablespoons plain low-fat yogurt
Salt and freshly ground black pepper
Crumbled feta cheese (optional)

In a large bowl, thoroughly mix all the ingredients except the feta. Divide the mixture into 6 burgers and grill, broil, or sauté about 6 minutes on each side. Crumble some feta cheese on top of each patty 1 minute before they're done.

YIELD: 6 small burgers
PER SERVING: 192 calories, 15 g protein, 14 g fat, 2 g carbohydrate, 47 mg sodium, 51 mg cholesterol

Garden Turkey Burgers

Preparation time: 5 minutes
Cooking time: about 8 to 12 minutes

Grated zucchini adds a touch of sweetness to these fresh-tasting patties.

1 pound ground turkey
2½ tablespoons grated onion
1 large egg yolk
1 teaspoon finely chopped garlic (optional)
⅓ cup grated zucchini
2 tablespoons bread crumbs
Salt and freshly ground black pepper

In a bowl, mix all the ingredients thoroughly. Divide into 6 burgers and grill, broil, or sauté until done, about 4 to 6 minutes on each side.

YIELD: 6 small burgers
PER SERVING: 147 calories, 14 g protein, 9 g fat, 2 g carbohydrate, 63 mg sodium, 74 mg cholesterol

Asian Turkey Burgers

Preparation time: 5 minutes
Cooking time: 8 to 12 minutes

Top with slices of red bell pepper and serve with hoisin sauce, tamari, or low-sodium soy sauce.

    1 **pound ground turkey**
    1½ **teaspoons grated fresh ginger or ½ teaspoon ground**
    2 **tablespoons finely chopped red bell pepper**
    2 **tablespoons finely chopped scallions**
    2 **tablespoons low-sodium soy sauce or tamari**
    1 **teaspoon dark sesame oil**

In a large bowl, mix all the ingredients thoroughly. Form into 6 burgers and grill, barbecue, or sauté until cooked, about 4 to 6 minutes on each side.

YIELD: 6 small burgers
PER SERVING: 137 calories, 14 g protein, 8 g fat, 1 g carbohydrate, 176 mg sodium, 38 mg cholesterol

Maya's Chicken Fingers with
Two Dips

Preparation time: 15 minutes
Cooking time: 16 minutes

The chicken for this wonderful kid's favorite is baked instead of fried, so it's fairly low in fat and not too greasy (but keep some napkins on hand, just in case). Children will also love the salsa and barbecue dips—one is savory, the other sweet.

2 whole skinless, boneless 16-ounce chicken breasts
2 large eggs, lightly beaten
2 tablespoons low-fat milk
Salt and freshly ground black pepper
1½ cups plain or seasoned bread crumbs

SALSA DIP:
1 cup low-fat sour cream or plain yogurt
3 to 5 tablespoons mild salsa
1 tablespoon lime juice (optional)

BARBECUE DIP:
½ cup catsup
2 tablespoons honey or maple syrup
½ teaspoon ground cinnamon
Pinch nutmeg
Dash hot pepper sauce (optional)

Preheat the oven to 400 degrees. Cut the chicken into thin, finger-size strips.

In a small bowl, beat the eggs, milk, salt, and pepper. Add the chicken strips and let them soak for about 5 minutes. Place the bread crumbs on a plate. Lightly dredge the chicken in the bread crumbs.

Place the chicken strips on an ungreased baking sheet and bake for 8 minutes, until golden brown. Remove from the oven and flip over. Bake another 8 minutes, until golden brown on this side as well. (If you have cut them very thin, they may need to cook for only 12 to 14 minutes total.) Serve hot or at room temperature.

To make the salsa dip, in a small bowl, mix the sour cream or yogurt with the salsa and lime juice if using. Taste and add more salsa if needed.

To make the barbecue dip, in a small bowl, mix the catsup, honey, cinnamon, nutmeg, and hot pepper sauce if using. Taste and add more spices or hot sauce if needed. Serve cold or at room temperature.

YIELD: 4 to 6 servings

PER SERVING: 376 calories, 31 g protein, 8 g fat, 45 g carbohydrate, 830 mg sodium, 156 mg cholesterol

Chicken Satay

Preparation time: 35 minutes
Marinating time: 30 minutes or more
Cooking time: 10 minutes

Satay, or barbecue, is popular throughout Southeast Asia. This one features chicken and a peanut butter sauce.

4 whole skinless, boneless 16-ounce chicken breasts, cut into 2-inch-wide strips
⅓ cup soy sauce
¼ cup lemon juice

SAUCE:

1 cup chunky peanut butter
1 large clove garlic, finely chopped
2 tablespoons sugar
5 tablespoons fresh lemon or lime juice
5 tablespoons soy sauce or tamari
3 tablespoons peanut or vegetable oil
¼ cup water
Hot pepper sauce (optional)

Place the chicken, soy sauce, and lemon juice in a large bowl, cover, and let marinate at least 30 minutes or overnight in the refrigerator.

Meanwhile, prepare the sauce. Mix together the peanut butter, garlic, and 1 tablespoon of the sugar. Stir in the lemon or lime juice, soy sauce or tamari, oil, and water and blend until smooth. Taste and add the remaining sugar and hot pepper sauce if desired.

Preheat the broiler or prepare a charcoal fire in an outdoor grill. If you are using wooden skewers, soak them in cold water for 15 minutes. Place the chicken strips on skewers and broil or grill about 5 minutes on each side, or until cooked through. Serve hot with the sauce on the side.

YIELD: 6 servings
PER SERVING: 471 calories, 38 g protein, 30 g fat, 17 g carbohydrate, 1,608 mg sodium, 66 mg cholesterol

Broiled Chicken

Preparation time: 5 minutes
Cooking time: about 30 minutes

Sometimes there is nothing more satisfying than broiled chicken. This is a dish my kids beg for time and time again. The chicken can be made from start to finish in about 30 minutes. If you make a pot of rice and steam some green beans while the chicken is broiling, you'll have dinner ready in no time.

1 chicken (3 to 3½ pounds), cut into small serving pieces
¼ cup low-sodium soy sauce
¼ cup balsamic vinegar
1 tablespoon chopped garlic
Dash hot pepper sauce (optional)
1 tablespoon flour
½ cup chicken broth or water

Preheat the broiler. Place the chicken, skin side up, in a large cast-iron skillet or broiler tray and sprinkle with the soy sauce, vinegar, garlic, and hot pepper sauce if using. Broil for 10 minutes about 6 inches from the flame. Flip the chicken pieces and broil for another 10 minutes. Turn the chicken again and broil for 5 to 10 minutes, or until the skin is crisp and the chicken is cooked through.

Remove the chicken to a warm platter and place the skillet or tray on the stove over moderate heat. Skim off any excess fat. Stir the flour into the remaining juices to create a thick paste, and cook for about 1 minute. Slowly pour in the broth or water, whisking to create a smooth gravy. Let the gravy simmer for 3 to 5 minutes, or until flavorful. Season to taste and serve over the hot chicken.

YIELD: 4 servings
PER SERVING: 414 calories, 46 g protein, 22 g fat, 4 g carbohydrate, 859 mg sodium, 143 mg cholesterol

Roast Chicken with Zucchini and Peppers

Preparation time: about 15 minutes
Cooking time: about 1 hour 15 minutes

The chicken in this simple dish is surrounded by spears of zucchini, strips of red peppers, and small new potatoes, and roasted until golden brown. The whole dish can be made in a little over an hour, and there's only one dish to clean at the end of the night.

1 chicken (2½ to 3 pounds)
1 lemon
2 zucchini, cut lengthwise into quarters
2 red or green bell peppers, cored and cut into thick slices
12 small new potatoes
6 cloves garlic, peeled and left whole (optional)
Salt and freshly ground black pepper
About ½ cup dry red or white wine

Preheat the oven to 425 degrees. Remove any excess fat from the chicken, particularly at the opening of the cavity. Cut an *X* in the side of the lemon and place it inside the cavity. Place the chicken in a large casserole and surround it with the zucchini, peppers, potatoes, and garlic if using. Sprinkle everything generously with salt and pepper. Pour the wine over the bird and roast for 15 minutes.

Reduce the temperature to 350 degrees and roast another 45 minutes to an hour, basting the bird every 15 minutes or so. Roast until tender, or until the juices run yellow, not pink, when a thigh is pierced with a small sharp knife. Remove the lemon and serve the chicken thinly sliced, accompanied by the potatoes and vegetables.

YIELD: 4 servings
PER SERVING: 594 calories, 44 g protein, 32 g fat, 31 g carbohydrate, 162 mg sodium, 159 mg cholesterol

Tomato-Chicken Stew

Preparation time: 20 minutes
Cooking time: about 20 minutes

Parenting *Executive Editor Bruce Raskin contributed this recipe—ideal for putting together a last-minute meal. "The original recipe called for veal," he reports, "but when our kids stopped eating red meat, we substituted chicken—and it tastes just as good."*

Double the recipe and refrigerate or freeze the extra; it is equally delicious the second time around. Serve over rice.

2 whole skinless, boneless 16-ounce chicken breasts, split

½ cup flour

¼ teaspoon each salt, freshly ground black pepper, onion powder, and paprika

1 tablespoon vegetable oil

1 onion, chopped

1 green bell pepper, cored and chopped

1 cup canned or homemade tomato sauce

½ to 1 cup chicken stock or white wine

Cut the chicken into 1-inch cubes and pound until tender. Place the flour on a large plate and mix in the salt, pepper, onion powder, and paprika. Dredge the chicken pieces in the seasoned flour.

In a medium skillet or a shallow flameproof casserole, heat the oil over moderate heat. Add the onion and green pepper and sauté for about 5 minutes, or until the onion is soft. Remove the vegetables from the skillet and set aside.

Add the chicken to the skillet and brown on both sides. Return the vegetables to the skillet and pour the tomato sauce over everything. Add the stock, cover, and simmer until tender, approximately 10 to 15 minutes.

YIELD: 4 servings

PER SERVING: 253 calories, 31 g protein, 5 g fat, 19 g carbohydrate, 741 mg sodium, 68 mg cholesterol

Sour Cream and Salsa Chicken

Preparation time: 2 minutes
Cooking time: 20 to 25 minutes

"My husband and I whip this dish together when we're tired but want a proper meal," says *Leah Hennen, Associate Editor at* Parenting. *"We invented the sauce as a homemade equivalent to premade sauces, and now it's a standard at our house."* Serve on a bed of rice or pasta.

1½ teaspoons vegetable oil
4 skinless, boneless chicken breast halves
½ cup homemade (see page 444) or bottled salsa
½ cup low-fat sour cream
Salt and freshly ground black pepper

In a large skillet, heat the oil over moderate heat. Add the chicken and cook until browned, about 3 to 4 minutes on each side. While the chicken cooks, mix together the salsa and sour cream. Pour over the chicken, reduce the heat, and simmer for about 10 to 15 minutes, turning the chicken once. Add salt and pepper to taste.

YIELD: 4 servings
PER SERVING: 190 calories, 28 g protein, 5 g fat, 6 g carbohydrate, 427 mg sodium, 78 mg cholesterol

Honey-Glazed Chicken Wings

Preparation time: 5 minutes
Marinating time: 5 hours or overnight
Cooking time: about 16 minutes

You'll have enough sauce to coat 16 chicken wings or a 3-pound chicken cut into pieces. Marinate the chicken in the morning before you leave for work and you can cook it in no time once you get home.

16 chicken wings
½ cup soy sauce
½ cup honey
Juice of 2 lemons

Place the chicken pieces in a shallow pan. Mix all of the remaining ingredients in a medium bowl and pour over the chicken, turning several times to coat. Cover and refrigerate for at least 5 hours or overnight.

Preheat the broiler or prepare a charcoal fire in an outdoor grill. Broil or grill the chicken for about 10 minutes on each side.

YIELD: 4 servings
PER SERVING: 293 calories, 21 g protein, 15 g fat, 20 g carbohydrate, 1,091 mg sodium, 63 mg cholesterol

Seafood Shish Kebabs

Preparation time: 30 minutes
Marinating time: 10 minutes to several hours
Cooking time: 6 to 10 minutes

You can marinate the fish and shellfish before you leave for work in the morning, and you'll have thoroughly tender shish kebabs for dinner. However, this is one of the few cases where the dish is equally good if you marinate the seafood for only about 10 minutes. Serve with lemon or lime wedges, rice, a large green salad, and rolls or a warm loaf of French bread.

MARINADE:
> ⅓ **cup olive oil**
> **Juice of 1 large lemon**
> ¼ **cup dry sherry or white wine**
> **1 tablespoon white wine vinegar**

> **12 medium shrimp, peeled and deveined**
> **6 large sea scallops, cut in half horizontally, or 12 bay scallops left whole**
> **1 pound swordfish, haddock, or other firm-fleshed fish, cut into small cubes about the size of the scallops**
> **1 zucchini, thinly sliced**
> **1 red or green bell pepper, cut into thin strips**
> **Fresh basil (optional)**

In a small bowl, mix all the ingredients for the marinade. Place the shrimp, scallops, and swordfish in a large bowl, pour the marinade on top, and turn gently. Let marinate for at least 10 minutes, or cover and refrigerate for several hours.

Preheat the broiler or prepare a charcoal fire in an outdoor grill. Divide the seafood and vegetables among 6 large skewers, placing a leaf of fresh basil, if desired, next to each piece of scallop. Broil or grill for about 3 to 5 minutes on each side, depending on the thickness of the fish, brushing with the marinade. Test with a fork; the seafood and vegetables should be tender, and the shrimp pink.

YIELD: 6 servings

PER SERVING: 195 calories, 22 g protein, 10 g fat, 3 g carbohydrate, 123 mg sodium, 59 mg cholesterol

Grilled Fish Steak

Preparation time: 5 minutes
Marinating time: 5 hours, or overnight
Cooking time: 8 to 10 minutes

Swordfish is ideal for this dish, but any firm-fleshed fish, such as salmon, halibut, or tuna, will work. If you marinate the fish in the morning, the dish will take under 15 minutes to put together.

1 pound fresh swordfish steak, about 1 inch thick
¼ cup fresh lemon or lime juice
2 tablespoons olive oil
Coarsely ground black pepper
1 lemon or lime, cut into wedges

Place the swordfish in a shallow baking dish. Pour the lemon juice and olive oil on top and sprinkle with the pepper. Turn to coat the fish thoroughly. Let marinate, covered and refrigerated, for at least 5 hours or overnight.

Preheat the broiler or prepare a charcoal fire in an outdoor grill. Remove the fish from the marinade and place under the broiler or on the grill for about 4 to 6 minutes on each side, until the center is opaque, brushing with the marinade. Be careful not to overcook. Serve with lemon or lime wedges.

YIELD: 2 to 4 servings

PER SERVING: 205 calories, 27 g protein, 10 g fat, 1 g carbohydrate, 121 mg sodium, 53 mg cholesterol

Fish Cakes

Preparation time: about 5 to 10 minutes
Cooking time: 8 minutes

Any variety of fish will do—cod, flounder, bluefish, or snapper, for example. The fish and potatoes must be precooked, so plan accordingly. Serve with lemon wedges, tartar sauce, and hot sauce if desired.

1 pound cooked fish
2 cooked potatoes, peeled
2 large eggs
1½ tablespoons chopped fresh parsley
1 tablespoon Dijon mustard
2 teaspoons grated fresh ginger or 1 teaspoon ground
Salt and freshly ground black pepper
1 cup cornmeal

In a bowl, mash the fish and potatoes together with a fork. Add all the remaining ingredients except the cornmeal and mix well.

Place the cornmeal on a plate. Divide the mixture into 8 small patties. Coat each patty thoroughly with the cornmeal and grill, broil, or sauté about 4 minutes on each side.

YIELD: 8 small fish cakes
PER SERVING: 173 calories, 17 g protein, 2 g fat, 21 g carbohydrate, 119 mg sodium, 84 mg cholesterol

Grilled Swordfish with Buttermilk-Thyme Sauce

Preparation time: about 8 minutes
Marinating time: 15 minutes or more
Cooking time: 15 to 20 minutes

Years ago I discovered that marinating swordfish in milk tenderizes it and creates a creamy sauce. In this dish I decided to try buttermilk and top the fish with thin slices of scallions and fresh thyme. The result is a deliciously moist treat. For very young children, you may want to omit the scallions. Serve with rice or mashed potatoes and a steamed green vegetable.

1½ **pounds swordfish steak**
½ **cup buttermilk**
½ **cup very thinly sliced scallions**
1½ **teaspoons chopped fresh thyme or** ½ **teaspoon dried**
Freshly ground black pepper
1 lemon, cut into wedges

Place the fish in a flameproof shallow casserole or baking pan. Pour the buttermilk on top and let marinate at least 15 minutes or cover and refrigerate for up to 24 hours.

Preheat the oven to 400 degrees. Sprinkle the scallions, thyme, and pepper on the fish and bake for 10 minutes. Place the fish under the broiler and broil for 5 to 10 minutes, depending on the thickness of the fish, or until tender when tested with a fork. Serve hot with lemon wedges.

YIELD: 3 to 4 servings
PER SERVING: 228 calories, 35 g protein, 7 g fat, 5 g carbohydrate, 188 mg sodium, 68 mg cholesterol

Baked Swordfish with a Spinach Glaze

Preparation time: 15 to 20 minutes
Marinating time: 15 minutes or more
Cooking time: 15 to 17 minutes

The swordfish is topped with a garlicky spinach topping and then baked until tender. Serve with boiled or baked potatoes and roasted red peppers for a colorful presentation.

1 pound swordfish steak
¾ cup low-fat milk
1 pound fresh spinach, stemmed
1 teaspoon olive oil
1 clove garlic, finely chopped
Salt and freshly ground black pepper
1 lemon, cut into wedges

Place the swordfish in a flameproof shallow casserole or baking pan and pour the milk on top. Let marinate for at least 15 minutes or cover and refrigerate for up to several hours.

Meanwhile, wash the spinach and place in a large pot. Steam over high heat with the water still clinging to the leaves, about 4 to 5 minutes, or until tender. Drain and refresh under cold water. With your hands, squeeze out all the excess water. Finely chop the spinach.

In a medium skillet, heat the oil over moderate heat. Add the garlic and sauté about 10 seconds. Add the chopped spinach, salt, and pepper and cook, stirring, about 3 minutes. (The recipe can be made several hours ahead of time up to this point.)

Preheat the oven to 400 degrees. Spoon the spinach over the swordfish and bake for about 10 to 12 minutes, or until almost tender. Place under the broiler and broil about 5 minutes, or until tender. Serve with lemon wedges.

Yield: 4 servings
Per serving: 186 calories, 26 g protein, 6 g fat, 5 g carbohydrate, 190 mg sodium, 46 mg cholesterol

Mediterranean Salmon

Preparation time: 10 minutes
Cooking time: about 15 minutes

This dish is elegant enough for any dinner party, yet so simple it can be put together for Tuesday night's dinner. The salmon fillets are baked with the flavors of the Mediterranean—garlic, onion, fresh lemon juice, and olive oil. Capers and roasted red pepper strips are then placed on top of the fish, and just before serving, a touch of heavy cream is added to the bottom of the dish to make a simple sauce. Serve with boiled new potatoes and a sautéed green vegetable.

1½ teaspoons olive oil
1 pound salmon fillets
1 clove garlic, very thinly sliced
2 tablespoons very finely chopped onion
Juice of 1 lemon
Freshly ground black pepper
2 tablespoons capers, drained
8 strips roasted red or yellow pepper (see recipe, page 442) or
**   pimiento, drained**
¼ to ⅓ cup heavy cream
1 lemon, cut into wedges

Preheat the oven to 400 degrees. Place 1 teaspoon of the oil in the bottom of a flame-proof shallow casserole or baking pan. Add the salmon. Gently insert the garlic slices into the fish and sprinkle the top with the onion. Pour the remaining olive oil and the lemon juice on top and sprinkle with pepper.

Bake the fish for 10 minutes. Place the capers and pepper strips on the fish and pour the cream on top. Bake another 5 minutes, then place under the broiler until golden brown and bubbling. Serve with lemon wedges.

Yield: 4 servings
Per serving: 269 calories, 23 g protein, 17 g fat, 6 g carbohydrate, 184 mg sodium, 86 mg cholesterol

Sole with Sautéed Almonds and Lime

Preparation time: 5 minutes
Cooking time: 15 minutes

The fish is sautéed and then topped with crunchy almond slivers and a squeeze of lime juice.

Flour for dredging (about 1 cup)
¼ teaspoon salt
⅛ teaspoon freshly ground black pepper
1½ pounds sole or flounder fillets (about 4 to 6 fillets)
1 tablespoon safflower or vegetable oil
1 tablespoon butter
½ cup slivered almonds
1½ tablespoons lime juice
1 lime, cut into wedges

Place the flour on a large plate and mix in the salt and pepper. Lightly dredge both sides of the fish fillets in the seasoned flour, then shake the fillets to make sure only a small bit of flour adheres.

In a large nonstick skillet, heat the oil over moderately high heat. Working in batches, sauté the fillets for about 3 minutes on each side, or until golden brown and cooked through. Keep the fillets warm on a plate or serving platter loosely covered with foil while sautéing the remaining fish; add more oil if needed.

Add the butter to the skillet and sauté the almonds over moderate heat for about 3 minutes, stirring constantly. Pour the lime juice over the nuts and simmer for 1 minute. Sprinkle the almonds on top of the sole and serve with the lime wedges.

YIELD: 4 to 6 servings
PER SERVING: 354 calories, 37 g protein, 17 g fat, 13 g carbohydrate, 213 mg sodium, 89 mg cholesterol

Broiled Scallops with Basil and Lemon

Preparation time: 10 minutes
Cooking time: about 7 minutes

Serve with rice and lemon wedges.

1½ tablespoons olive oil
1 pound bay scallops
2 cloves garlic, chopped
2 tablespoons thinly shredded fresh basil
Salt and freshly ground black pepper
Sweet Hungarian paprika
¼ cup bread crumbs
1 tablespoon grated lemon zest

Preheat the broiler. Place ½ tablespoon of the oil in a flameproof gratin dish, baking pan, or pie plate. Add the scallops, garlic, basil, salt, pepper, and a generous pinch of paprika and mix. Drizzle with the remaining oil.

Broil the scallops for 5 minutes. Mix the bread crumbs and lemon zest and sprinkle over the scallops. Broil another 2 minutes, or until cooked through and tender.

YIELD: 4 servings
PER SERVING: 175 calories, 20 g protein, 6 g fat, 8 g carbohydrate, 241 mg sodium, 37 mg cholesterol

Broiled Shrimp with Coconut-Lime Marinade

Preparation time: 5 minutes if using canned coconut milk
and 15 minutes if using a fresh coconut
Cooking time: about 5 minutes

Fresh coconut milk is obtained by cracking open a fresh coconut or by using a hammer and screwdriver to pierce a hole in it and drain the juice. Pour the milk through a sieve to remove any debris. Or substitute canned unsweetened coconut milk. Serve the shrimp with steamed white rice, lime wedges, and the Pineapple Salsa on page 446.

1 pound large shrimp
2 cloves garlic, finely chopped
¾ cup fresh coconut milk
1 teaspoon olive oil
Juice of 1 large or 2 medium limes
2 scallions, very finely chopped (both white and green parts)

Place the shrimp in a large bowl. Add the remaining ingredients and toss well to thoroughly coat the shrimp.

Preheat the broiler or prepare a charcoal fire in an outdoor grill. Place the shrimp and marinade in a shallow broiler pan or, if you are grilling, in a double thickness of aluminum foil. Broil or grill for about 2 to 3 minutes, or until pink. Flip over and grill another 2 minutes, until pink, firm, and cooked throughout. Serve hot in shell or peeled.

YIELD: 2 to 4 servings
PER SERVING: 139 calories, 25 g protein, 3 g fat, 2 g carbohydrate, 198 mg sodium, 186 mg cholesterol

Baked Potato Wedges with Dipping Sauce

Preparation time: 5 minutes
Cooking time: 40 minutes

Large baking potatoes are cut into thick wedges, tossed with olive oil, salt, pepper, and paprika, and baked until crisp and brown. These wedges make ideal party food, particularly when they're served with the salsa sour cream. They also make a great quick dinner served with thin cucumber slices. Make extra—they tend to disappear quickly.

4 large baking potatoes, each cut into 6 wedges
2½ tablespoons olive oil
Salt and freshly ground black pepper
Sweet Hungarian paprika
Dried herbs, such as basil, thyme, oregano, sage, or rosemary (optional)
Salsa Dipping Sauce (see recipe, page 445) (optional)

Preheat the oven to 400 degrees. Place the potato wedges in a bowl and pour the olive oil over them. Toss well to coat all sides thoroughly. Place the greased potatoes on a baking sheet, baking tray, or very shallow casserole, skin side down. Sprinkle liberally with the salt, pepper, paprika, and herbs if using.

Bake the potatoes for 30 minutes. Remove from the oven and turn over so the skin side is up. Season with more salt, pepper, paprika, and herbs and bake another 5 minutes. Remove from the oven, flip them over again, and bake another 5 minutes, or until the potatoes are well browned and tender throughout. Serve hot with the salsa dipping sauce.

YIELD: 6 servings
PER SERVING: 188 calories, 3 g protein, 6 g fat, 32 g carbohydrate, 10 mg sodium, 0 mg cholesterol

Baked Potatoes with Broccoli-Cheese Topping

Preparation time: 20 minutes
Cooking time: 45 to 60 minutes, depending on the size of the potatoes

Give kids their own baked potato topped with a broccoli and cheese sauce, then let them spoon on their own choice of toppings. Cook the potatoes ahead of time and then heat them up in a low oven until warm.

By inserting a metal skewer through the potatoes, you can speed up the cooking time by at least 20 minutes, making this an easy weeknight supper. Or start the potatoes in a microwave oven for 10 minutes, then finish them in the oven for about 30 minutes.

6 medium-sized baking potatoes
1 head broccoli, cut into small florets
1 tablespoon butter or margarine
1 tablespoon flour
1 cup low-fat milk
Salt and freshly ground black pepper
½ cup grated mild cheese

TOPPINGS:
About 1 cup finely chopped scallions or chives
1 cup low-fat sour cream
1 cup chopped walnuts
1 cup chopped fresh tomatoes

Preheat the oven to 350 degrees. Pierce the potatoes with a sharp knife in one or two spots and place on a baking sheet. Bake for about 45 to 60 minutes, depending on the size, or until tender when tested with a fork.

Meanwhile, in a saucepan fitted with a steaming basket, steam the broccoli over moderate heat until just tender, about 3 to 5 minutes; be careful not to overcook. Drain and set aside.

To make the cheese sauce, melt the butter in a medium saucepan over moderate heat. Stir in the flour and cook for about a minute, whisking constantly. Slowly add the milk and whisk until smooth and thick. Let the sauce come to a gentle simmer, then add salt and pepper to taste. Remove from the heat and stir in the grated cheese. Once the cheese is melted, add the broccoli.

To serve, cut the potatoes in half. Place a half or whole potato on a serving plate and top with the sauce. Put the toppings in small bowls and let everyone help themselves.

YIELD: 6 servings

PER SERVING: 274 calories, 10 g protein, 6 g fat, 47 g carbohydrate, 141 mg sodium, 17 mg cholesterol

Potato Pie

Preparation time: 15 minutes
Cooking time: 45 to 60 minutes

A cross between a quiche and a creamy, layered potato dish, this pie can be served as a main course or as a side dish with roasts and grilled chops.

3 large baking potatoes, peeled and thinly sliced
1 prepared 9-inch pie crust
¾ cup grated Swiss, Gruyère, Cheddar, or Parmesan cheese
1 large egg
1½ cups low-fat milk
1 tablespoon chopped fresh thyme or basil or 1 teaspoon dried
Salt and freshly ground black pepper

Preheat the oven to 350 degrees. Layer the potatoes in the crust, sprinkling the cheese between the layers. In a bowl, mix the egg, milk, thyme, salt, and pepper. Pour the egg mixture over the potatoes and cheese and bake for 45 to 60 minutes, or until the potatoes are tender and golden brown.

YIELD: 4 to 6 servings
PER SERVING: 371 calories, 13 g protein, 19 g fat, 39 g carbohydrate, 320 mg sodium, 61 mg cholesterol

Mexican Sweet Potato Tortillas

Preparation time: about 15 minutes
Cooking time: about 5 minutes

This unusual tortilla is a great way to use up leftover cooked sweet potatoes and turkey from a holiday feast. The filling is particularly popular with kids because the potato is so sweet. (If your leftovers have melted marshmallows or another topping, simply scrape off before proceeding.) Spread the potato mixture onto a warm tortilla and serve with a dollop of salsa and an assortment of fresh garnishes.

3 tablespoons olive oil
2 cooked large sweet potatoes, peeled and mashed (about 3 cups)
2 cups shredded cooked turkey
2 to 3 pickled jalapeño peppers or 1 fresh, chopped (optional)
Salt
8 corn tortillas
Salsa, bottled or homemade (see recipe, page 444)

GARNISHES:
Shredded lettuce
Chopped tomatoes
Grated cheese
Chopped onions

In a medium saucepan, heat the oil over moderately low heat. Add the mashed sweet potatoes, turkey, and half of the jalapeños if desired. Heat through and add salt to taste. If you want the mixture to be spicier, add the remaining jalapeños.

Heat the tortillas in a low oven for about 1 minute on each side, or until warm but not brittle. Spread some of the sweet potato mixture on each tortilla, roll it up, and serve with the salsa and garnishes.

YIELD: 4 to 8 servings
PER SERVING: 384 calories, 18 g protein, 10 g fat, 55 g carbohydrate, 110 mg sodium, 36 mg cholesterol

Garlic Cheese Bread

Preparation time: 10 minutes
Cooking time: 10 minutes

Use a good loaf of crusty French bread for this melt-in-your-mouth side dish.

3 tablespoons butter
2 cloves garlic, finely chopped
1 loaf French bread
½ cup grated Parmesan or other hard cheese

Preheat the oven to 400 degrees. Place the butter and garlic in a small skillet and heat over low heat for 5 minutes.

While the garlic is cooking, slice the bread thinly and, keeping the slices in order so that you can reassemble the loaf, place the bread on a large sheet of aluminum foil. Using a pastry brush or the back of a spoon, lightly spread the melted garlic butter on each slice of bread, then reassemble the loaf. Sprinkle the Parmesan cheese on top of the bread, wrap tightly in the foil, and bake for about 10 minutes, or until warmed through.

YIELD: 4 to 6 servings
PER SERVING: 435 calories, 14 g protein, 15 g fat, 60 g carbohydrate, 965 mg sodium, 31 mg cholesterol

Some Thoughts About . . .
Vegetable Pancakes

Pancakes offer a wonderful way to entice your children to eat vegetables. The logic is simple: kids are less likely to turn up their noses at a crispy little cake that happens to contain some grated beets than at the genuine, unadorned article. All kinds of vegetables can be worked into a pancake—from asparagus to zucchini. All you need to do is mix them with some flour, egg, and seasonings, and fry the pancakes in a minimum of oil (if the oil is hot enough, they will cook quickly and soak up less grease).

These recipes make 12 to 14 small pancakes, enough to serve as a side dish for a family of four. My children have come to love them so much that I often double the recipe and serve them as a main course, with a green salad and perhaps another vegetable on the side. Keep in mind that the batter for vegetable pancakes should be freshly mixed and cooked immediately. If it sits around too long, it can become watery and discolored. But if you get everything ready ahead of time, these pancakes can be put together at the last minute.

Beet Pancakes

Preparation time: 10 minutes
Cooking time: about 10 minutes (does not include cooking time for beets)

The bright pink color of these pancakes grabs kids' attention, and the naturally sweet taste hooks them. Try to find fresh dill for this recipe; it makes a big difference. The beets need to be cooked a day ahead of time.

3 large eggs
3 medium beets, cooked, peeled, and grated
½ cup flour
Pinch sugar
3 tablespoons finely chopped fresh dill or 1½ teaspoons dried
Salt and freshly ground black pepper
Vegetable oil
Sour cream

In a medium bowl, whisk the eggs. Mix in the grated beets, flour, sugar, dill, and salt and pepper to taste.

Heat about ¼ inch of oil in a large skillet over moderately high heat. For each pancake, place a heaping tablespoon of batter in the hot skillet. Use a spatula to press down on the batter to form flat pancakes, and cook about 1½ minutes on each side. Serve with sour cream.

YIELD: about 12 to 14 pancakes
PER SERVING: 204 calories, 7 g protein, 11 g fat, 19 g carbohydrate, 95 mg sodium, 159
   mg cholesterol

Carrot and Ginger Pancakes

Preparation time: about 10 minutes
Cooking time: about 10 minutes

Serve a bowl of plain low-fat yogurt on the side with these light, fresh-tasting pancakes.

3 large eggs
2¼ cups grated carrots
3 teaspoons grated fresh ginger or 1 teaspoon ground
¾ cup plus 2 tablespoons bread crumbs
Salt and freshly ground black pepper
Vegetable oil

In a medium bowl, whisk the eggs. Stir in the grated carrots, ginger, ¾ cup of the bread crumbs, and salt and pepper to taste. Add another tablespoon or two of bread crumbs as needed to hold the mixture together.

Heat ¼ inch of oil in a large skillet over moderately high heat until it is just starting to smoke. For each pancake, drop a heaping tablespoon of batter into the hot oil and flatten with a spatula. Cook about 1½ minutes on each side.

YIELD: about 12 to 14 pancakes
PER SERVING: 229 calories, 8 g protein, 12 g fat, 23 g carbohydrate, 230 mg sodium, 160 mg cholesterol

Chinese-Style Scallion Pancakes

Preparation time: 10 minutes
Cooking time: 5 to 10 minutes

Make a simple dipping sauce to serve with the pancakes by combining ½ cup soy sauce with 1 tablespoon grated ginger and 1 tablespoon chopped scallions.

3 large eggs
12 scallions, thinly sliced (both white and green parts)
1½ teaspoons dark sesame oil
1½ teaspoons soy sauce or tamari
¾ cup regular or coarsely ground cornmeal
Vegetable oil

Beat the eggs in a bowl. Add the scallions, sesame oil, soy sauce, and cornmeal.

Heat about ¼ inch of vegetable oil in a large skillet over moderately high heat. For each pancake, drop a heaping tablespoon of the batter into the hot oil, flatten with a spatula, and cook about 1½ minutes on each side.

YIELD: about 12 to 14 pancakes
PER SERVING: 178 calories, 8 g protein, 6 g fat, 23 g carbohydrate, 178 mg sodium, 160 mg cholesterol

Basic Baked Asparagus

Preparation time: 5 minutes
Cooking time: 12 to 25 minutes

Most cooks rely on blanching or steaming for best results, but baking asparagus has two advantages: the vegetable loses fewer vitamins, and it develops a distinctive smoky taste that's often lost when boiled or steamed. In fact, the taste is so rich that you and your kids may forgo adding butter. Serve plain or sprinkled with fresh lemon juice or grated Parmesan cheese.

1½ tablespoons olive oil
1 pound fresh asparagus, bottoms trimmed
1 large clove garlic (optional)
1 lemon, cut into wedges

Preheat the oven to 350 degrees. Pour 1 tablespoon of the oil into a shallow baking dish, casserole, or thick piece of aluminum foil. Add the asparagus and sprinkle with the garlic if desired and the remaining ½ tablespoon of oil. Cover tightly with foil and bake for 12 to 25 minutes, depending on the thickness of the asparagus, or until just tender. Serve with the lemon wedges.

YIELD: 4 servings
PER SERVING: 65 calories, 2 g protein, 5 g fat, 5 g carbohydrate, 2 mg sodium, 0 mg cholesterol

Plain and Simple Boiled Beans

Preparation time: 5 minutes
Cooking time: about 10 minutes

When beans are at their summer peak, there's no better way to serve them than boiled and buttered. If you want to avoid extra fat, you can replace the butter with about 1 tablespoon lemon juice.

1 pound beans, trimmed
About 2 tablespoons butter
Salt and freshly ground black pepper

Bring a pot of lightly salted water to boil. Add the beans and stir. Cook until tender, about 5 to 7 minutes, depending on the thickness. Drain and refresh under cold running water.

Heat the butter in a medium saucepan. Toss the beans in the butter, add salt and pepper to taste, and serve hot. If you want to use lemon juice, simply drain the beans and toss with lemon juice, salt, and pepper.

YIELD: 4 servings
PER SERVING: 82 calories, 2 g protein, 6 g fat, 7 g carbohydrate, 65 mg sodium, 16 mg cholesterol

Stir-fried Garlic Green Beans with Ground Turkey

Preparation time: 10 minutes
Cooking time: about 12 to 15 minutes

Quick and simple, this stir-fry can be served with white or brown rice.

1 teaspoon vegetable oil
1 to 2 cloves garlic, finely chopped
⅓ pound ground turkey or 2 sweet or hot sausages, thinly sliced
1 pound green beans, trimmed
About 1½ tablespoons soy sauce or tamari
About 1½ tablespoons water
Chinese chile paste (optional)

Heat the oil in a wok or large skillet over moderately high heat. Add the garlic and turkey or sausage and sauté about 5 minutes if using turkey and 10 minutes if using sausage; stir frequently to prevent burning. Add the beans and 1 tablespoon each of the soy sauce and water, and cook for about 3 minutes, or until the beans are just tender. They should still have a slight crunch to them. Add the remaining soy sauce and water if you want more sauce. Serve as is or add chile paste to taste.

YIELD: 4 servings
PER SERVING: 99 calories, 9 g protein, 4 g fat, 8 g carbohydrate, 427 mg sodium, 27 mg cholesterol

Beans in Curry Cream Sauce with Curried Almonds

Preparation time: 10 minutes
Cooking time: about 25 minutes

These richly flavored beans can be served as a main course with white rice or couscous, or as an accompaniment to pork chops, fish, or chicken.

2 tablespoons butter
½ cup slivered almonds
3 teaspoons curry powder
1 tablespoon vegetable oil
1 large onion, thinly sliced
2 teaspoons ground cumin
1 pound green or wax beans, trimmed
2 cups chicken broth
¼ cup heavy cream
Salt and freshly ground black pepper

In a small skillet, heat 1 tablespoon of the butter over moderate heat. Add the almonds and 1 teaspoon of the curry powder and sauté 4 minutes, stirring constantly to prevent burning. Drain the nuts on paper towels.

In another skillet or saucepan, heat the remaining tablespoon of butter and the oil over moderate heat. Add the onion and sauté about 4 minutes, stirring frequently. Stir in the remaining 2 teaspoons curry powder and the cumin and cook another minute. Add the beans and sauté 1 minute. Pour in the broth and let the mixture come to a boil. Reduce the heat, cover, and simmer until the beans are tender, about 8 minutes. Remove the beans with a slotted spoon, place on a warm plate, and cover loosely to keep warm.

Add the cream to the saucepan, raise the heat, and boil until reduced to about 1 cup, about 5 minutes. Add salt and pepper to taste. Pour over the beans and sprinkle with the almonds.

YIELD: 4 servings
PER SERVING: 308 calories, 8 g protein, 25 g fat, 17 g carbohydrate, 576 mg sodium, 36 mg cholesterol

Green Beans and Ham

Preparation time: 15 minutes
Cooking time: 10 minutes

In this colorful side dish, the ham adds a nice accent to the fresh flavors of the corn, green beans, and peppers without overwhelming them. You can easily omit the ham to make this a vegetarian dish.

½ pound green beans, trimmed and cut into ½-inch pieces
2 large ears corn or 1 package (10 ounces) frozen corn kernels
1½ tablespoons butter
3 shallots, chopped
½ green bell pepper, cored and diced
⅓ cup diced ham
1½ tablespoons chopped fresh thyme or 1 teaspoon dried
Freshly ground black pepper

In a saucepan fitted with a steaming basket, steam the beans for 3 minutes over moderate heat. Meanwhile, if you're using whole ears of corn, cut the kernels off the cob with a sharp knife. Add the corn to the basket and steam for 1 minute if using fresh, or 3 minutes if using frozen. Remove from the heat. Refresh the vegetables by rinsing them under cold running water, then drain.

In a medium skillet, melt 1 tablespoon of the butter over moderate heat. Add the shallots and sauté for about 2 to 3 minutes, stirring frequently. Add the green pepper, ham, and thyme and sauté for 2 minutes. Add the beans and corn and the remaining ½ tablespoon of butter and toss to warm. Transfer to a serving bowl and sprinkle with freshly ground pepper.

Yield: 2 servings as a main dish; 4 to 6 as a side dish
Per serving: 264 calories, 10 g protein, 13 g fat, 33 g carbohydrate, 425 mg sodium, 37 mg cholesterol

Marinated Green Beans

Preparation time: 10 minutes
Cooking time: 5 to 7 minutes
Marinating time: 30 minutes or up to 8 hours

Accompanied by a good loaf of bread, these beans make a light summer meal. Make the dish in the morning and let it marinate until dinnertime.

2 pounds string beans, trimmed
About ½ cup pitted black olives, preferably oil cured (if olives are
    large, cut in half)
1 teaspoon prepared mustard
1 tablespoon soy sauce
1 green or red bell pepper, cored and chopped
½ cup lemon juice
2 tablespoons chopped onion or scallions
2 tablespoons red wine vinegar
5 to 6 tablespoons olive oil
Salt and freshly ground black pepper

In a saucepan fitted with a steaming basket, steam the beans over moderate heat about 5 to 7 minutes, or until just tender but not limp. Refresh under cold running water and drain thoroughly. Dry with paper towels and arrange the beans and olives on a serving plate or in a bowl.

To make the vinaigrette, whisk together all the remaining ingredients and taste for seasoning. Pour on top of the beans and olives, cover, and refrigerate for at least 30 minutes and up to 8 hours before serving. Serve cold or at room temperature.

YIELD: 6 to 8 servings
PER SERVING: 147 calories, 2 g protein, 12 g fat, 10 g carbohydrate, 248 mg sodium, 0 mg
    cholesterol

Haricots Verts Provençal

Preparation time: 5 minutes
Cooking time: about 20 to 25 minutes

Look for the thinnest, freshest green beans you can find. This dish is delicious served hot, but it can also be served at room temperature mixed with a few teaspoons of vinaigrette. The fresh mint adds a fresh, bright flavor. These beans go particularly well with chicken and lamb dishes.

1 pound thin green beans (*haricots verts*), trimmed
1½ teaspoons olive oil
1 onion, very thinly sliced
1 clove garlic, chopped
Salt and freshly ground black pepper
1 ripe tomato, finely chopped
1 to 2 tablespoons finely chopped fresh mint (optional)

Bring a few inches of water to a boil in a large pot. Add the green beans and steam for about 3 to 5 minutes, depending on the thickness of the beans, or until *almost* tender. Drain and refresh under cold running water. Drain again.

In a large skillet, heat the oil over low heat. Add the onion and sauté for about 8 minutes, or until tender but not brown. Add the garlic, drained beans, and salt and pepper to taste. Raise the heat to moderate and sauté the beans, stirring constantly, for about 3 minutes. Add the tomato and sauté another 5 minutes, or until the tomato is warm but not completely broken down. Serve on a warm platter and sprinkle with the fresh mint if desired.

YIELD: 4 to 6 servings
PER SERVING: 56 calories, 2 g protein, 2 g fat, 10 g carbohydrate, 8 mg sodium, 0 mg cholesterol

White Beans Provençal

Preparation time: 10 minutes
Cooking time: 10 minutes

This simple recipe shows how to transform canned beans into a luscious, buttery dish. Serve with roast chicken, pork, or beef or as a main course accompanied by salad and crusty bread.

1 tablespoon olive oil
1 onion, finely chopped
1 clove garlic, finely chopped
2 cups canned white beans, rinsed and drained
1 ripe tomato, cored and cut into small cubes (optional)
1 teaspoon dried thyme or 1 tablespoon chopped fresh thyme
½ teaspoon crumbled dried rosemary or 1½ teaspoons chopped fresh
  rosemary
Salt and freshly ground black pepper
2 tablespoons dry white wine or water
⅓ cup finely chopped fresh parsley (optional)

In a large skillet, heat the olive oil over moderate heat. Add the onion and garlic and sauté for 5 minutes, stirring frequently to prevent browning. Add the beans, tomato, thyme, rosemary, salt, pepper, and white wine or water; simmer for 5 minutes. Sprinkle with the parsley if desired and serve hot.

YIELD: 4 servings
PER SERVING: 149 calories, 7 g protein, 4 g fat, 20 g carbohydrate, 265 mg sodium, 0 mg
  cholesterol

Corn Sauté

Preparation time: 5 to 10 minutes
Cooking time: about 10 minutes

It's hard to imagine ever getting tired of fresh corn on the cob, but by the middle of August many of us are looking for new ideas. In this simple sauté, corn kernels are cut off the cob and mixed with red bell pepper, fresh tomato, and onion. Serve with grilled foods or use to top garlic bread.

4 ears corn or 1½ cups frozen corn kernels, thawed
1 teaspoon vegetable oil
2 tablespoons finely chopped onion
Salt and freshly ground black pepper
1 red or green bell pepper, cored and chopped
1 small ripe tomato, cored and cubed
¼ cup chopped scallions or 2 tablespoons chopped fresh chives (optional)

If using fresh corn, cut the kernels off the cobs with a sharp knife.

In a medium skillet, heat the oil over moderate heat. Add the onion, salt, and pepper and sauté about 4 minutes, until soft but not brown. Add the bell pepper and sauté another 2 minutes. Remove from the heat and taste for seasoning, and sprinkle with the scallions if using. Add the tomato and corn and sauté about 3 minutes, until the corn is *just* cooked (to keep the fresh flavor, the kernels should be still a bit crisp). Remove from the heat and sprinkle with the scallions if using.

YIELD: 4 servings
PER SERVING: 72 calories, 2 g protein, 2 g fat, 14 g carbohydrate, 12 mg sodium, 0 mg cholesterol

Zucchini "Lasagna"

Preparation time: 15 minutes
Cooking time: 30 minutes

When my daughter was on a wheat-free diet a few years ago, I had to be very creative about what she ate. Instead of pasta, this "lasagna" is made with thin slices of zucchini layered with fresh tomatoes, thinly sliced onions, and cheese. You can use any type of cheese you want in this dish (grated Cheddar, Monterey Jack, or mozzarella, for example), but the first time I tried the recipe, I used crumbled goat cheese, which was a big hit. Best of all, this dish can be made from start to finish in about 40 minutes.

> **2 tablespoons olive oil**
> **4 large zucchini, thinly sliced lengthwise**
> **4 large ripe tomatoes, thinly sliced**
> **2 Vidalia onions, very thinly sliced**
> **2 tablespoons chopped fresh basil or 2 teaspoons dried**
> **1 tablespoon chopped fresh thyme or 1 teaspoon dried**
> **Salt and freshly ground black pepper**
> **About 1 cup grated cheese**

Preheat the oven to 400 degrees. Spread 1 tablespoon of the oil on the bottom of a large flameproof gratin dish or shallow casserole. Arrange half the zucchini over the bottom, then add a layer of half the tomatoes and then half the onions. Add half the basil and thyme and sprinkle with salt and pepper. Add half the cheese. Repeat the layers with the remaining ingredients, topping the remaining cheese. (The dish can be made an hour or two ahead up to this point.)

Bake the lasagna for about 30 minutes, or until the zucchini is tender and the cheese is melted. Place under the broiler for the last 3 minutes of cooking.

YIELD: 4 to 6 servings
PER SERVING: 257 calories, 11 g protein, 14 g fat, 26 g carbohydrate, 167 mg sodium, 24 mg cholesterol

Sautéed Zucchini with Dried Cranberries

Preparation time: 5 minutes
Cooking time: about 10 minutes

This colorful, festive side dish is perfect for serving around the holidays.

1 tablespoon olive oil
3 medium-sized zucchini, thinly sliced
1 clove garlic, finely chopped (optional)
⅓ cup dried cranberries or sun-dried tomatoes
Salt and freshly ground black pepper

Heat half of the oil in a large skillet over moderately high heat. Add the zucchini, spreading them out in a single layer if possible. Sauté about 3 minutes, or until golden brown. Add the remaining oil, flip the zucchini, and add the garlic if using. Sauté another 3 minutes, or until golden brown and tender. Sprinkle the cranberries, salt, and pepper on top and sauté another minute.

YIELD: 4 to 6 servings
PER SERVING: 62 calories, 1 g protein, 3 g fat, 9 g carbohydrate, 3 mg sodium, 0 mg cholesterol

Sautéed Zucchini and Tomatoes with Basil and Pine Nuts

Preparation time: about 8 minutes
Cooking time: about 15 minutes

In the summer, when zucchini are plentiful (often too plentiful) and tomatoes are ripe, this makes an ideal dish. Serve with crusty bread and a salad, or serve as a side dish or as a sauce over pasta or rice.

1 tablespoon olive oil
1 onion, chopped
2 cloves garlic, finely chopped
2 zucchini, chopped
1 tablespoon thinly shredded fresh basil
½ cup pine nuts
3 ripe tomatoes, cored and cubed
Salt and freshly ground black pepper

In a large skillet, heat the oil over moderate heat. Add the onion and garlic and sauté about 5 minutes, stirring constantly to make sure the onion doesn't burn. Add the zucchini and sauté about 5 to 8 minutes, or until almost tender. Add the basil and pine nuts and sauté 1 minute. Add the tomatoes, stir gently, and remove from the heat. (You don't really want the tomatoes to cook but simply to get heated through.) Add salt and pepper to taste and serve as suggested above.

YIELD: 4 servings
PER SERVING: 173 calories, 7 g protein, 13 g fat, 14 g carbohydrate, 13 mg sodium, 13 mg sodium, 0 mg cholesterol

Tomatoes Provençal

Preparation time: 10 minutes
Cooking time: 20 to 25 minutes

August is the time for these simple tomatoes. They should be ripe and as fresh as possible, and the basil should be fresh, not dried. This is a beautiful dish, with bright red tomatoes roasted with olive oil, fresh basil, and a spoonful of crème fraîche, surrounded by black olives and tiny croutons made from French bread. Serve with pasta or rice dishes, grilled foods, or on their own accompanied by a crusty loaf of French bread and a mixed salad.

1½ tablespoons olive oil
6 large ripe tomatoes, cut in half lengthwise
Salt and freshly ground black pepper
½ cup chopped fresh basil
½ cup crème fraîche or sour cream
1 cup pitted black olives, chopped
1 cup small cubes French bread with crusts

Preheat the oven to 350 degrees. Grease the bottom of a shallow casserole or oven-proof skillet with ½ tablespoon of the oil. Place the tomatoes on the greased surface, sprinkle the tops with salt and pepper and the basil, and dot with the crème fraîche. Bake for 15 minutes.

Remove from the oven and sprinkle the olives and bread cubes on top of and surrounding the tomatoes. Drizzle the entire dish with the remaining tablespoon of oil. Spoon the juices from the bottom of the pan over the tomatoes and roast another 10 to 15 minutes, or until very tender.

YIELD: 3 to 6 servings
PER SERVING: 164 calories, 3 g protein, 11 g fat, 17 g carbohydrate, 263 mg sodium, 8 mg cholesterol

Roasted Leeks with Parmesan Cheese

Preparation time: 5 minutes
Cooking time: about 25 minutes

Serve this creamy dish with any grilled or roasted food.

2 large leeks, ends trimmed
1 teaspoon olive oil
1 teaspoon dried thyme or 1 tablespoon chopped fresh thyme
Salt and freshly ground black pepper
About ¼ cup heavy cream
About ½ cup grated Parmesan cheese

Preheat the oven to 350 degrees. Cut the leeks lengthwise and rinse well under cold running water to remove any dirt caught between the leaves. Cut the leeks in half lengthwise again and then into 2-inch-long pieces.

Place the oil in the bottom of a flameproof gratin dish or baking pan. Add the leeks and toss with the oil. Sprinkle with the thyme, salt, and pepper. Roast for 10 minutes, tossing the leeks every few minutes. Add the cream, toss the leeks, and cook another 10 minutes. Add the cheese and place under the broiler for 5 minutes, or until the cheese is golden and bubbling. Serve hot.

YIELD: 4 servings
PER SERVING: 160 calories, 6 g protein, 10 g fat, 13 g carbohydrate, 209 mg sodium, 28 mg cholesterol

Creamed Spinach

Preparation time: 15 minutes
Cooking time: about 20 minutes

This classic dish can be made with endless variations; see the ideas below. It's a particular favorite at holiday meals.

2 pounds fresh spinach, stemmed
¼ to ½ cup heavy cream
Salt and freshly ground black pepper
1½ teaspoons ground nutmeg
½ teaspoon ground allspice
1 tablespoon butter, cut into small cubes (optional)

Wash the spinach leaves and place in a large pot with the water still clinging to the leaves. Steam over high heat until soft, about 5 to 8 minutes. Drain and rinse under cold running water. Drain again, pressing the spinach between 2 plates to remove any excess water.

Place the spinach in a food processor and process with ¼ cup of the cream and the salt, pepper, nutmeg, and allspice. Taste for seasoning. If you want the spinach to be creamier, add the remaining ¼ cup cream and process until smooth.

Heat and serve as is or place in a lightly buttered casserole and dot with the butter cubes. (This dish can be made several hours ahead of time up to this point.) Preheat the oven to 350 degrees and bake for about 15 minutes, or until bubbling hot.

YIELD: 4 to 6 servings
PER SERVING: 94 calories, 4 g protein, 7 g fat, 5 g carbohydrate, 104 mg sodium, 25 mg cholesterol

Creamed Spinach Variations

- Add 1 clove chopped garlic to the spinach before processing.
- Top with toasted slivered nuts.
- Add interesting herbs or spices, such as fresh cilantro, thyme, cinnamon, or ginger.

Stir-fried Broccoli with Hoisin Sauce

Preparation time: 10 minutes
Cooking time: about 12 to 15 minutes

Consider this a master recipe of sorts and create variations by adding pieces of leftover cooked chicken, pork, or beef; strips of red or green bell peppers; sliced water chestnuts and celery; and so on. The idea is to use the recipe as a quick, delicious, and wonderful way to use up leftovers or bits and pieces of raw vegetables lingering in your refrigerator vegetable bin. This dish is also excellent sprinkled with ¼ cup chopped walnuts or almonds. Serve with brown or white rice.

- 1 teaspoon safflower or vegetable oil
- 1 tablespoon minced fresh ginger or 1 teaspoon ground
- ½ cup finely chopped scallions
- 1 cup thinly sliced carrot sticks
- 1 head broccoli, cut into small florets
- ½ to 1 cup diced cooked leftover beef, pork, or chicken (optional)
- 1 tablespoon low-sodium soy sauce or tamari
- 1 tablespoon rice wine (optional)
- 1 tablespoon hoisin sauce
- 1 tablespoon water

In a wok or large heavy skillet, heat the oil over high heat. Add half the ginger and sauté for about 5 seconds. Add half the scallions and sauté another 10 seconds. Add the carrots and cook about 3 minutes, stirring constantly. Add the broccoli and remaining ginger and cook another 3 minutes, stirring frequently. Add the cooked meat if using. Add the soy sauce, rice wine, hoisin sauce, water, and remaining scallions, mixing everything in the bottom of the wok with a spoon, and toss the mixture well to coat everything. Cook another 2 to 5 minutes, or until the vegetables are tender but not overly soft. (If the sauce seems thin, remove the vegetables with a slotted spoon and reduce the sauce over high heat for a minute or two.) Serve over rice.

YIELD: 4 servings
PER SERVING: 92 calories, 6 g protein, 2 g fat, 16 g carbohydrate, 289 mg sodium, 0 mg cholesterol

Honey-Kissed Greens

Preparation time: 5 minutes
Cooking time: about 20 to 25 minutes

Stephanie Hamilton, a Parenting *Senior Editor, is the mother of two sons and a daughter. "For years, I have tried to be a vegetarian without success," Hamilton admits. "Now that I have kids, my biggest challenge is to show my young carnivores that even leafy green vegetables can be lip-smacking good—without hunks of pork floating around in them in the finest southern tradition." This dish, which combines turnips, onions, and beet greens with vinegar and honey, is, in Hamilton's words, "exactly the sort of dish that is just as good to you as it is for you."*

> **2 tablespoons safflower or vegetable oil**
> **1 small onion, chopped**
> **1 medium-small turnip, washed, unpeeled, and chopped**
> **1 chicken bouillon cube**
> **1 bunch turnip, mustard, or collard greens, washed, dried, and roughly chopped**
> **½ cup water**
> **2 to 2½ teaspoons cider vinegar**
> **1 tablespoon honey**
> **1 bunch beet greens, washed, dried, and roughly chopped (optional)**

Heat the oil in a large pot or Dutch oven over moderate heat. Add the onion and turnip and sauté for about 3 minutes. Add the bouillon cube and mash it into the sautéed vegetables until it blends in.

Stir in the greens (not the beet greens—save them for last). Pour in the water and vinegar, stir in the honey, and cover. Simmer over moderately low heat until done: for turnip and mustard greens, about 5 to 7 minutes; for collard greens, about 10 to 15 minutes. Just before you remove the pot from the heat, stir in the beet greens and cover. Cook for 5 minutes and serve.

YIELD: 4 servings
PER SERVING: 123 calories, 2 g protein, 7 g fat, 15 g carbohydrate, 412 mg sodium, 0 mg cholesterol

Other Ideas for Quick Dinners

The following dishes from other chapters will all work well for a weeknight dinner if you do some preparation work ahead of time. In many cases you simply need to marinate a dish before you leave for work; in other cases you can take care of a few steps in preparing the dish the night before serving.

- French-Style Vegetable Soup (page 101)—make ahead and reheat before serving.
- Granny's Turkey-Vegetable-Rice Soup (page 103)—make the turkey broth ahead of time and put together the soup before serving.
- Basic Chicken Soup (page 434)—make ahead and reheat before serving.
- Chicken Fricassee (page 250)—make the chicken soup ahead of time and finish off the dish before serving.
- Country-Style Pork Ribs in Sweet-and-Sour BBQ Sauce (page 273)—marinate the ribs the night before and bake them when you get home from work.
- Grilled Marinated Pork Tenderloin (page 134)—marinate the night before serving.
- Baked Salmon with Roasted Pecan Crust (page 277)—prepare the pecan crust ahead of time.
- Spaghetti and Turkey Meatballs (page 254)—make the meatballs a day ahead of time.

- Light Macaroni and Cheese (page 115)—make the night before serving and bake before serving.
- Ground Meat, Spinach, and Ricotta Lasagna (page 280)—make ahead of time and heat before serving (can be made without meat).
- Portuguese Potatoes with Linguica Sausages and Peppers (page 294)—make the mashed potatoes and roast the peppers ahead of time and assemble just before serving.
- Sweet Potato and Vegetable Croquettes (page 302)—mash the potatoes and prepare the vegetables ahead of time and assemble the dish before serving.
- Cheese Fondue (page 279)—grate the cheese and cut up the dipping ingredients ahead of time.
- Cheese and Herb Pancakes (page 121)—grate the cheese ahead of time.
- Vegetable Shish Kebab (page 124)—assemble the kebabs in the morning and grill them when you get home from work.
- Bean Bundles (page 286)—precook the beans and assemble the dish before serving.
- Ginger Beets (page 128)—cook the beets ahead of time and sauté before serving.

---— ❧ ——---

Family Dining: The Importance
of Eating Together

"Dinner!" I can still hear my mother's booming voice announcing the evening meal. Every night at six o'clock on the dot, my two brothers and I would run downstairs, wolf down our meat loaf, mashed potatoes, frozen peas, and canned fruit chunks in about eight minutes (ten minutes if we were feeling particularly chatty), and bolt from the table. Our mother would then clear the dishes and begin cooking the "real" dinner, the one she would eat with my father when he arrived home from work. I got the message early on that food wasn't something to be savored or shared and that mealtime was certainly not a priority in our family.

I assumed that everyone ate this way until the third grade, when my best friend invited me to her house for dinner one night. Not only was her entire family seated around the table, but most shocking of all, we ate in the dining room. (In my home the dining room was reserved exclusively for my parents' occasional dinner parties.) The meal itself was divided into actual courses, beginning with homemade soup and crusty bread, followed by roast chicken with potatoes and fresh vegetables. We sat around that table for what seemed like hours, but despite my own conditioning, I wasn't the least bit restless. I sat in awe as I listened to my friend's family engage in an unfamiliar form of communication—dinner-table conversation. They talked about school, work, and upcoming vacations. I felt as if I had discovered a new religion, or at least a new culture.

To be sure, mealtimes form some of our most vivid childhood memories. In many households, in fact, the evening meal is the only time of day when everyone can actually be together and catch up on each other's lives. I recently met a man who told me about his father's mealtime quizzes. Whenever he was home for dinner, the father required his four sons to give a full ten-minute report on a U.S. president. Then, in order to "earn" their dessert, they had to pretend that they were giving a stranger directions from one part of town to another without ever using the words "up" or "down." Sound bizarre? This man claims to have loved the ritual because it meant that his entire family was together and that his father, who spent a good deal of time on the road as a traveling salesman, was paying attention to him.

Sadly, however, my friend hasn't been able to continue this nightly tradition with his own family. He and his wife get home from work so late that his children usually end up eating dinner with a babysitter. Apparently, they are not alone. Stories in the news and images on television tell of families in which everyone eats at different times, grabbing whatever they can find in the refrigerator. Major food companies even cater to the idea of young children fending for themselves, with frozen "kids' meals" that can be zapped in a microwave oven in less than ten minutes.

It's true that keeping a family connected these days can be a real struggle. Between work, school, activities, and daycare, just getting to the grocery store sometimes seems like a major accomplishment, let alone setting food on the table. But overloaded schedules are not the only thing keeping families apart in the evening. The pace of modern life has transformed the very idea of what it means to eat a meal. We've become so used to the idea of fast food, for instance, that standing at a pizza counter and downing a slice or picking up a quick burger and fries now passes for dinner. And with so much ready-made processed food available at supermarkets, even eating at home can be the same kind of last-minute, eat-on-the-run experience.

Of course, one can't underestimate the impact of the chatty box that inhabits the living room in 98 percent of American homes—television. For millennia, families and friends have gathered around a table (or a mat on the floor) to share food together. But when the television set became a focal point of the household, mealtime was too often transformed from a cherished family gathering into just another opportunity to glaze out in front of the tube. According to a recent poll, while up to 80 percent of American families make some attempt to eat together, almost half of them do so while watching or listening to TV.

I was never more convinced of the power of this ubiquitous technology than when I traveled to China in the early 1980s and saw its effect on this most intimate of family rituals. At first the congenial Chinese dinner hour seemed to be in full flower everywhere I went. Large extended families gathered around tables eating enormous quantities of food. Children sat next to adults, chopsticks in hand, grabbing rice, vegetables, and meat out of huge communal bowls. What impressed me most was the gusto with which everyone talked while sharing their food.

Then, in one small village near Hong Kong, I visited a family living in a mud hut. The dwelling was extremely primitive, but inside its brown earthen walls, next to the cots and the wok set over a wood-fire burner, was a tiny black-and-white television set. The family sat on bamboo mats, huddled around the set, bowls of rice in hand, perfectly speechless. I was speechless too. Evidently, TV had the same effect on this rural Chinese family as it does on millions of American families.

Modern technology aside, even under the best of circumstances mealtime can be one of the roughest adjustments to family life for couples who are used to dining only with other adults. Suddenly, long, leisurely meals are replaced by chaotic, noisy affairs with a hungry, demanding child wanting this now, and that without the cheese, and the soup not so hot. One woman I know claims that her husband refuses to eat with their two toddlers because he winds up with a serious case of indigestion every time. Another friend tells me that dinner in his house is so crazy that it generally lasts only five minutes.

Whatever it is that's keeping your family apart at dinnertime, a few simple tricks and adjustments can make eating a meal with the kids—even infants and toddlers—not only possible but enjoyable. Once your family becomes used to eating together, you'll find it's a habit that's hard to break. If my family, for instance, goes for more than two or three days without gathering for a meal, I feel a definite sense of loss. I grow hungry—both physically and spiritually—for the joy and sense of completeness I experience sitting at a table and sharing food with my children and husband.

If you're one of those families that hasn't been breaking bread together at night, it's never too late to start. Bear in mind that, like any new experience, this one may be awkward and difficult at first, but don't be put off by lapses in the conversation or the fact that you feel as if you're in the middle of a three-ring circus. My mother once tried to civilize our family meal by instigating what she called "the Kennedy routine." According to a magazine she had read, the Kennedys had a nightly custom of going around the table and having each member of the family report on an incident that occurred that day. The ritual failed in our family, however, because it felt forced and unnatural.

The point is, every evening meal does not have to conform to some ideal of the perfect family scene. As soon as you relax and take things at your own pace, you'll start to see changes occur in your family, changes that you probably never thought would be so easy to achieve. In the warm, supportive atmosphere of the family dinner table, children who once seemed devoted to fast foods or who would only eat from a limited menu may start—without even knowing it—to eat more balanced meals. Food tastes better when it's being shared, and the kids' enthusiasm may actually give you new inspiration in the kitchen. Even more important, there will be new opportunities for conversation, a chance for you to silence the clamor of the outside world and really listen to what your kids have to say about their days and their lives.

When you take the time to sit down with your children, you're telling them that they matter and that good eating is more than just a slogan. Even if they're too young to appreciate the camaraderie now, you'll be starting a tradition that's bound to pay off in the years to come.

———————— ∾ ————————

Tips for Making Family Meal Time Easier

• Don't feel that you have to prepare a three-course gourmet meal to create a successful family dinner. Having your family seated around a table eating and talking is as important as what you serve. In fact, with kids, the simpler the better. A pot of spaghetti with a hunk of bread and a salad is as fancy as you ever need to get.

• When kids come home at the end of the day, they're hungry. Moving your own dinnertime up to 6:00 or 6:30 may seem like a punishment at first, but eventually you may come to enjoy it, since you'll have more time to digest your food and spend a leisurely evening together. If you work late hours, try to get home early once or twice a week, or have the kids eat a substantial late-afternoon snack to tide them over until dinnertime.

• According to current nutrition wisdom, the worst thing a parent can do is force a child to eat. (See Picky Eaters essay on page 93 for more on this subject.) Creating battles over food can lead to unhealthy eating habits and even serious eating disorders in the future. As long as you offer children a range of healthy options, they'll eventually get the nutrients they need.

• It's hard for most four-year-olds to sit still for an hour, but you'll find that if you let them come and go as they please—or at least after the main dish is eaten—they'll be drawn back to the table after a while and will want to rejoin the conversation. They might even request another serving of food.

• Don't get into the habit of cooking separate meals for children; you can always spice up a portion of the main dish for the adults. If your kids are particularly finicky, let them choose the menu two or three times a week.

• Europeans have a wonderful custom of placing little plates of food— olives, vegetables, dips, cubes of local cheese, and so forth—on the table as soon as customers arrive at the restaurant. These tidbits take the edge off people's hunger so that they don't get cranky waiting for the meal. At home, simple snacks will do the trick for kids. Try an assortment of raw vegetables with yogurt dip, crackers, or slices of ripe melon.

Chapter Seven

Weekend Dinners

❧

Saturday and Sunday nights are a time when many parents cook something a bit more elaborate and celebratory. This is also the time of the week when we entertain friends and extended family, invite other families and children over, and dinnertime becomes party time. There are dozens of recipes here for all these occasions. You'll find some old favorites like Spaghetti and Meatballs, Coq au Vin, and the best Standing Rib Roast, as well as some interesting new ideas for Baked Salmon with Roasted Pecan Crust, a creamy Pumpkin Risotto, and French-Style Braised Lamb Shanks.

> *Granny's Turkey-Lemon-Rice Soup*
> *Cream of Baked Squash Soup*
> *Coq au Vin*
> *Roast Chicken with Lemon-Almond-Rice Stuffing*
> *Roast Chicken and Winter Squash Stew*
> *Roast Chicken with Red Wine and Cream Sauce*
> *Chicken Fricassee*
> *Chicken and Sausage Paella*
> *Spaghetti and Turkey Meatballs*
> *Spaghetti Squash and Turkey Meatballs*
> *Asian Chicken Wrapped in Lettuce Leaves*
> *French-Style Braised Lamb Shanks*
> *Rack of Lamb with Almond-Cornmeal Crust*
> *Standing Rib Roast*

Granny's Turkey-Lemon-Rice Soup

Preparation time: 10 minutes
Cooking time: about 15 to 20 minutes

A soothing, comforting soup, this is the ideal meal for a cold winter's night.

6 cups turkey broth (see recipe, page 435), or chicken broth
3 carrots, cut into small chunks
3 stalks celery, cut into small chunks
1 large onion, peeled and quartered
½ cup finely chopped fresh parsley
1 large egg yolk
1½ tablespoons heavy cream
3 tablespoons fresh lemon juice
Salt and freshly ground black pepper
1 cup cooked white rice
1 cup cubed cooked turkey meat (optional)

In a large pot, heat the broth over high heat. Add the carrots, celery, onion, and parsley and bring to a boil. Reduce the heat and let simmer about 10 minutes.

In a small bowl, whisk the egg yolk with the cream, lemon juice, salt, and pepper. Add 1 cup of the hot soup to the cream mixture and whisk. Slowly add the mixture to the soup pot and cook over low heat until the soup is slightly thickened and warm. Add the cooked rice, making sure to break up any clumps. Stir in the turkey meat if using, and taste for seasoning.

YIELD: 4 servings
PER SERVING: 199 calories, 9 g protein, 7 g fat, 32 g carbohydrate, 236 mg sodium, 61 mg
  cholesterol

Cream of Baked Squash Soup

Preparation time: 10 minutes
Cooking time: about 1 hour 15 minutes

What makes this recipe so special is that the squash is baked with several cloves of garlic and then pureed into a creamy, satisfying soup. Baking squash brings out its natural sweetness, and the garlic imparts a mellow flavor that even the most finicky eater won't object to. To toast the walnuts, if using, place them on a baking sheet in a 350-degree oven for 5 minutes.

Serve this hearty soup as a first course at holiday meals or for lunch or dinner, accompanied by a loaf of crusty bread and lots of salad.

1 large acorn squash
4 large cloves garlic, peeled
¼ cup dry white wine or water
1½ tablespoons olive or vegetable oil
2 onions, chopped
2 tablespoons chopped fresh thyme or 1 teaspoon dried
6 tablespoons chopped fresh chives or parsley
Salt and freshly ground black pepper
3½ cups chicken or vegetable broth
½ cup heavy cream
½ cup walnut halves, toasted and chopped (optional)

Preheat the oven to 350 degrees. Cut the squash in half and scoop out the seeds and pulp. Place in a baking dish and surround with the garlic. Add about ¼ cup water to the bottom of the pan to prevent the squash from drying out while baking. Bake for 45 minutes to 1 hour, or until soft. Remove from the oven and add the wine or water to the hot pan, scraping up any bits that are clinging to the pan.

Meanwhile, in a large pot, heat the oil over moderate heat. Add the onions and sauté for about 8 minutes, or until soft but not brown. Remove the squash meat from the shells and discard the shells. Add the squash and roasted garlic to the onion mixture. Add the thyme and half the chives or parsley. Season with salt and pepper and sauté about 2 minutes. Raise the heat to high and add the deglazing liquid from the baking dish along with the broth and bring to a boil. Reduce the heat and simmer, covered, for about 10 minutes.

Puree the soup in a blender or food processor. (The soup can be refrigerated for several days or frozen for several months.) Add the cream and heat through. (Or whip the cream into soft peaks and swirl it through the soup just before serving.) Garnish each bowl of soup with the remaining chives or parsley and chopped walnuts if desired.

YIELD: 4 to 6 servings
PER SERVING: 234 calories, 4 g protein, 15 g fat, 22 g carbohydrate, 717 mg sodium, 33 mg cholesterol

Coq au Vin

Preparation time: 25 minutes
Cooking time: about 1½ hours

This French classic is one of the most satisfying dishes imaginable and a whole lot simpler to make than you might think. Make it a day ahead of time and let it sit overnight; it always seems to taste better the next day. Serve with French Mashed Potatoes (page 292), Edwin Potatoes (page 293), or wide egg noodles.

The wine and the juices from the chicken create a rich sauce, but don't be turned off by the generous amount of wine in this recipe. Much of the alcohol burns off during the lengthy cooking process. Have the butcher cut the chickens into eight pieces; small pieces are much more appealing and easier for younger children to eat.

2 to 3 tablespoons olive oil
10 cloves garlic, 2 thinly sliced and 8 peeled and left whole
2 leeks or onions, thinly sliced
2 shallots, peeled and quartered
About 1 cup flour
Salt and freshly ground black pepper
2 teaspoons dried thyme
2 chickens (2½ to 3 pounds each), cut into 8 pieces
3 cups dry red wine or 1½ cups wine and 1½ cups chicken broth
2 cups quartered mushrooms
1 cup finely chopped fresh parsley

In a large flameproof casserole or deep sauté pan, heat 1 tablespoon of the oil over moderate heat. Add the 2 sliced cloves of garlic, the leeks, and the shallots and sauté, stirring constantly, about 10 minutes, or until golden but not brown. Remove the sautéed vegetables to a plate.

Place the flour on a large plate and add a generous amount of salt and pepper and half the thyme. Dredge the chicken pieces in the flour, coating all sides. In the casserole, heat 1 tablespoon of the oil over moderately high heat. Add the chicken in batches and brown about 3 minutes on each side. Add more oil as needed. Transfer chicken pieces to a plate and remove any excess oil from the bottom of the casserole (the oil will be dark brown).

Return the sautéed vegetables and chicken to the casserole and set over moderately high heat. Add the wine, the remaining teaspoon of thyme, and the whole garlic cloves and slowly bring to a boil. Reduce the heat, partially cover the casserole, and let simmer over low heat for about 1½ hours, stirring gently, or until the chicken is very tender. Add the mushrooms and half the parsley about 30 minutes before the chicken is done. Serve steaming hot, sprinkled with the remaining parsley just before serving.

YIELD: 6 to 8 servings

PER SERVING: 743 calories, 64 g protein, 42 g fat, 24 g carbohydrate, 220 mg sodium, 217 mg cholesterol

Roast Chicken with Lemon-Almond-Rice Stuffing

Preparation time: 40 minutes
Cooking time: 1 hour 15 minutes

This dish is festive enough for a special occasion but simple enough to serve for an every-day meal. If you prepare the stuffing ahead of time, the chicken can be put together in no time at all. This one-dish dinner presents chicken stuffed with a savory rice mixture surrounded by slices of sweet parsnips. You could substitute zucchini wedges, winter squash, mushrooms, onions, or a combination of a few vegetables for the parsnips.

STUFFING:
Salt
1 cup white rice
1 tablespoon olive oil
1 small onion, finely chopped
1 clove garlic, chopped
1 tablespoon chopped fresh thyme or 1 teaspoon dried
1 stalk celery, finely chopped
1 chicken liver, cut into small pieces (optional)
½ cup slivered almonds
1 tablespoon thin julienne strips lemon zest
2 tablespoons lemon juice
Freshly ground black pepper
½ cup finely chopped fresh parsley

CHICKEN AND PARSNIPS:
1 chicken (about 3 pounds), excess fat removed
3 large parsnips, peeled and cut into 2- to 3-inch pieces
About ½ cup dry white wine, red wine, or Cinzano
Freshly ground black pepper
Hungarian paprika

To make the stuffing, bring 2 cups water and a pinch of salt to a boil in a medium saucepan over high heat. Add the rice and bring to a boil. Reduce the heat to low, stir the rice to prevent sticking, cover, and let cook about 10 to 15 minutes, or until the rice is cooked and all the liquid is absorbed. Remove and let cool slightly. Place the rice in a large bowl, breaking up any clumps.

Meanwhile, heat the oil in medium skillet over moderate heat. Add the onion, garlic, and thyme and sauté for 3 minutes. Add the celery and liver if using and sauté another 3 minutes. Remove from the heat and stir in the almonds and lemon zest. Add to the bowl of rice and mix well. Add the lemon juice, salt, pepper, and parsley. Taste for seasoning. (The stuffing can be prepared 12 hours ahead of time up to this point.)

Preheat the oven to 400 degrees. Place the stuffing inside the cavity of the chicken, pressing to fit in as much as possible without overfilling the bird. Place the remaining stuffing in a lightly greased small casserole. Close the bird's cavity using toothpicks or a small wooden skewer, or tie the drumsticks together with butcher's twine to enclose the cavity. Place the parsnips around the bird and pour half the wine or Cinzano on top. Sprinkle with pepper and paprika and roast for 30 minutes. Add the remaining wine, basting the bird and the parsnips with the pan juices. Continue roasting for a total cooking time of 1 hour 15 minutes, or until a drumstick is loose when wiggled and the juices run clear, not pink, when a thigh is pierced with a small sharp knife. Place the casserole of rice stuffing in the oven 15 to 20 minutes before the chicken is done. Remove the stuffing from the cavity of the bird and carve the chicken. Serve hot, topped with pan juices and parsnips.

YIELD: 4 servings

PER SERVING: 895 calories, 52 g protein, 48 g fat, 64 g carbohydrate, 191 mg sodium, 174 mg cholesterol

Roast Chicken and
Winter Squash Stew

Preparation time: 20 minutes
Cooking time: 1 hour 20 minutes

Here is the perfect dish for cool autumn nights when you crave something hearty. Serve with crusty bread and a green salad.

1 chicken (about 3 pounds), cut into 8 small pieces
2 large onions, peeled and quartered
4 stalks celery, cut into 2-inch pieces
4 carrots, cut into 2-inch pieces
2 leeks, washed and cut into 2-inch pieces
1 butternut squash, peeled, seeded, and cut into large chunks
2 cloves garlic, peeled
3 large potatoes, well scrubbed and cut into chunks
2 scallions, thinly sliced
Salt and freshly ground black pepper
1 tablespoon chopped fresh thyme or 1½ teaspoons dried
1½ tablespoons chopped fresh basil or 1½ teaspoons dried
4¼ cups low-sodium chicken broth
6 ripe tomatoes, cored and cut into quarters
2 tablespoons flour

Preheat the oven to 400 degrees. In a large roasting pan, arrange the chicken pieces, onions, celery, carrots, leeks, squash, garlic, potatoes, and scallions. Distribute the vegetables evenly in the pan, sprinkle with the salt, pepper, thyme, and basil, then add ¼ cup of the chicken broth. Roast for 45 minutes, stirring once or twice. Remove the pan from the oven and reduce the temperature to 350 degrees. Add the tomatoes and return the pan to the oven to roast an additional 15 minutes.

Remove the pan from the oven and place it across 2 burners on moderately high heat. Remove the chicken and vegetables from the pan and set them aside on a separate plate while you make the sauce.

Skim the excess fat from the juices that have accumulated in the pan, then stir in the flour. Cook for 1 minute, stirring constantly. Gradually add the remaining 4 cups of broth and bring to a boil. After 1 or 2 minutes, turn off the heat and season the sauce to taste. Return the chicken and vegetables to the pan and coat them with the sauce. Return the pan to the oven and roast for another 15 minutes, or until the sauce is thickened and the chicken, squash, and potatoes are thoroughly cooked.

YIELD: 4 to 6 servings
PER SERVING: 628 calories, 42 g protein, 24 g fat, 62 g carbohydrate, 233 mg sodium, 122 mg cholesterol

Roast Chicken with Red Wine and Cream Sauce

Preparation time: 10 minutes
Cooking time: about 1 hour 25 minutes

Don't be misled by this sophisticated-sounding name. This is a simple roast chicken doused with a bit of red wine and surrounded with chunks of carrots and garlic cloves. The carrots become sweet when roasted, and the garlic takes on a mellow, buttery flavor. Once the chicken is roasted, the pan juices are reduced with a touch of heavy cream and chicken stock to make a rich sauce.

1 chicken (about 3 pounds), excess fat removed
½ lemon
2 cloves garlic, peeled and left whole
1 tablespoon chopped fresh sage or thyme or 1 teaspoon dried
Salt and freshly ground black pepper
4 large carrots, cut into large chunks
1 head garlic
About 1 cup dry red wine
1½ tablespoons flour
1 cup chicken broth
3 tablespoons heavy cream

Preheat the oven to 425 degrees. Clean the inside of the chicken and place in a large roasting pan. Place the lemon, 2 garlic cloves, half of the sage, and salt and pepper in the cavity. Surround the bird with the carrots and whole head of garlic. Sprinkle with the remaining sage and salt and pepper and pour about ⅓ cup wine on top.

Roast the chicken for 15 minutes, then reduce the temperature to 350 degrees, basting the bird with the pan juices and adding more wine if needed. Roast for another 45 minutes to an hour, basting the bird every 20 minutes and adding more wine if the bottom of the pan gets dry. The chicken is done when the juices run yellow, not pink, when a thigh is pierced with a small sharp knife. Remove the chicken to a warm platter and cover loosely with foil.

Remove any excess fat from the bottom of the pan. Place the pan over 1 or 2 burners on moderate heat and sprinkle in the flour. Let cook 1 minute. Whisk in the broth and raise the heat to moderately high. Let simmer 2 minutes. Add the cream and salt and pepper to taste and let simmer about 5 minutes, or until somewhat reduced and flavorful. Carve the chicken and serve with the roast carrots and garlic on the side. Top the meat with the sauce and serve.

YIELD: 4 servings
PER SERVING: 633 calories, 46 g protein, 40 g fat, 21 g carbohydrate, 458 mg sodium, 189 mg cholesterol

Chicken Fricassee

Preparation time: 10 minutes
Cooking time: 10 minutes for the fricassee; about 1 to 1½ hours for the soup

My mother-in-law taught me this old family favorite. It is one of those dishes that is so soothing and comforting that I will cook a pot of chicken soup just so I can make this dish. The chicken and broth from the chicken soup is mixed with a creamy lemon sauce and then served over a bed of white rice. My kids started eating this when they were toddlers, and it's still one of the most requested dishes in our home.

SOUP:
> 1 chicken (about 3 pounds)
> 4 carrots, cut into chunks
> 4 stalks celery, cut into chunks
> 3 onions, peeled and quartered
> ½ cup finely chopped fresh parsley
> 1 bay leaf
> 6 peppercorns
> Salt

FRICASSEE:
> 1 cup white rice
> Salt
> 1 tablespoon butter
> 1 tablespoon flour
> 1 large egg yolk
> 2 tablespoons heavy cream
> Freshly ground black pepper
> Juice of 1 lemon

Place all the ingredients for the soup into a large pot and just cover the chicken with cold water. Bring to a boil over high heat, reduce the heat, cover partially, and let simmer for about 1 hour or 1½ hours, or until the soup is flavorful and the chicken is tender. Taste for seasoning. If the soup tastes weak, remove the chicken from the pot and vigorously simmer the broth until flavorful. Return the chicken to the pot. The soup can be made several days ahead of time and refrigerated until ready to use.

To make the fricassee, in a medium saucepan, mix 2 cups water and a pinch of salt and bring to a boil. Add the rice, reduce the heat to low, cover, and simmer about 8 to 10 minutes, or until all the liquid has been absorbed and the rice is cooked. Set aside.

Meanwhile, in a large skillet, heat the butter over moderate heat. Add the flour and stir together to make a paste; let cook for 1 minute. Slowly whisk in 4 cups of the chicken broth from the soup and let simmer for about 5 minutes, or until somewhat thickened.

In a small bowl, beat the egg yolk, cream, salt, and pepper. Add a few tablespoons of the simmering broth from the skillet to the cream mixture and then slowly whisk the mixture into the skillet. Add the vegetables from the soup. Cut the chicken into pieces; it should be almost falling apart and very tender. Add the chicken pieces to the skillet. Reduce the heat and stir in the lemon juice. Taste the sauce and add more salt, pepper, or lemon juice if needed. Serve with the rice.

YIELD: 4 servings

PER SERVING: 689 calories, 48 g protein, 28 g fat, 60 g carbohydrate, 217 mg sodium, 203 mg cholesterol

Chicken and Sausage Paella

Preparation time: about 30 minutes
Cooking time: 30 minutes

The classic rice dish from Spain is traditionally made with a variety of seafood, along with chicken and sausage. This version is easier and more affordable. Have the butcher cut the whole chicken breast into four parts, each thigh into two parts, each wing into two parts, and leave the drumsticks whole.

4 cups chicken broth
2 tablespoons olive oil
1 large chicken (3 to 4 pounds), cut up (see note above)
Salt and freshly ground black pepper
2 cloves garlic, finely chopped
4 sweet or hot sausages, cut into ½-inch slices
1 onion, chopped
1 red bell pepper, cut into thin strips
1½ cup short-grain white rice
3 tablespoons chopped fresh parsley
1 bay leaf
2 cups fresh or frozen peas, thawed if frozen
1 teaspoon paprika
1 lemon, cut into wedges

Preheat the oven to 325 degrees. In a saucepan, heat the broth over moderate heat; keep warm.

In a large, shallow skillet or a paella pan, heat 1 tablespoon of the oil over moderate heat. Sprinkle the chicken pieces with salt and pepper, add to the skillet, and sauté for about 5 minutes on each side, or until golden brown. Remove and drain. Add the garlic and sausage slices to the pan and sauté for about 2 to 3 minutes on each side, or until brown. Remove the sausage, drain on paper towels, and set aside.

Place the skillet back over moderate heat and add the remaining tablespoon of oil if needed. Add the onion and red pepper and sauté for about 5 minutes, or until the onion is golden brown. Add the rice and stir to coat it well with the oil and vegetables. Add the parsley and the bay leaf and stir in the warm broth and the peas. Bring to a boil and cook, uncovered, over moderately high heat for about 10 minutes, stirring occasionally. Mix in the chicken and sausage. Sprinkle the dish with paprika.

Place the paella in the oven and bake, uncovered, for about 20 minutes or until the rice is cooked. Serve with lemon wedges.

YIELD: 6 servings

PER SERVING: 760 calories, 51 g protein, 37 g fat, 54 g carbohydrate, 1,278 mg sodium, 146 mg cholesterol

Spaghetti and Turkey Meatballs

Preparation time: about 20 minutes
Cooking time: about 40 minutes

When I was growing up, my mother always made spaghetti and meatballs on Halloween night, just before we went out trick-or-treating. There was never any explanation for this meal (my mother had not been served spaghetti and meatballs as a child, and we aren't Italian), but it became a cherished tradition.

Each October, as my children put on their costumes and makeup, I keep the tradition going. Although these are not the meatballs of my childhood (see page 150 for a more traditional version), they are the ones my kids love most. Low-fat ground turkey is combined with sautéed onions, parsley, chopped black olives, and seasoned bread crumbs. Serve with garlic bread and a salad.

The meatballs and sauce can be prepared several hours ahead of time and reheated while the pasta water simmers.

1½ tablespoons olive or vegetable oil
1 onion, finely chopped
1 clove garlic, chopped
Salt and freshly ground black pepper
1 teaspoon dried oregano
1 cup very finely chopped fresh parsley
1 pound ground turkey or low-fat ground beef
2 large eggs, beaten
½ cup chopped pitted black olives
About 1 cup seasoned bread crumbs
4 cups homemade or canned tomato sauce
½ cup dry red or white wine
1 bay leaf
1 pound spaghetti or linguine
Grated Parmesan cheese

In a large skillet, heat ½ tablespoon of the oil over moderately low heat. Add the onion, garlic, salt, pepper, oregano, and half of the parsley and sauté about 10 minutes, or until soft and sweet but not brown, stirring frequently. Remove from the heat and let cool slightly.

In a large bowl, mix the turkey, eggs, sautéed onion, olives, about ¾ cup of the bread crumbs, the remaining parsley, and salt and pepper. Mix well to incorporate all the ingredients, adding the remaining ¼ cup of bread crumbs if the mixture doesn't hold together well. (You should be able to form the meatballs without having the mixture fall apart.) Using your hands, form the mixture into about 24 small (golf ball size) meatballs.

Heat the remaining 1 tablespoon oil in the skillet over moderately high heat. Working in batches, brown the meatballs about 3 minutes on each side. Remove with a slotted spoon and drain on paper towels. Remove any excess fat from the skillet (blot it up with a few paper towels). Add the tomato sauce and wine and bring to a boil. Reduce the heat to low and gently return the meatballs to the skillet. Add the bay leaf to the sauce and let simmer over low heat for about 35 minutes. Remove the bay leaf.

Bring a large pot of lightly salted water to a boil. Boil the pasta for about 8 to 12 minutes, depending on the type of pasta you use, and drain. Place on a large platter or bowl and top with the meatballs and sauce. Pass the cheese separately.

YIELD: 6 servings

PER SERVING: 606 calories, 30 g protein, 14 g fat, 86 g carbohydrate, 1,599 mg sodium, 126 mg cholesterol

Spaghetti Squash and Turkey Meatballs

Preparation time: 20 minutes
Cooking time: 1 hour, 15 minutes

Kids will get a real kick out of this vegetable version of one of their favorite foods.

1 spaghetti squash (about 2 to 2½ pounds)
1 pound ground turkey
1 large egg, lightly beaten
2½ tablespoons bread crumbs
1 tablespoon finely chopped fresh basil or 1 teaspoon dried
Salt and freshly ground black pepper
1 tablespoon olive oil
1 onion, finely chopped
4 cups homemade or canned tomato sauce
1 bay leaf
Grated Parmesan cheese

Preheat the oven to 350 degrees. Make several small *X*'s in the skin of the squash and place it on a sheet of aluminum foil. Bake for about 1 hour to 1 hour 15 minutes, or until tender when pierced with a fork.

Meanwhile, in a medium bowl, mix the ground turkey, egg, bread crumbs, basil, and salt and pepper to taste. Form into small meatballs.

In a large skillet, heat the oil over moderate heat. Add the onion and sauté for about 2 minutes, or until it begins to soften. Add the meatballs and brown them on all sides. Add the tomato sauce and bay leaf and reduce the heat to moderately low. Partially cover the skillet and let the meatballs and sauce simmer for 30 to 45 minutes, or until the meatballs are firm and thoroughly cooked. Taste the sauce for seasoning. (The meatballs and sauce can be cooked up to 24 hours ahead and refrigerated. Reheat for 10 minutes before serving.)

Remove the squash from the oven, cut it in half, and spoon out the seeds. Scrape the flesh out with a fork; the "spaghetti" will pull off in long strands. Place the spaghetti squash in a large bowl or on a serving platter and toss with salt and pepper and a few tablespoons of the sauce. Top with the meatballs and the remaining sauce and sprinkle with the grated Parmesan.

YIELD: 4 servings

PER SERVING: 296 calories, 21 g protein, 12 g fat, 29 g carbohydrate, 1,331 mg sodium, 109 mg cholesterol

Asian Chicken Wrapped in Lettuce Leaves

Preparation time: 40 minutes (including marinating time)
Cooking time: 15 minutes

Lettuce makes a crisp and refreshing wrapper for stir-fried chicken and vegetables. If all the prep work is done ahead of time, this dish takes only about 10 minutes to assemble.

1 pound skinless, boneless chicken breast, cut into thin 2-inch strips
3 teaspoons light soy sauce
3 teaspoons dry sherry
2 tablespoons vegetable or peanut oil
1 large carrot, cut into thin 2-inch strips
2 small zucchini, cut into thin 2-inch strips
1 large, green, red, or yellow bell pepper, cut into thin 2-inch strips
½ cup thinly sliced mushrooms
½ cup thinly sliced water chestnuts or chopped walnuts
2 tablespoons finely chopped fresh mint (optional)
1 head iceberg lettuce, separated into individual leaves

GARNISHES:
1 cup chopped walnuts or cashews
½ cup finely chopped scallions
¼ cup hoisin sauce
¼ cup finely chopped fresh mint (optional)

Place the chicken in a small bowl with 2 teaspoons of the soy sauce and 2 teaspoons of the sherry and marinate for 30 minutes.

In a wok or large skillet, heat 1 tablespoon of the oil over high heat. Add the chicken and stir-fry for 1 minute. Remove the chicken with a slotted spoon and set aside. Discard the oil and wipe the wok clean.

Heat the remaining oil in the wok over high heat. Add the carrot and cook 1 minute. Add the zucchini, bell pepper, mushrooms, and water chestnuts and stir-fry another 3 to 5 minutes, or until the vegetables are just tender. Add the reserved chicken and the remaining teaspoon of soy sauce and teaspoon of sherry and cook 1 minute. Stir in the chopped mint if using. Place on a serving platter, surrounded with the garnishes.

To serve, spoon 3 to 5 tablespoons of filling onto individual lettuce leaves, roll each leaf to form a cone, and top the open end with garnish of choice.

YIELD: 6 servings

PER SERVING: 355 calories, 24 g protein, 18 g fat, 21 g carbohydrate, 850 mg sodium, 44 mg cholesterol

French-Style Braised Lamb Shanks

Preparation time: about 35 minutes
Cooking time: 2½ to 3 hours

This is one of those deeply satisfying dishes that leaves everyone taking a hunk of bread and mopping up the last precious juices—always a sign of a great meal. Lamb shanks are a relatively unknown cut of meat in this country, which is strange, since they are so flavorful, reasonably priced, and available in most supermarket meat sections.

The stew cooks for several hours in the oven, filling your kitchen with an enticing, beguiling scent. It is an ideal dish to cook in the morning, as it can cook slowly for hours while you go out and attend to chores, soccer games, Little League, whatever. When you come home, everything is ready to eat. Serve with Edwin Potatoes (page 293) or French Mashed Potatoes (page 292) so you can sop up the rich gravy, plus a green salad and crusty bread. Don't be concerned about the amount of red wine in this dish; due to the long cooking time, a good deal of the alcohol burns off.

This dish was adapted from a recipe in James Villas's wonderful book, The French Country Kitchen *(Bantam, 1992).*

> **7 meaty lamb shanks (about 8 to 10 pounds total)**
> **8 cloves garlic, 2 thinly sliced, 6 left whole**
> **4 tablespoons finely chopped fresh rosemary or 4 teaspoons dried**
> **Salt and freshly ground black pepper**
> **About 1 cup flour**
> **1 to 2 tablespoons vegetable oil**
> **6 shallots or small onions, cut in half**
> **1 bottle (750 ml) good-quality dry red wine**
> **6 carrots, cut into small chunks**
> **2 cups low-sodium beef or chicken broth**
> **1 cup finely chopped fresh parsley**

Preheat the oven to 300 degrees. Using a small knife, cut a small incision in each shank and insert a sliver of garlic. Rub each shank with half the rosemary and salt and pepper and then lightly dredge in the flour, coating all sides.

In a large flameproof casserole or sauté pan, heat 1 tablespoon of the oil over moderately high heat. Add the shanks in 2 batches, and brown about 3 to 4 minutes on each side, or until nicely browned, adding more oil if necessary. Remove to a large plate. When all the meat is browned, remove the casserole from the heat and use a paper towel to blot up all but about a teaspoon of the oil left in it.

Place the casserole back over moderately high heat. Add the shallots and whole garlic cloves and sauté about 2 minutes in the tiny bit of remaining fat. Remove from the casserole and place on the plate with the meat. Raise the heat to high and add the wine, allowing it to come to a boil. Let simmer until reduced to 2 cups. (After about 5 minutes, remove from the heat and measure it.) Return the shanks, shallots, and garlic to the casserole along with the carrots and broth and bring to a boil. Remove from the heat, cover, and place in the oven.

Let the lamb cook for about 2½ to 3 hours, or until it is very tender and the sauce is quite flavorful. Taste for seasoning. (If you want the sauce to thicken, remove the meat to a platter, place the sauce over high heat, and reduce until thickened.) Sprinkle the stew with the parsley and serve piping hot.

Yield: 8 servings

Per serving: 614 calories, 50 g protein, 35 g fat, 22 g carbohydrate, 222 mg sodium, 177 mg cholesterol

Rack of Lamb with Almond-Cornmeal Crust

Preparation time: 15 minutes
Cooking time: 35 to 45 minutes

This is definitely not everyday fare, but you don't have to wait for a holiday to serve a rack of lamb. Essentially, a rack of lamb is a few lamb chops still connected together. If you serve lamb chops to your family, why not try a rack of lamb?

A thin coating of mustard is "painted" on the meat, and a simple topping made from garlic, cornmeal, rosemary, sun-dried tomatoes, and almonds is pressed down onto it. As the lamb roasts, the topping becomes a kind of crust, crunchy and flavorful. Serve with polenta or roast potatoes and spinach. You can also surround the lamb with wild or button mushrooms—lightly doused in olive oil and salt and pepper—or with fresh tomatoes cut into quarters.

    1 teaspoon olive oil
    1 rack of lamb (1½ to 2 pounds), excess fat trimmed (about 8 chops)
    2 tablespoons Dijon mustard
    1 tablespoon chopped fresh rosemary or 1 teaspoon dried
    Salt and freshly ground black pepper
    About ½ cup dry white or red wine

TOPPING:
    2 cloves garlic, chopped
    1 small shallot, chopped
    1 tablespoon chopped fresh rosemary or 1 teaspoon dried
    2 tablespoons chopped sun-dried tomatoes (optional)
    ¼ cup slivered or chopped almonds
    Salt and freshly ground black pepper

Spread the oil in the bottom of a medium roasting pan and place the lamb on top. Using the back of a spoon or a barbecue or pastry brush, rub or "paint" the mustard onto the top and sides of the chops. Sprinkle the mustard with the rosemary and salt and pepper.

Place all the ingredients for the topping in a food processor or blender and process just a few seconds, until chopped but not too finely. Gently press the topping onto the mustard coating on the lamb. (The dish can be prepared up to 2 hours ahead of time up to this point. Cover and refrigerate until ready to roast. Be sure to bring the meat to room temperature before roasting.)

Preheat the oven to 400 degrees. Roast the lamb for about 15 minutes, then splash some of the wine on top. Add another splash of wine after another 10 minutes. Roast for a total of about 35 to 45 minutes, depending on how pink you like your meat. Let the lamb sit for 5 minutes, then slice into chops. Serve with pan juices on top.

YIELD: 4 servings

PER SERVING: 257 calories, 21 g protein, 15 g fat, 3 g carbohydrate, 253 mg sodium, 64 mg cholesterol

Standing Rib Roast

Preparation time: 25 minutes
Cooking time: about 2¼ hours
Sitting time: 15 minutes

A standing rib roast is the ultimate beef dinner—a prime cut of roast beef studded with garlic and surrounded with onions and potatoes—ideal for a holiday dinner or any special occasion. Serve with a simple green vegetable (string beans with slivered almonds, Brussels sprouts, or spinach). Of course, the classic accompaniments are Yorkshire pudding, popovers, and ground horseradish.

Always choose well-aged top-quality prime *beef. Have the butcher trim off any excess fat (you want a thin layer of fat to act as a natural baster during roasting and provide a crispy exterior) and tie the roast with string.*

1 well-aged standing rib roast, about 3 ribs (5 pounds)
2 cloves garlic, very thinly sliced
Freshly ground black pepper
Hungarian paprika
20 new potatoes or 8 to 10 baking potatoes, peeled and quartered
About 20 small onions, peeled and left whole
Salt
1 tablespoon chopped fresh thyme or 1 teaspoon dried

Preheat the oven to 450 degrees. Using a small sharp knife, make several slits in the fat along the top of the roast and gently insert the garlic slices. Season the top of the roast liberally with the pepper and paprika.

Place the roast on a rack or directly into a large roasting pan and surround the beef with the potatoes and onions. Season with the salt, pepper, and thyme. Roast for 15 minutes, spoon the vegetables around gently, and reduce the temperature to 325 degrees. The beef will need to roast for about 20 to 25 minutes per pound, or until it reaches an internal temperature of 125 degrees for rare or 140 for medium. Baste the beef and the vegetables every 20 minutes or so, being careful not to leave the oven door open for too long. Remove the roast from the oven and let sit about 15 minutes before carving. Remove any excess fat from the pan juices and serve with the juices poured on top and the vegetables on the side.

Yield: 8 to 10 servings

Per serving: 721 calories, 33 g protein, 56 g fat, 19 g carbohydrate, 109 mg sodium, 137 mg cholesterol

Brisket with Roasted Vegetables

Preparation time: about 20 minutes
Cooking time: about 3 to 3½ hours

This brisket is surrounded with a variety of vegetables—onions, leeks, carrots, celery, parsnips—and placed in the oven until naturally juicy and tender. The meat can be prepared up to three days before serving. Simply cook the beef, cool it thoroughly, cover, and refrigerate. Rewarm the meat in a 250-degree oven for about 15 to 20 minutes, or until warm throughout. Serve with fresh horseradish and applesauce.

About 1 cup flour
Salt and freshly ground black pepper
1 large beef brisket (about 5 to 6 pounds), trimmed of excess fat
1½ tablespoons safflower oil
10 onions, cut in half
2 leeks, cut lengthwise, then into 3-inch pieces
2 shallots, cut in half
3 cloves garlic, coarsely chopped
8 carrots, cut into thin 3-inch pieces
1 large bunch celery, cut into 3-inch pieces
3 parsnips, cut into 3-inch pieces
1 cup chopped fresh parsley
2 bay leaves
3 tablespoons tomato puree
About 1 cup water
About 1 cup dry red wine

Preheat the oven to 400 degrees. Place the flour on a large plate and season well with the salt and pepper. Dredge both sides of the meat in the flour, shaking off any excess.

In a large roasting pan or flameproof shallow casserole, heat half the oil over moderately high heat. Add the brisket and brown for about 5 minutes, or until it turns a nice brown color. Add the remaining oil and brown the meat on the other side. Remove the pan from the heat and turn the brisket fat side up. Place the onions, leeks, shallots, garlic, carrots, celery, parsnips, parsley, and bay leaves around the meat. Using a spoon, spread the tomato puree on top of the brisket and pour 1 cup of the water and 1 cup of the wine around, *not on top of,* the meat. Season with salt and pepper and cover the pan with aluminum foil if you don't have a lid.

Roast for 10 minutes, reduce the temperature to 325 degrees, and roast for a total of about 3 to 3½ hours, basting the meat and vegetables with the juices every half hour or so. The meat should be very tender. (At this point, the meat can be covered and refrigerated for 1 to 3 days. Reheat in a 250-degree oven for about 20 minutes.)

Remove the brisket to a warm serving platter, surround with the vegetables, and slice the meat on the diagonal. Place the juices in the pan over moderately high heat and bring to a boil. Taste for seasoning and serve the juices in a gravy boat or drizzled over each serving.

YIELD: 8 servings

PER SERVING: 657 calories, 60 g protein, 22 g fat, 54 g carbohydrate, 332 mg sodium, 158 mg cholesterol

Old-Fashioned Meat Loaf

Preparation time: about 20 minutes
Cooking time: 1 hour to 1 hour 15 minutes

A favorite food of the 1950s, this meat loaf mixes ground meat with sautéed onions and peppers, catsup, rolled oats, and a touch of Chinese hoisin sauce or fruit marmalade. The meat loaf is then topped with a sweet catsup-based sauce and covered with strips of bacon, which baste the dish as it bakes and add a crispy topping. Serve with potatoes and a steamed green vegetable.

1 teaspoon vegetable oil
1 onion, finely chopped
1 green bell pepper, finely chopped
1 clove garlic, finely chopped
1½ teaspoons dried thyme
Salt and freshly ground black pepper
2 large eggs
1½ pounds low-fat ground meat
⅓ cup rolled oats
¼ cup catsup
1½ tablespoons hoisin sauce or fruit marmalade

TOPPING:
⅓ cup catsup
1 tablespoon hoisin sauce or fruit marmalade
Salt and freshly ground black pepper or dash of hot pepper sauce
3 strips of bacon (optional)

In a medium skillet, heat the oil over a moderately low heat. Add the onion, bell pepper, garlic, ½ teaspoon of the thyme, and salt and pepper and sauté about 10 minutes, stirring frequently, or until the vegetables are soft.

In a bowl, whisk the eggs. Add the ground meat, oats, catsup, hoisin sauce, remaining thyme, salt, pepper, and the sautéed vegetables; mix well. If the mixture seems too moist, add a few more tablespoons of oats so the meat loaf holds together. Form the mixture into a meat loaf shape and place in the middle of a baking pan or shallow casserole.

In a small bowl, combine the topping ingredients except the bacon. Using the back of a spoon or a pastry brush, "paint" the sauce onto the top and sides of the meat loaf. Place the strips of bacon over the meat loaf lengthwise if desired. (At this point, the meat loaf can be covered and refrigerated for up to 8 hours.)

Preheat the oven to 350 degrees. Bake the meat loaf for about 1 hour to 1 hour 15 minutes, or until it is cooked through. Baste with any juices that may have accumulated in the bottom of the pan after about 45 minutes. Remove the strips of bacon and cut the meat loaf into slices.

YIELD: 4 servings
PER SERVING: 412 calories, 24 g protein, 26 g fat, 18 g carbohydrate, 384 mg sodium, 156 mg cholesterol

Easter Ham with a
Clove, Rum, and Orange Glaze

Preparation time: 10 minutes
Marinating time: 4 to 48 hours
Cooking time: about 2 hours

Find a high-quality smoked country ham, follow this recipe, and get ready for the best Easter dinner you've ever had. It may seem odd to cook a ham with rum when you know you'll be serving children, but virtually all of the alcohol has long burned off by the time the ham gets to the table. The combination of the orange juice, rum, cranberry juice, and shallots is irresistible and creates a gorgeous glaze. This recipe is in honor of my friend, Gene Brown, who has hosted our family for Easter dinner ever since our children were babies. Serve with hot cross buns, asparagus, potatoes (or macaroni and cheese), and applesauce.

1 fully cooked smoked country ham, bone in (about 10 pounds)
½ cup whole cloves
About 4 cups freshly squeezed orange juice or old-fashioned type with
**   pulp**
1 cup cranberry juice
About 1 cup light rum
12 shallots, peeled and left whole

Place the ham in a large roasting pan. Insert the cloves into the top of the ham (the side with the most fat) at about 2-inch intervals. Pour the orange juice, cranberry juice, and rum over the ham and let marinate, covered and refrigerated, for at least 4 hours or up to 48 hours, turning the ham once or twice.

Preheat the oven to 325 degrees. Add the shallots to the roasting pan and roast the ham until the internal temperature reaches 140 degrees, about 12 minutes per pound, for a total cooking time of 2 hours. The marinade should now be a thick gooey glaze. Baste the ham every 15 minutes, making sure the glaze is not drying out. If the glaze gets too thick and appears to be burning, add more orange juice and/or rum or water.

Remove the roast from the oven. Place the ham on a carving board and let sit, loosely covered with aluminum foil, for 10 to 15 minutes before carving.

Discard any excess fat from the pan. Place the roasting pan over 2 burners on the stove. Heat the sauce and the shallots over moderately low heat and bring to a gentle simmer, scraping up any browned juices. Add another ¼ cup orange juice or water if necessary to thin the sauce a bit.

Cut the ham into thin slices. Serve topped with the sauce and roasted shallots.

YIELD: 12 servings

PER SERVING: 169 calories, 17 g protein, 5 g fat, 14 g carbohydrate, 1,219 mg sodium, 40 mg cholesterol

Roast Pork with White Beans and Cider

Preparation time: 10 minutes
Cooking time: about 1 hour 10 minutes

This is a terrific dish for the fall, when those first cool nights signal a need for heartier, comforting foods. From start to finish, it takes about 1 hour 15 minutes.

1 teaspoon olive oil
3 cups cooked white beans, drained
3 pounds boneless loin of pork
2 cloves garlic, very thinly sliced
Salt and freshly ground black pepper
3 tablespoons chopped fresh rosemary or 3 teaspoons dried
1 tablespoon chopped fresh thyme or 1 teaspoon dried
About 1 cup apple cider

Preheat the oven to 425 degrees. Grease the bottom of a shallow casserole or baking pan with the oil. Place the beans in the casserole, and the meat in the center of the beans. Using a small sharp knife, make several small incisions on top of the meat and insert a thin slice of garlic in each. Spread the rest of the garlic around the meat on top of the beans. Sprinkle the meat and beans with the salt, pepper, rosemary, and thyme and pour ½ cup cider on top. Stir the beans to incorporate the seasonings.

Roast for 15 minutes. Reduce the oven temperature to 350 degrees and cover loosely with aluminum foil. After about 30 minutes, add the remaining ½ cup cider, baste the meat, and stir the beans. Cover and continue roasting for a total of about 1 hour 10 minutes, or until the pork reaches an internal temperature of 150 degrees when tested with a meat thermometer. Remove from the oven and let sit for about 5 minutes. Thinly slice and serve with the beans on the side.

YIELD: 4 to 6 servings
PER SERVING: 725 calories, 65 g protein, 36 g fat, 34 g carbohydrate, 145 mg sodium, 172 mg cholesterol

Country-Style Pork Ribs in Sweet-and-Sour BBQ Sauce

Preparation time: 10 minutes
Marinating time: 1 to 48 hours
Cooking time: about 1 hour 15 minutes

A thick, gooey sauce makes these ribs so tender that they practically fall off the bone. Mashed potatoes are a must (particularly topped with a spoonful of barbecue sauce), and be sure to supply plenty of napkins. Marinate the ribs in the morning and pop them in the oven when you get home in the early evening.

SAUCE:

> 1 cup catsup
>
> 2 tablespoons soy sauce
>
> 1½ tablespoons balsamic or red wine vinegar
>
> ½ to 1 teaspoon Chinese chili paste or hot pepper sauce
>
> ¼ cup maple syrup or honey
>
> 1 tablespoon chopped fresh ginger or 1 teaspoon ground

THE RIBS:

> 3½ to 4 pounds country-style pork ribs

Mix all the ingredients for the sauce in a shallow casserole, broiler pan, or large gratin dish. Add the ribs, cover, and let marinate in the refrigerator for at least 1 hour, preferably overnight, or up to 48 hours.

Preheat the oven to 325 degrees. Remove a little more than half the sauce from the ribs and place in a small saucepan. Bake the ribs for 30 minutes. Meanwhile, place the pot of sauce over moderately low heat and let simmer. Flip the ribs and add half the remaining sauce. Bake another 30 minutes. Flip the ribs again and add the remaining sauce. Bake another 15 to 30 minutes, or until the ribs are very tender.

YIELD: 4 to 6 servings
PER SERVING: 662 calories, 40 g protein, 43 g fat, 24 g carbohydrate, 1,143 mg sodium, 160 mg cholesterol

Chris's Somewhat Low-Fat
Louisiana Gumbo

Preparation time: about 1 hour
Cooking time: about 2 hours

My friend Chris Williams grew up in Cajun country, and gumbo, in its many guises, was an integral part of her childhood. One wintery afternoon she visited my New England kitchen and taught me the basics of making a real gumbo, but this being the nineties, we cut out a whole lot of the fat.

This is the perfect dish to make for a crowd. Although it takes several hours to put together, the whole gumbo can be made a day ahead of time and simply reheated before serving. (Chris insists that, like most soups and stews, the gumbo tastes better the longer it sits.) Gumbo can be made from just about anything—shrimp, chicken, catfish, sausage, and okra or other vegetables. This version uses a variety of sausages and pieces of chicken mixed with leeks and what the Cajuns call "the holy trinity"—garlic, onions, and bell peppers.

The gumbo is served in a big bowl over a bed of rice, and everyone takes a sweet potato and buries it in their serving. The natural sweetness of the potato cuts the rich spiciness of the gumbo. Then everyone tops their stew with finely chopped parsley, scallions, and gumbo filé (a powder of ground sassafras leaves).

You will need a very large pot for this dish; if you don't have one, you can use two large pots and make the gumbo in batches. You can also cut this recipe in half for a smaller party.

> **About 1½ cups all-purpose flour**
> **About 2 to 3 tablespoons olive or vegetable oil**
> **6 andouille or other type of spicy sausage, cut into bite-size chunks (a low-fat variety if available)**
> **6 mild turkey, chicken, or pork sausages, cut into bite-size chunks (a low-fat variety if available)**
> **3 whole skinless, boneless chicken breasts, cut into bite-size chunks**
> **6 to 8 chicken drumsticks or wings**
> **⅓ to ½ cup chopped fresh thyme or ¼ cup dried**
> **1 large leek, finely chopped**
> **3 large onions, chopped**
> **10 cloves garlic, finely chopped**

5 scallions, finely chopped

3 red bell peppers, cored and chopped

2 green bell peppers, cored and chopped

6 stalks celery, finely chopped

6 cups low-sodium chicken broth or water

12 peppercorns tied in cheesecloth

4 bay leaves

Cayenne pepper or hot pepper sauce

Salt and freshly ground black pepper

ACCOMPANIMENTS:

16 small sweet potatoes or 8 large

3 cups white rice

Pinch salt

1½ tablespoons vegetable oil

1½ cups finely chopped scallions

1½ cups finely chopped parsley

About ⅓ cup filé powder

Hot pepper sauces

Preheat the oven to 300 degrees. Bring a small saucepan of water to a simmer. Spread the flour in a thin layer in a shallow broiling pan or a baking sheet and cover loosely with tin foil or a lid. Place the pan on the middle shelf of the oven and bake for about 20 to 30 minutes, stirring frequently and checking to make sure the flour isn't burning. To test the flour, sprinkle a few teaspoons of the flour into the simmering water and stir. The water will turn a golden or chocolate brown. Keep testing, using fresh water, until the water is a rich, mahogany brown. This indicates the color the gumbo will turn when the flour is mixed in.

In a large pot, heat 1 tablespoon of the oil over moderately high heat. Add the sausages in batches and brown on both sides, about 5 minutes. Remove with a slotted spoon and set aside. Add another tablespoon of oil if needed and add the chicken pieces and some of the thyme. Brown on both sides, about 5 minutes, and set aside.

Add another tablespoon of oil if the pot is dry and add the leek, onions, half the garlic, and the scallions. Sauté, stirring frequently, about 5 minutes. Add more of the thyme, the bell peppers, and the celery and cook, stirring frequently, for about 15 minutes.

When testing the flour produces a rich, chocolate brown color, remove it from the oven. Add about a cup of the flour to the pot, stirring well to coat all the vegetables, and let cook about 5 minutes. Add the chicken broth and bring to a simmer. Add the sautéed sausages and chicken pieces and add enough water to cover all the ingredients. Add the peppercorns, bay leaves, and a sprinkle of cayenne or hot pepper sauce. Bring to a boil, reduce the heat, and let simmer, partially covered, for about 2 hours. The final consistency of the gumbo should be like slightly thickened chicken soup. Taste for seasoning and add more cayenne, salt, and pepper if desired. (The dish can be made ahead of time up to this point. Cover and keep in the refrigerator or a very cool spot.)

An hour before you are ready to eat, preheat the oven to 350 degrees. Bake the sweet potatoes for about 45 minutes to 1½ hours, depending on the size, or until tender throughout. Meanwhile, mix the rice with 6 cups of water, a pinch of salt, and the oil in a large saucepan. Bring to a boil, stir well, and then reduce the heat and let cook about 10 minutes, or until all the water has been absorbed and the rice is tender and dry. Keep warm over low heat.

Place the sweet potatoes in a large bowl. Place the chopped scallions, parsley, and the filé powder in small bowls, and set everything on the table.

To serve, heat the gumbo until simmering and hot throughout. Remove the peppercorn bundle and bay leaves and discard. For each serving, place a ladleful of rice in the bottom of a large bowl. Top with the gumbo and let each person place a potato (or half a potato) in the middle of the gumbo and sprinkle with the parsley, scallions, and filé. Serve hot sauces on the side and let everyone season their stew to taste.

YIELD: 16 servings

PER SERVING: 725 calories, 38 g protein, 26 g fat, 84 g carbohydrate, 737 mg sodium, 107 mg cholesterol

Baked Salmon with Roasted Pecan Crust

Preparation time: about 10 minutes
Cooking time: about 20 minutes

The Tyler Place, on the shores of Lake Champlain in Highgate Springs, Vermont, is a family camp where adults and children vacation together. One of the outstanding features of the camp is the food they serve; it is always fresh, seasonal, and has the unique quality of pleasing both adults and kids.

This salmon recipe, which comes from chef Jamie West, is definitely on the sophisticated side, but kids will be lured in by the rich, crunchy pecan topping. For an extra-nutty taste, roast the pecans on a baking sheet in a 350-degree oven for about 5 minutes, making sure they don't burn. This is an ideal dish for a dinner party. Be sure to make plenty, because the leftovers are delicious the next day served in a cold salad.

½ teaspoon vegetable or olive oil
1½ pounds salmon fillet
Salt and freshly ground black pepper
1½ cups chopped pecans
2½ tablespoons butter, melted
1 tablespoon fresh lemon juice
1 teaspoon Worcestershire sauce

Preheat the oven to 350 degrees. Grease a medium roasting pan or large ovenproof skillet with the oil. Place the salmon fillet in the pan, skin side down, and sprinkle with the salt and pepper.

In a small bowl mix the pecans, melted butter, lemon juice, and Worcestershire sauce. Spread the nut topping on the salmon. Place on the middle shelf of the oven and bake for about 20 minutes, or until cooked through.

YIELD: 4 servings
PER SERVING: 583 calories, 37g protein, 46 g fat, 8 g carbohydrate, 162 mg sodium, 113 mg cholesterol

Grilled Trout Stuffed with
Fresh Figs and Wrapped in Bacon

Preparation time: 15 minutes
Cooking time: about 20 minutes

This is one of the best fish dishes I've ever tasted. Fresh trout are stuffed with thin wedges of fresh figs and sprigs of fresh rosemary and then wrapped in thin pieces of bacon or prosciutto and grilled over an open fire or on a barbecue. The fish can also be roasted at a high temperature and then placed under the broiler just before serving.

This is an ideal dish for an outdoor family gathering. The fresher the ingredients, the better the dish. Serve with roast or grilled potatoes.

4 trout, cleaned
Freshly ground black pepper
2 tablespoons chopped fresh rosemary, or 2 teaspoons dried
2 ripe figs, cut into quarters, or 4 dried figs, soaked in hot water for
   10 minutes and drained
4 thin slices of prosciutto or cured ham or 4 slices bacon

Lay the fish on a clean work surface, open up the cavity, and sprinkle with pepper. Divide the rosemary and figs evenly among the fish and place inside the cavities. Place the prosciutto or bacon on the work surface and "roll" around each fish, covering as much of the outside surface of the fish as possible. Tie in the center with a piece of string or butcher's twine. Place on a rack if grilling and in a broiler pan if roasting in oven.

Prepare a charcoal fire in an outdoor grill or preheat the oven to 400 degrees. Grill the trout for about 10 minutes on each side, depending on the thickness of the fish and the intensity of the fire. Or roast the fish in the oven for 10 to 15 minutes, then place under the broiler for another minute or two, until the fish feels soft and flakes easily when tested with a sharp knife or fork. The outside will become slightly blackened, but be careful not to overcook the fish.

YIELD: 4 servings
PER SERVING: 227 calories, 35 g protein, 7 g fat, 5 g carbohydrate, 239 mg sodium, 97 mg
   cholesterol

Cheese Fondue

Preparation time: about 30 minutes
Cooking time: 15 minutes

Although you could serve this fondue on a weeknight, it is such fun to make and eat that it calls for something of a celebration. Each person is given a fondue fork or wooden skewer with a different color at the tip, and dips a wide assortment of vegetables, cubed bread, potatoes, and fruit into a bubbling pot of melted cheese. (Get the kids to help paint the ends of wooden skewers if you don't have fondue forks.)

To keep the cheese from hardening, the fondue must be kept hot over a Sterno burner or small candle, or you can prepare it in a chafing dish. Traditional cheese fondue is made with white wine, but I've found that apple cider works just as well.

FONDUE:
- **1 cup apple cider or white wine**
- **¾ pound Gruyère, Cheddar, Emmentaler, or Swiss cheese or a combination, grated**
- **1 tablespoon flour**
- **Freshly ground black pepper**

DIPPING CHOICES:
- **1 loaf French or Italian bread, cubed**
- **About 4 cups vegetables cut into bite-size pieces (zucchini, cauliflower, celery, carrots, broccoli, etc.), raw or lightly steamed**
- **4 cooked small new potatoes, cut into bite-size pieces (optional)**
- **1 cup apples and pears cut into bite-size pieces (optional)**

Pour the cider or wine into a large pot or chafing dish and bring to a boil. In a small bowl, mix the cheeses with the flour. Reduce the heat and slowly add the grated cheeses to the pot, stirring constantly, until melted. Season with pepper and serve bubbling hot with the assortment of foods for dipping.

YIELD: 4 servings
PER SERVING: 388 calories, 26 g protein, 27 g fat, 9 g carbohydrate, 288 mg sodium, 94 mg cholesterol

Ground Meat, Spinach, and
Ricotta Lasagna

Preparation time: about 1 hour
Cooking time: 30 to 45 minutes

There are several steps involved in this recipe, but if you prepare the dish ahead of time, it can simply be popped in the oven to bake for about 30 to 45 minutes. (Because the preparation for this dish is lengthy, I like to double the recipe and freeze half for later.) Serve with garlic bread and a tossed salad. If you want to make this a vegetarian dish, double the amount of spinach and omit the meat.

SPINACH LAYER:

> **20 ounces spinach, stemmed**
> **1 tablespoon olive oil**
> **2 cloves garlic, chopped**
> **Salt and freshly ground black pepper**
> **Pinch ground nutmeg**
> **½ teaspoon ground cinnamon**

GROUND MEAT LAYER:

> **1 teaspoon vegetable oil**
> **1 onion, finely chopped**
> **2 cloves garlic, finely chopped**
> **1 teaspoon dried thyme**
> **1 teaspoon dried oregano**
> **½ teaspoon ground cinnamon**
> **Salt and freshly ground black pepper**
> **Dash hot pepper sauce**
> **1 pound ground beef**
> **1 cup canned or homemade tomato sauce**

RICOTTA LAYER:

> **2 large eggs**
> **4 cups (32 ounces) low-fat ricotta cheese**

½ cup grated Parmesan cheese
Salt and freshly ground black pepper
1 teaspoon ground cinnamon
½ cup tomato sauce

LASAGNA LAYER:
10 to 12 lasagna noodles
1 cup tomato sauce
2 cups grated mozzarella cheese
Freshly ground black pepper

To prepare the spinach, wash the leaves well and place in a large pot with the water still clinging to the leaves. Steam over high heat until tender, about 5 minutes, stirring constantly. Rinse the spinach under cold running water and squeeze all the water out by pressing between 2 plates.

Finely chop the spinach. In a medium skillet, heat the oil over moderate heat. Add the garlic and cook 1 minute. Add the spinach, salt, pepper, nutmeg, and cinnamon and sauté about 3 minutes. Set aside.

To prepare the meat, in a large skillet, heat the oil over moderate heat. Add the onion and garlic and sauté about 5 minutes, being careful not to let it brown. Add the thyme, oregano, cinnamon, salt, pepper, and hot pepper sauce. Add the meat and cook until there is no sign of pinkness, about 10 to 15 minutes. Drain off any excess fat by tipping the skillet slightly to the side and blotting any fat up with a paper towel. Add the tomato sauce and set aside.

To prepare the ricotta mixture, in a large bowl, whisk the eggs. Add the ricotta cheese, Parmesan, salt, pepper, cinnamon, and tomato sauce and mix well. Set aside.

To assemble the lasagna, bring a large pot of lightly salted water to a boil over high heat. Add the lasagna noodles, placing them in the boiling water crisscross style (one going one way, the next going the other way). Boil for about 12 to 15 minutes, until just tender, or follow the directions on the package. Drain and place in cold water to stop the cooking. Drain and pat dry with paper towels or a clean tea towel.

While the noodles are cooking, spread about ⅓ cup of the tomato sauce on the bottom of a 13-by-9-inch pan or lasagna pan. Preheat the oven to 350 degrees.

Line the bottom of the pan with 5 lasagna noodles placed crosswise. Add the spinach mixture, spreading it out in an even layer across the noodles. Sprinkle with one-third of the mozzarella cheese and top with half of the ricotta mixture. Spread the meat over the ricotta layer and spoon the remaining ricotta cheese on top. Sprinkle with another third of the mozzarella. Cover the cheese with the remaining 5 strips of lasagna, making sure to trim the edges so that none of the pasta hangs over the edge. (Any overhanging pasta will burn.) Spread the remaining tomato sauce over all the pasta and sprinkle with the remaining mozzarella and a grinding of pepper. (The recipe can be prepared ahead of time up to this point; cover and refrigerate for up to 2 days or freeze for up to 2 months.) Bake for about 30 to 45 minutes, or until the cheese is golden brown and bubbling.

YIELD: 10 servings

PER SERVING: 480 calories, 32 g protein, 24 g fat, 35 g carbohydrate, 822 mg sodium, 121 mg cholesterol

SOME THOUGHTS ABOUT . . .
Popeye's Favorite: Spinach

Despite what you've heard for years, children do not hate spinach. Oh, sure, there are kids out there who will turn their nose up at just about any green food. In a very unscientific poll taken among a group of four- and seven-year-olds, over 50 percent of the children I interviewed admitted that, in fact, they do like spinach. "So what's the big deal?" one boy asked.

Spinach, like so many other foods, needs to be presented in the right context. It's never a good idea to serve your child a dish and say, "I know you don't like this, but why don't you give it a try." Instead, serve spinach with other foods your child enjoys— raisins, cream, spices, or bread crumbs—and encourage her in a positive way to experience this delicious, nutritious vegetable.

Spinach is full of vitamins and calcium and is available fresh year round. It can be tossed into salads (it's particularly good topped with nuts), baked in quiche (see page 160) or lasagna (see page 280), used as a pasta sauce, or incorporated into soufflés (page 284) and omelettes. It's simple to stir-fry or sauté or cream (page 227) and adds wonderful color to sandwiches (either steamed or raw) and soups.

The basic technique for cooking fresh spinach is simple. Because spinach tends to be sandy, always wash the leaves well under cold running water. Place in a large pot with the water still clinging to the leaves. Cover and steam over high heat until tender, about 6 minutes, depending on the quantity and freshness of the spinach. Place in a colander and rinse under cold running water; this process (called refreshing) stops the cooking so that the spinach doesn't get overcooked, and helps to preserve its bright green color. To remove all the excess water from the spinach (there's nothing worse than soggy spinach), place it between 2 large plates and press down hard to remove the water, or squeeze out the water using your hands. Chop the spinach and proceed with the recipe. This technique also applies to fresh kale, Swiss chard, and other hearty greens.

Spinach Soufflé Roll Stuffed with Roasted Red Peppers

Preparation time: 45 minutes
Cooking time: 10 minutes

The red and green colors of this spectacular soufflé make it perfect holiday fare. Once the advance prep is completed, all you do at the last minute is beat the egg whites, fold them in, and bake.

1½ tablespoons butter or margarine
2 tablespoons olive or vegetable oil
1 large onion, chopped
1 pound fresh spinach, steamed and finely chopped (see page 283), or frozen spinach, thawed
¼ teaspoon ground nutmeg
Salt and freshly ground black pepper
4 large eggs
⅔ cup grated Parmesan cheese
2 large roasted red bell peppers (see page 442), cut into thin slices, or the equivalent amount of pimientos, drained
2 tablespoons chopped scallions or fresh chives

Place a piece of wax paper on the bottom and an inch up the sides of a large shallow baking dish. Fold the paper at the corners to create a kind of shallow box. Butter the paper with ½ tablespoon of the butter and set the baking dish aside.

In a large skillet, heat the remaining tablespoon of butter and 1 tablespoon of the oil over moderate heat. Add the onion and sauté about 3 minutes, over moderate heat, then add the spinach and sauté another 2 minutes. Remove from the heat and add the nutmeg, salt, and pepper. Let cool slightly. (The recipe can be prepared a day ahead of time up to this point. Refrigerate the spinach mixture and the peppers in separate containers, then let sit at room temperature for several minutes when you're ready to proceed.)

Preheat the oven to 400 degrees. Separate the eggs. Whisk the egg whites until soft peaks form.

Whisk the yolks and add one at a time, to the cooled spinach mixture and stir to incorporate. Gently fold in the beaten egg whites. Spread the mixture evenly in the pre-pared baking dish and sprinkle with half of the cheese. Bake on the top oven shelf for about 10 minutes, or until the soufflé has risen and is firm to the touch.

Meanwhile, heat the other tablespoon of oil in a medium skillet over moderate heat. Add the pepper strips, scallions, and salt and pepper to taste.

Remove the soufflé from the oven and gently turn it upside down onto a baking sheet or a piece of wax paper. Peel the paper from the soufflé and spread the peppers over the surface. Roll the soufflé up into a fat log shape, sprinkle with the remaining cheese, and serve.

YIELD: 6 to 8 servings

PER SERVING: 158 calories, 9 g protein, 11 g fat, 7 g carbohydrate, 248 mg sodium, 132 mg cholesterol

Bean Bundles

Preparation time: 25 minutes
Cooking time: about 11 minutes

This is one of my favorite ways to prepare fresh green beans. The beans are cooked for a minute, drained, and gathered into little bundles rolled in a slice of prosciutto ham. A garlic butter is poured on top, and the dish is finished off under the broiler with a thin grating of cheese. This dish is especially good for parties, as it can be done ahead of time.

¾ pound thin green beans, trimmed
½ pound prosciutto, sliced paper thin
3 tablespoons butter
1 tablespoon olive oil
3 cloves garlic, minced
Freshly ground black pepper
⅓ cup grated Parmesan cheese

Bring a pot of water to a boil over moderately high heat, add the beans, and cook until *almost* tender, about 4 minutes. Drain and rinse under cold water. Drain again. Gather beans into small bundles of 8. Trim the ends so they are all of equal size.

Cut the prosciutto slices in half lengthwise. Put 1 bean bundle at a short end of each piece of prosciutto. Roll the prosciutto around the bundles and place in a baking dish or ovenproof skillet.

In a small saucepan, heat the butter and olive oil over moderate heat. Add the garlic and let simmer about 2 minutes. Pour the garlic mixture over the beans and sprinkle with pepper. Bake for 10 minutes. Remove and sprinkle the beans with the cheese. Broil for about 1 minute, or until the cheese is golden brown and bubbling.

YIELD: 4 servings
PER SERVING: 293 calories, 20 g protein, 22 g fat, 6 g carbohydrate, 1,264 mg sodium, 74 mg cholesterol

Baked Leeks with Olive Puree
and Goat Cheese

Preparation time: 10 minutes
Cooking time: 20 minutes

Leeks are blanketed in olive oil, creamy goat cheese, and tapenade (black olive paste, which is available in specialty goods stores)—a fabulous combination. Serve this dish on its own, hot and bubbling from the oven, or as an accompaniment to roast chicken, beef, or fish. Leftovers are delicious served at room temperature and tossed with a simple vinaigrette (see page 448).

> **1 tablespoon plus 1 teaspoon olive oil**
> **4 leeks, sliced lengthwise, then into 2-inch-long pieces**
> **Salt and freshly ground black pepper**
> **½ cup crumbled goat cheese**
> **¼ cup tapenade or olive puree**

Preheat the oven to 350 degrees. Place ½ tablespoon of the oil in the bottom of a flameproof shallow casserole or baking pan. Add the leeks and drizzle with another ½ tablespoon of olive oil and sprinkle with salt and pepper. Toss well to thoroughly coat the leeks. Roast for 15 minutes, tossing every 5 minutes to make sure the leeks cook evenly. (If they start to brown lightly, cover the casserole with a lid or a sheet of aluminum foil.)

Sprinkle the cheese over the leeks and add the olive puree in a line down the center of the dish. Drizzle with the remaining teaspoon of olive oil and bake another 5 minutes. Place under the broiler for a minute if desired, until the cheese is golden brown and bubbling.

YIELD: 4 servings
PER SERVING: 184 calories, 6 g protein, 11 g fat, 17 g carbohydrate, 389 mg sodium, 15 mg cholesterol

New Year's Day Roast Beet Salad

Preparation time: 15 minutes
Cooking time: 1 hour

This salad pleases the palate, the eye, and the spirit. Beets, with their earthy maroon color and sweet taste, are roasted and then tossed with a simple vinaigrette. Leeks, a totally underrated vegetable, are roasted separately with a touch of heavy cream. And pecans are sautéed in butter and then drizzled liberally with honey to create gooey, caramelized nuts. The beets, leeks, and pecans are presented on a bed of mixed greens. This festive dish is a very colorful, delicious, and healthy way to say Happy New Year, but it can be served at any time of year. The recipe makes enough to serve a large crowd, but the quantities can easily be reduced.

BEETS:

10 medium beets, washed but unpeeled
1 tablespoon Dijon mustard
Salt and freshly ground black pepper
¼ cup red wine vinegar
½ cup plus 3 tablespoons good-quality olive oil
2 tablespoons chopped fresh dill or chives (optional)

LEEKS:

1 teaspoon olive oil
2 thin leeks, sliced lengthwise, then into 2-inch-long pieces
Salt and freshly ground black pepper
¼ cup heavy cream

HONEY-GLAZED PECANS:

2 tablespoons butter
8 ounces pecan halves
¼ to ⅓ cup good-quality honey

THE SALAD AND VINAIGRETTE:

About 3 to 4 cups mixed greens cut into bite-size pieces
1 tablespoon Dijon mustard
Salt and freshly ground black pepper
¼ cup red wine vinegar
7 to 8 tablespoons olive oil

Preheat the oven to 400 degrees. To prepare the beets, wrap them tightly in a large piece of aluminum foil. Roast for about 1 hour, or until tender when tested with a small sharp knife or fork. Remove from the oven and let cool until just cool enough to handle. Use a small knife to cut off the root end of each beet and then, using your fingers (or the knife), remove the peel. (When the beets are warm, this is quite simple. If the beets cool too much, the peel won't loosen easily and you may need to cut it off with a knife.)

In a large bowl, mix the mustard, salt, and pepper. Add the vinegar, then whisk in the oil and the dill or chives. Taste for seasoning. Cut the beets into large cubes or thin slices and add to the vinaigrette. Toss well. (This can be done up to 4 hours before serving.)

To prepare the leeks, place the oil in a small gratin dish or ovenproof skillet and add the leek strips. Toss to coat. Add the salt and pepper and the cream. Roast for about 15 minutes, or until tender. Remove and set aside. (The leeks can be roasted at the same time as the beets.)

To prepare the pecans, in a large skillet, melt the butter over moderate heat. Add the nuts and sauté about 3 minutes, stirring to prevent browning. Add the honey and stir continually for about 5 minutes, or until the pecans are coated with the honey mixture and the honey has caramelized on the nuts. Remove from the heat and let cool.

Arrange the beets in the center of a large platter. Place the salad greens around the outside. Place the leeks around the beets and sprinkle the pecans around the leeks. Mix the mustard, salt, pepper, vinegar, and oil and serve this vinaigrette on the side or lightly sprinkled over the greens.

YIELD: 10 to 12 servings
PER SERVING: 455 calories, 3 g protein, 41 g fat, 22 g carbohydrate, 133 mg sodium, 13 mg cholesterol

Vegetable Risotto

Preparation time: 5 minutes
Cooking time: 40 minutes

A creamy accompaniment to fish, poultry, or beef entrees, risotto can also star as the main dish.

1 tablespoon olive or vegetable oil
1 small onion, finely chopped
Salt and freshly ground black pepper
5 asparagus spears, ends trimmed, cut into 2-inch pieces
1 cup arborio or short-grain rice
2 to 3 cups chicken or vegetable broth
½ cup freshly grated Parmesan cheese
2 tablespoons finely chopped fresh parsley (optional)

In a medium heavy-bottomed pan, heat the oil over moderate heat. Add the chopped onion and sauté for about 5 minutes, or until tender but not browned. Add the salt and pepper and the asparagus pieces and sauté for another 2 minutes. Add the rice and sauté for 2 minutes more. Add the stock, about ¼ cup at a time, stirring until each addition is absorbed. Continue adding the stock until the rice is creamy and tender and has a very slight crunch, about 20 to 30 minutes.

Remove the risotto from the heat and stir in the cheese, a few tablespoons at a time. Season with salt and pepper to taste and garnish with the parsley if desired. Serve immediately.

YIELD: 4 servings
PER SERVING: 296 calories, 11 g protein, 8 g fat, 44 g carbohydrate, 845 mg sodium, 10 mg cholesterol

Pumpkin Risotto

Preparation time: 10 minutes
Cooking time: about 30 to 35 minutes

This is a rich, creamy rice dish, just right for a cool autumn night. The pumpkin gives the rice a slightly sweet flavor and a beautiful orange hue. (My younger daughter told me the dish looked a lot like macaroni and cheese but "tasted yummier.") Choose a small sugar pumpkin, slice it in half, and cut the flesh from the skin. Use a cheese grater to grate the pumpkin.

2 cups chicken broth
1 tablespoon olive or vegetable oil
1 onion, finely chopped
1½ cups grated pumpkin
1 tablespoon chopped fresh sage or 1 teaspoon dried
1 cup short-grain rice, preferably arborio
About 2 cups chicken or vegetable broth
1 cup grated Parmesan cheese
Salt and freshly ground black pepper

Heat the broth in a medium saucepan over moderately low heat and keep at a simmer.

In a large saucepan, heat the oil over moderate heat. Add the onion and sauté about 8 minutes, or until soft but not brown. Add the pumpkin and sauté another 5 minutes. Stir in the sage. Add the rice and sauté, stirring constantly, for about a minute. Slowly add the broth, about ¼ cup at a time, stirring frequently. Don't add more broth until all the liquid has been absorbed. After the 2 cups of broth have been absorbed, the rice should be tender; add more broth if needed. Slowly stir in the cheese and add salt and pepper to taste. Serve hot.

YIELD: 4 servings as a main course; 6 as a side dish
PER SERVING: 347 calories, 14 g protein, 11 g fat, 48 g carbohydrate, 875 mg sodium, 16 mg cholesterol

French Mashed Potatoes

Preparation time: 25 minutes
Cooking time: 45 minutes

These mashed potatoes are enriched with ½ cup crème fraîche, a thickened cultured French cream. If you can't find crème fraîche in your grocery store, sour cream is a reasonable substitute.

12 medium boiling potatoes, peeled and cut in half
2 tablespoons plus 1 teaspoon olive oil
½ cup low-fat milk
½ cup crème fraîche
Salt and freshly ground black pepper

Bring a large pot of water to boil over high heat. Add the potatoes and boil for about 20 minutes, or until tender when tested with a fork or small knife. Drain the potatoes and return to the pan. Mash the potatoes with a large fork, masher, or spoon. Add the 2 tablespoons of olive oil, the milk, and a generous pinch of salt and pepper. Stir in half the crème fraîche. Mash until (mostly) smooth and taste for seasoning.

Grease the bottom of a medium or large casserole or ovenproof skillet with the teaspoon of oil. Scoop the potatoes into the casserole, smoothing down the top. Spoon the remaining crème fraîche down the middle of the dish and season the top with salt and pepper. (The dish can be made to this point up to 6 hours ahead of time. Cover and refrigerate until ready to serve.)

Preheat the oven to 350 degrees. Bake the potatoes for about 30 minutes, or until golden brown on top and warm throughout. You can also put the casserole under a hot broiler for a few minutes just before serving to give the potatoes a golden "crust."

YIELD: 6 servings
PER SERVING: 364 calories, 7 g protein, 14 g fat, 53 g carbohydrate, 45 mg sodium, 17 mg cholesterol

Edwin Potatoes

Preparation time: about 20 minutes
Cooking time: 1 hour 15 minutes

These potatoes are a favorite in our house because they go well with just about everything. We like them so much that sometimes we eat them without anything else for dinner. Thin slices of potatoes are layered with butter, a very light sprinkling of flour, and salt and pepper, then covered with milk and baked until creamy, golden brown, and bubbling. Traditionally these are called scalloped potatoes, but I was first introduced to this dish by our friend Edwin Child, so in our house they are always referred to as "Edwin Potatoes."

4 tablespoons butter, cut into small cubes
8 medium potatoes, peeled and thinly sliced
About 2 tablespoons flour
Salt and freshly ground black pepper
3 tablespoons chopped fresh thyme or 3 teaspoons dried
About 1½ to 2 cups low-fat or whole milk

Preheat the oven to 350 degrees. Lightly grease the bottom and sides of a shallow casserole, gratin dish, or ovenproof skillet with a tablespoon of the butter. Place about a third of the potatoes in a single layer on the bottom. Sprinkle with about a tablespoon of flour, a liberal pinch of salt and pepper, a tablespoon of the thyme, and a tablespoon of butter cubes. Place another layer of potatoes on top and repeat with the remaining tablespoon of flour, salt and pepper, 1 tablespoon of thyme, and another tablespoon of butter. Place the remaining potatoes on top and add salt, pepper, and the remaining thyme and butter. (The dish can be made several hours ahead of time up to this point. Cover and refrigerate.)

Pour 1½ cups of the milk over the potatoes, sprinkle the top with salt and pepper, and bake for 1 hour to 1 hour 15 minutes, occasionally basting the potatoes and breaking up any bubbles that form on the top. If the potatoes appear to be drying out, add the additional milk on top. The potatoes are done when they tender, golden brown, and bubbling.

YIELD: 6 to 8 servings

PER SERVING: 247 calories, 6 g protein, 7 g fat, 40 g carbohydrate, 109 mg sodium, 20 mg cholesterol

Portuguese Potatoes with Linguica Sausage and Peppers

Preparation time: about 10 minutes
Cooking time: about 21 minutes

Try this belly-warming dish on a cold winter night; it's a blend of soothing potatoes, sweet peppers, and spicy sausage. The peppers can be roasted ahead of time, and the potatoes mashed in advance as well.

3 cups mashed potatoes
Salt and freshly ground black pepper
1 fresh linguica, chorizo, or Italian sausage, thinly sliced (about 1 pound)
2 roasted large red or green bell peppers, thinly sliced (page 442), or 2 cups bottled roasted peppers
Paprika
¼ cup freshly grated Parmesan cheese

Preheat the oven to 350 degrees. Season the potatoes with salt and pepper, then spread them over the bottom of a lightly oiled medium shallow baking pan. Top with the sausage slices, peppers, paprika, and cheese. Bake for about 20 minutes, or until the potatoes are warmed through and the sausage is totally cooked. Brown under the broiler for 1 minute.

YIELD: 4 servings
PER SERVING: 404 calories, 14 g protein, 26 g fat, 30 g carbohydrate, 994 mg sodium, 51 mg cholesterol

Roast Potatoes with Caramelized Pears

Preparation time: 5 minutes
Cooking time: 1 hour

I was roasting potatoes one night and felt like doing something a bit unusual. I had a bowl of beautiful pears sitting on the kitchen counter and decided to cut them up and roast them along with the potatoes. Sometimes my experiments have dubious results, but this one turned out to be quite wonderful. The potatoes were golden brown and crispy, and the pears became caramelized and added a subtle sweetness to the dish that my children found irresistible. Try it.

10 medium new potatoes
2 just ripe pears, cored and quartered
1 tablespoon olive oil
1 teaspoon dried thyme or 1 tablespoon chopped fresh thyme
Salt and freshly ground black pepper

Preheat the oven to 350 degrees. Place the potatoes and pears in a large ovenproof skillet or shallow casserole. Drizzle the olive oil on top and sprinkle with the thyme and salt and pepper. Shake the pan to coat the potatoes and pears on all sides. Roast for 15 minutes, then turn the potatoes and pears over. Roast another 30 minutes and turn them again so they brown on each side. If the potatoes and pears seem dry, add another ½ tablespoon oil. Roast for 1 hour, or until the potatoes and pears are tender and golden brown.

YIELD: 4 to 5 servings
PER SERVING: 211 calories, 4 g protein, 3 g fat, 43 g carbohydrate, 14 mg sodium, 0 mg cholesterol

Potato Pancakes

Preparation time: about 15 minutes
Sitting time: about 10 minutes
Cooking time: about 20 minutes

This is the traditional food of Chanukah. It's a classic accompaniment to brisket, but it goes equally well with any roast poultry or meat. You can make a whole meal out of these addictive little pancakes; serve with applesauce, sour cream, and/or horseradish.

2 pounds baking potatoes, peeled
About 2 tablespoons flour
1 large onion, finely chopped
1 large egg
Salt and freshly ground black pepper
Vegetable oil or shortening
Sour cream, applesauce, and horseradish

Finely grate the potatoes by hand or with a food processor and place in a large bowl. Let stand about 10 minutes, until a watery liquid forms. There are several ways to remove the water: drain the potatoes in a fine sieve and press down with the back of a spoon; drain the potatoes by wringing them in a dish towel; carefully spoon off all the water; or blot the potatoes dry with paper towels. Stir the flour, onion, and egg into the potatoes, adding more flour if needed to bind the mixture together.

In a large skillet, heat about ¼ inch of oil over moderate heat until it just starts to smoke. For each pancake, carefully drop about ¼ cup batter into the skillet and flatten with a spatula. Cook about 1½ minutes on each side, or until golden brown. Serve with the sour cream, applesauce, and horseradish on the side.

YIELD: 8 servings
PER SERVING: 125 calories, 3 g protein, 4 g fat, 19 g carbohydrate, 14 mg sodium, 27 mg cholesterol

Potato and Chestnut Gratin

Preparation time: 20 minutes if using canned chestnuts; 50 minutes if using fresh

Cooking time: 1 hour 25 minutes

Sitting time: about 10 to 15 minutes

Savor the rich, earthy scent that fills the kitchen when chestnuts are roasting in the oven. To save time, slice the potatoes in a food processor instead of by hand.

1½ cups fresh chestnuts or 1 can (10 ounces) unsweetened chestnuts, drained

3 tablespoons butter or margarine plus 1 teaspoon, cut into small pieces

4 baking potatoes, peeled and thinly sliced

Salt and freshly ground black pepper

2 onions, thinly sliced

About 2 tablespoons flour

About 3 cups whole or low-fat milk

To prepare the fresh chestnuts, preheat the oven to 400 degrees. Using a small sharp knife, cut an *X* into the flat side of each chestnut; place them on a baking sheet or shallow baking dish. Roast about 12 to 15 minutes, or until they begin to pop through the opening. Using a pot holder, peel the chestnuts while still warm. (The more they cool, the harder they are to peel. You can reheat them in the oven if necessary.) Thinly slice the chestnuts and set aside. (If you are using canned chestnuts, thinly slice and set aside.)

Grease the bottom of a large shallow casserole or gratin dish with 1 tablespoon of the butter. Arrange half of the potatoes in the casserole, overlapping the edges slightly. Season well with salt and pepper. Scatter half of the onions on top. Sprinkle lightly with 1 tablespoon of the flour and top with 1 tablespoon of the butter. Repeat with a second layer. Place the chestnuts on top, and dot with the remaining teaspoon of butter. Slowly pour the milk over the potatoes and chestnuts until they are almost completely covered.

Lower the oven temperature to 350 degrees, place the casserole on a baking sheet, and bake in the lower third of the oven for 1 hour 10 minutes, checking periodically to make sure the milk hasn't all been absorbed. (Add more milk if necessary.) Raise the temperature to 375 degrees and bake an additional 10 to 15 minutes, or until golden brown. Let sit for 10 to 15 minutes before cutting and serving.

YIELD: 6 to 8 servings
PER SERVING: 249 calories, 7 g protein, 10 g fat, 35 g carbohydrate, 124 mg sodium, 29 mg cholesterol

Mashed Sweet Potatoes with Honey-Glazed Pecans

Preparation time: about 45 minutes
Cooking time: 30 minutes

This is a rich dish that is ideal for the holidays. Sweet potatoes are boiled until soft and then mashed with a touch of maple syrup, butter, and ground ginger. The potatoes are then placed in a casserole and topped with pecans that have been caramelized in a honey butter. This recipe makes enough to serve about 15 people—a large holiday crowd—and still have some left over for noshing on in the days to come.

8 large sweet potatoes, peeled and cut into large chunks
4 tablespoons butter
¼ cup maple syrup or honey
2 teaspoons ground ginger
Salt and freshly ground black pepper

PECAN TOPPING:
3 tablespoons butter
½ pound shelled pecan halves
3 tablespoons good-quality flowery honey

Bring a large pot of water to a boil over high heat. Add the potatoes and boil for about 25 minutes, or until the potatoes are very tender when tested with a small sharp knife. Drain the potatoes and mash them with a masher, a fork, or the back of a large spoon. Mash in the butter, maple syrup, ginger, and salt and pepper to taste.

Lightly butter a large casserole and place the mashed potatoes in it. (The recipe can be made up to a day ahead of time up to this point.)

To prepare the pecans, in a medium skillet, heat the butter over moderate heat. Add the pecans and sauté about 2 minutes. Pour the honey on top and sauté, stirring frequently, for about 5 minutes, or until the nuts are well coated with the caramelized honey butter and turn golden brown. Spoon the pecans on top of the sweet potatoes and cover with a lid or aluminum foil. (The recipe can be done an hour ahead of time up to this point.)

Preheat the oven to 350 degrees. Bake the casserole for about 30 minutes, or until hot throughout.

YIELD: about 15 servings
PER SERVING: 313 calories, 3 g protein, 16 g fat, 42 g carbohydrate, 72 mg sodium, 14 mg cholesterol

Sweet Potatoes with Maple-Nutmeg Butter

Preparation time: 1 hour, 15 minutes
Cooking time: 15 to 20 minutes

The sweetness of maple syrup balanced with the pungency of nutmeg creates a memorable blend. This dish goes particularly well with pork dishes. You can turn it into a holiday classic by sprinkling the potatoes with miniature marshmallows and baking them until golden brown.

4 large sweet potatoes
1 stick butter (½ cup)
2 teaspoons ground nutmeg
½ cup maple syrup
Salt and freshly ground black pepper
1 to 1½ cups miniature marshmallows (optional)

Preheat the oven to 350 degrees. Pierce the sweet potatoes in several places, wrap in foil, and bake for about 1 hour, or until soft in the center.

Let the potatoes cool slightly, then peel. Puree in a food processor or mash by hand with a large fork or potato masher.

Melt the butter over moderate heat in a large casserole or an attractive baking dish. Add the nutmeg and sauté for about a minute. Add the pureed sweet potatoes and stir well. Drizzle in the syrup and season to taste with salt and pepper. Smooth out the top of the potatoes. Bake for about 15 minutes, or until warmed through. Sprinkle with the marshmallows if using, and bake another 5 minutes, or until the marshmallows are golden brown.

YIELD: 8 servings
PER SERVING: 285 calories, 2 g protein, 12 g fat, 43 g carbohydrate, 135 mg sodium, 31 mg cholesterol

Sweet Potato and Vegetable Croquettes

Preparation time: about 30 minutes
Chilling time: 2 to 24 hours
Cooking time: about 10 to 15 minutes

These croquettes—small, deep-fried balls of mashed sweet potatoes, sautéed onions, nutmeg, and vegetables—are delicate morsels that melt in the mouth. They're an adaptation of the classic Italian arancini, *which are fried balls of rice stuffed with peas and cheese. Serve as an hors d'oeuvre, first course, or alongside meat and poultry dishes. Make a lot. They go fast.*

1 tablespoon butter
1 small onion, finely chopped
Salt and freshly ground black pepper
Pinch ground nutmeg
**½ cup peas, finely cubed zucchini, diced red or green bell pepper, or a
    combination**
1½ cups mashed cooked sweet potatoes
1 large egg yolk
1 tablespoon low-fat milk
About 1 cup all-purpose flour
About 1 cup bread crumbs
2 large eggs
Peanut oil

In a large skillet, melt the butter over moderate heat. Add the onion and a sprinkling of salt, pepper, and nutmeg and sauté for about 2 minutes. Add the peas or other vegetables and sauté for about 5 minutes, or until the vegetables are just tender but not brown.

Place the vegetables in a large bowl. Add the mashed potatoes, egg yolk, and milk and mix together. Season generously with salt, pepper, and nutmeg. Cover and refrigerate for several hours or overnight, until well chilled.

Place the flour on a large plate and the bread crumbs on another plate. Whisk the eggs in a bowl and season with salt and pepper.

To form the croquettes, take about a tablespoon of the sweet potato mixture in your hands and form into a ball. Roll the ball in the flour; shake off the excess. Dip each ball into the egg and coat it thoroughly, then roll it in the bread crumbs. Place the prepared croquettes on a large plate while you heat the oil.

Add 2½ inches of oil to a large deep skillet or deep-fat fryer and heat to 375 degrees. (If you don't have a thermometer, simply add a pinch of bread crumbs to the oil; when it's hot enough, it will sizzle vigorously.) Fry the croquettes a few at a time for 2 to 3 minutes, or until golden brown. Remove, drain on paper towels, and serve warm.

YIELD: about 12 to 14 croquettes

PER SERVING: 530 calories, 13 g protein, 19 g fat, 76 g carbohydrate, 266 mg sodium, 169 mg cholesterol

Herbed Popovers

Preparation time: 15 minutes
Cooking time: about 35 minutes

Although the batter can be made ahead, popovers are best served hot from the oven. You may want to double the recipe because these popovers often get gobbled up before they make it to the table.

1½ cups all-purpose flour
1 tablespoon chopped fresh rosemary or ½ teaspoon dried
1 tablespoon chopped fresh thyme or ½ teaspoon dried
¼ teaspoon salt
1½ cups whole or low-fat milk
3 large eggs
2½ tablespoons butter, melted

In a medium bowl, mix the flour, herbs, and salt. Make a well in the center and add the milk, eggs, and 1 tablespoon of the melted butter. Mix until the batter is smooth. (The recipe can be made ahead of time up to this point. Cover and store in the refrigerator.)

Preheat the oven to 400 degrees. Generously butter a 12-cup muffin pan or iron popover pan and place in the oven for 5 minutes.

Pour the batter into the hot muffin or popover cups until they are two-thirds full. Pour a little of the remaining butter into the center of each cup and bake 15 minutes. Reduce the temperature to 350 degrees and bake an additional 15 to 20 minutes, or until the popovers are golden brown. Serve immediately with plenty of sweet butter.

YIELD: 12 popovers
PER SERVING: 133 calories, 4 g protein, 7 g fat, 14 g carbohydrate, 120 mg sodium, 69 mg cholesterol

Buttermilk-Scallion Corn Bread

Preparation time: 15 minutes
Cooking time: 25 minutes

This moist, flavorful bread is chock full of scallions and flecks of black pepper. It's a particularly good accompaniment to barbecued spareribs, or serve with a pot of tea and herbal butter. For a holiday treat, serve with the cranberry butter on page 454. This bread also makes a great stuffing for turkey, chicken, or duck. Bake the corn bread a day ahead of time, crumble into small pieces, and stuff the bird.

2 cups cornmeal
1 cup flour
1½ tablespoons sugar
1 tablespoon baking powder
Generous pinch of salt
1 stick butter (½ cup), cut into small cubes
3 large eggs
1½ cups buttermilk
½ cup thinly sliced scallions
Freshly ground black pepper

Preheat the oven to 350 degrees. Butter a large cast-iron or heavy-bottomed ovenproof skillet.

Mix the cornmeal, flour, sugar, baking powder, and salt. Add the butter and, using your hands or 2 knives, work the butter into the mixture until it is the size of small peas.

In a small bowl, whisk the eggs with the buttermilk. Add to the cornmeal mixture along with the scallions and a generous grinding of black pepper. Pour the batter into the buttered skillet and bake about 25 minutes, or until a toothpick inserted in the center comes out clean. Cut into thin triangles and serve warm or at room temperature.

YIELD: 8 to 10 servings
PER SERVING: 309 calories, 8 g protein, 13 g fat, 39 g carbohydrate, 356 mg sodium, 101 mg cholesterol

---~o~---

Entertaining with Kids,
Or How to Have a Dinner Party
Without Losing Your Mind

The role my brothers and I played at our parents' parties was strictly ornamental. Long before the guests arrived, we were fed, bathed, and dressed in our nicest pajamas. We were allowed to watch television until bedtime, when we would be marched downstairs, as though in a scene from *The Sound of Music*, to say goodnight to the assembled crowd.

These days entertaining has changed dramatically. Kids are often invited to help with preparations and cooking and are expected to be an integral part of the festivities. Many parents today don't feel comfortable excluding their children from social events, particularly when these parties occur in their own home.

The ironic upshot of this open policy is that many parents have stopped entertaining. Ever notice that once your friends became parents they stopped inviting you to dinner? Or that the best party you've attended in the last year was your four-year-old son's birthday? The truth is that many parents entertain less and less, even after their kids are old enough to help out or be a part of the party.

I spoke with dozens of parents about their entertaining habits. One woman I know was so nervous about entertaining while her children were home that she allowed her boys to do something she would never normally permit. "We had another couple over for dinner a few months ago. I let the kids watch three videos in a row. It worked out just fine!" Then I heard a story about a couple who let their kids eat take-out pizza in the playroom while the adults dined on a three-course dinner. The dinner party ended abruptly when a toddler had an uncontrollable temper tantrum.

Many parents recalled the days when they were single or just a couple and had total control over the parties they gave. "I had the luxury of spending a few hours shopping for the best ingredients," one woman explained. "I could spend time planning the menu, flowers, and guest list. Now I'm lucky if I can get the shopping done before the guests arrive." The biggest complaint I heard was summed up by one father: "I figure if I can't give a party the way I used to, then I just won't do it anymore."

But there are ways to entertain successfully—with your children—so that everyone has a good time. Here are some tips to keep in mind while planning your party.

- The first step to successful family entertaining is to be realistic about the kind of party you can give.
- Keep things simple. Don't get overly ambitious or set yourself up for disappointment. Choose dishes that can be prepared completely or partially ahead of time (see menu suggestions below). Don't be embarrassed to serve something as simple as roast chicken or spaghetti and meatballs.
- Never cook something for the first time when you're entertaining, particularly when you're inviting children. This is not the occasion for experimentation and culinary surprises.
- Think about inviting a few friends over and simply making more of what you normally serve to your family. Mark Bittman, father of three and an editor at *Cook's Illustrated,* says, "I used to try to impress people. Now when friends come to dinner, everyone gets what I'm cooking for the family. I try to cook good, simple stuff all the time. If I'm entertaining, I might add another vegetable or side dish just to make it feel a bit more special."
- Remember that it's not necessary to have everything ready and in perfect order when the guests arrive. Ask guests to help set the table or put the finishing touches on a dish.
- Decide ahead of time whether or not you want your children to be involved in preparing for the party. A casual get-together with a few close friends is an ideal time to ask the kids to help set the table, chop vegetables, or straighten up the kitchen. Ask your child to draw place cards with everyone's names on them and place them on the table. When children feel part of the event, they tend to be more enthusiastic about participating.
- When asking for your children's help, always make the preparations as anxiety-free as possible. If you're anxious about having everything perfect, your child will undoubtedly lose interest and resent being asked to help.
- Many parents agree that entertaining friends who are also parents can make a party much more relaxed and easy. Colman Andrews, an editor of *Saveur* magazine, says that he and his wife entertain a lot less since they became parents. "Now if we have people over, they usually have kids the same

age as ours." Parents don't seem to feel as much pressure when they're entertaining other parents. There is an unspoken understanding that anyone with
a child knows the realities of putting dinner on the table for family and friends.

• Another advantage to entertaining friends with children is that, once
kids reach a certain age, they can play together on their own. The ideal situa-
tion is when you can talk with your friends while the kids play with each other.

• When you're entertaining adults and children, be sure to consider a
menu that will appeal to both age groups. Always put a few simple foods on
the table that children enjoy—thin slices of cucumbers or pickles, wedges
of cheese, crackers, and such.

• There are several choices to consider when it comes to including
children at your party. Some parents I spoke to said that when they're having a party with friends, they invite the children to sit and have dinner with
everyone but then encourage the kids to be excused from the table when
they're done and go off and play.

• Remember that when a party is lively and the food is good, many
children choose to stay and be part of the action. John Mariani, a food
writer and father of two boys, has vivid memories of his parents' dinner parties. "We always sat at the table with my parents and their friends. I remember the riveting energy at the dinner table. My parents would talk and
scream about Joe McCarthy and communism and Nixon. And even though
I didn't understand everything that was being discussed, I remember learning a lot about the world and my parents, and how deeply and passionately
they felt about certain things."

• There are also times and occasions when you'll want to have an
adults-only party. When my children were four and seven, I longed to have
friends over without any interruptions—something I hadn't done since be-
coming a parent. At first I felt guilty, believing that somehow it was wrong
not to include the kids. But I decided to try it. I asked the kids' favorite
babysitter to take them out for a special evening on the town. While my
daughters enjoyed pizza and a movie, we had ten friends over for a sit-down
dinner with real "adult talk" and no interruptions.

• Remember that food, family, and friends are an equation that should
equal laughter, good times, and good eating. That, above all else, is the ob-
jective of entertaining.

Menu Ideas for Entertaining

Whatever type of party you choose to have—whether it's a family barbecue or a sit-down dinner for friends or business associates—remember to keep it simple.

• Make a large pot of pasta or have a pasta party (see page 420 for more information) with garlic bread and a salad to go along. Ask your friends to bring dessert, or make one of the simple fruit recipes in the dessert chapter.

• Have a summer barbecue and instead of grilling one dish, grill two or three. The morning of the party marinate a few foods to barbecue. Make a potato salad and freeze a few kinds of frozen fruit pops or ice cream. That night you will simply need to steam some corn on the cob, sauté a fresh vegetable, and throw the food on the grill.

• Soups and stews are ideal for lunch or dinner parties because they can be made ahead of time and their flavors actually improve with age.

• Marinating fish, pork, ribs, chicken, or beef in advance also gives you an advantage—all you need to do is throw the food on the grill or into the oven when your guests arrive, and dinner is ready in no time.

• Make a few batches of pizza dough the day before your party and set out an assortment of toppings in small bowls. Let your guests make their own pizza (see recipes, pages 87–90). The same idea can be applied to quesadillas: invite guest to choose among a few simple toppings and create their own quesadilla combination (see recipe, page 164).

• Virtually anything in the Quick Weekday Dinners chapter is ideal for quick, easy entertaining.

• For more elaborate affairs, choose from the Quick Weekend Lunches or Weekend Dinners chapters, or invite friends or family over for a weekend brunch and use some of the recipes in the Weekend Breakfasts chapter.

• See Chapter Thirteen for menu suggestions.

Chapter Eight

Desserts

❧

Dessert is a controversial topic in many households, with kids begging for more and parents insisting on less. In most homes, as well as most cookbooks, dessert means sugar in one form or another. This collection of recipes focuses on healthy and quick desserts, with an emphasis on fresh fruit and yogurt-based sauces and quick breads and cakes that use a minimum of sweeteners. But desserts for special occasions and weekends are not neglected: Peach Cobbler, French Vanilla Ice Cream, Frozen Cocoa, Devil's Food Cake, and more.

Devil's Food Cake

Devil's Food Cupcakes

Dark Chocolate Tangerine Crepes

The Ultimate Brownie

Aunt Mary's Squares

Marble Pumpkin Cheesecake

Becky's Pumpkin Roll

Peach-Honey Sauce for Cakes

Rhubarb-Strawberry Cake

Rhubarb-Strawberry Sauce

Peanut Butter Fondue

Vanilla Pudding

Orange and Ginger Rice Pudding

Impossible Pie

Apple Pie

Caramel Apples

Cranberry Applesauce

Cranberry-Apple Crisp

Quick Apple Crumble

Peach Cobbler

Fruit Kebabs with Yogurt Sauce

Two Seasons Ultimate Fruit Salad with Toppings

Marinated Oranges with Coconut

Caramelized Maple Banana Slices

Chocolate Bananas

Basic Butter Cookies

Gluck's Old-Fashioned Molasses Cookies

Andi's Coffee Tortoni

Andi's Coconut-Date Balls

Lemon Drop Cookies

SOME THOUGHTS ABOUT . . . *Making Homemade Frozen Fruit Pops*

Basic Frozen Fruit Juice Pops

Pineapple Crush Pops

Apple-Raspberry Pops

Strawberry Yogurt Pops

Creamy Frozen Fruit Pops

Chocolate-Covered Pudding Pops

SOME THOUGHTS ABOUT . . . *Making Your Own Ice Cream*

French Vanilla Ice Cream

Frozen Cocoa

Strawberry Yogurt Frappé

Orange-Lemon Ice

Frozen Peach Swirl

Nut and Orange Zest Sauté

Berry, Berry Good Sauce

Maple-Yogurt Sauce

Chocolate-Orange Sauce

Roasted Coconut and Raisin Sprinkle

Chocolate Buttercream

Simple Frosting

☙ Cooking with Kids: It May Be Messy But It Can Teach Them
a Lot About Food and Life

Devil's Food Cake

Preparation time: about 15 minutes
Cooking time: 45 to 50 minutes

The recipe for this rich, dense, and moist version of one of America's best-loved chocolate cakes comes from food writer Deirdre Davis. You can also use the recipe to make moist, chocolaty cupcakes (see the variation below).

3 ounces bittersweet chocolate
1 ounce unsweetened chocolate
½ cup unsalted butter, softened, plus butter for the pan
1½ cups sugar
½ teaspoon salt
1 tablespoon vanilla extract
2 large eggs
½ cup sour cream
2 cups sifted all-purpose flour
1 teaspoon baking soda
½ teaspoon baking powder
1 cup heavy cream

Place all the chocolate in a small bowl or double boiler and set over simmering water to melt, stirring occasionally until smooth. Set aside to cool.

Preheat the oven to 350 degrees. Generously butter a 10-inch cake pan and set aside.

In a large bowl, use an electric mixer to cream the butter, sugar, and salt until smooth and light, about 5 minutes. Add the vanilla and eggs and beat until smooth. Mix in the melted chocolate and sour cream and beat until smooth. Add half the flour and all of the baking soda and baking powder and gently mix on low to incorporate. Add the cream and mix on low to incorporate. Add the remaining flour and mix on low to incorporate.

Transfer the batter to the prepared pan and tap on the counter to settle the batter into the corners of the pan. Bake for 45 to 50 minutes on the middle rack, or until a knife inserted in the center of the cake comes out hot, with just a few crumbs clinging to it. The cake should spring back when touched.

Cool the cake in the pan and unmold. Using a long bread knife, split the cake into 2 layers with a sawing motion. Frost with Chocolate Buttercream (page 366) and serve.

YIELD: 12 to 16 servings

PER SERVING: 336 calories, 4 g protein, 19 g fat, 39 g carbohydrate, 213 mg sodium, 76 mg cholesterol

Devil's Food Cake Variation: Cupcakes

To make cupcakes, make the full recipe for Devil's Food Cake. Generously butter 24 muffin cups or line with paper cupcake liners. Spoon the batter into the cups until about three-quarters full. Bake for 20 to 25 minutes, using the same test for doneness as described above.

YIELD: 2 dozen cupcakes

Dark Chocolate Tangerine Crepes

Preparation time: 1 hour 15 minutes (including time for batter to sit)
Cooking time: about 15 minutes

This is a spectacular—and rich—dessert that's a thrilling treat for any child or adult. The crepes and the chocolate sauce can be prepared ahead of time and then assembled at the last minute.

CREPES:

> 1 ounce sweet dark chocolate
> 3 tablespoons unsalted butter
> ⅓ cup all-purpose flour
> 2 tablespoons sugar
> 2 tablespoons cocoa powder
> Pinch salt
> 2 large eggs
> ⅔ cup low-fat milk
> 1 teaspoon vanilla extract

CHOCOLATE SAUCE:

> 3 ounces sweet dark chocolate
> 1 cup low-fat milk or cream
> 1 tablespoon orange juice
> 1 teaspoon grated orange zest

GARNISHES:

> 4 small seedless tangerines, sectioned
> ¼ cup cocoa powder
> ¼ cup confectioners' sugar

To make the crepe batter, place the chocolate and butter in a small saucepan or in the top of a double boiler and heat over very low heat. Sift the flour, sugar, cocoa, and salt into a large bowl. Make a well in the center and add the eggs. Whisk the eggs, gradually incorporating the flour mixture, until the batter is smooth. Whisk in the milk, vanilla, and melted chocolate and butter and beat until smooth. Cover and refrigerate for an hour.

To make the chocolate sauce, in a medium saucepan, melt the chocolate over very low heat. Slowly add the milk or cream, orange juice, and orange zest and heat until smooth and warm.

To make the crepes, heat a 6-inch crepe pan or heavy skillet over moderately high heat. Add a small amount of oil and continue to heat until a drop of water spatters. Ladle about 4 to 5 tablespoons of batter into the hot pan, quickly tilt the pan to spread the batter. (The crepes should not be paper thin.) Cook until brown speckles appear on the bottom, about 60 seconds. Flip and cook about 30 seconds on the other side. Repeat the process with the remaining batter and stack the crepes on a plate. (They can be made ahead of time, covered, and refrigerated until needed. To reheat, simply heat the pan and let each crepe warm through for a few seconds on each side.)

To serve, place a few tablespoons of warm chocolate sauce on each dessert plate. Fold the crepe in half, then in quarters, and place in the center of the plate. Arrange a few tangerine sections along the sides of the crepe. Place the cocoa and confectioners' sugar in a sieve and lightly dust the top of each crepe before serving.

YIELD: 4 to 6 servings

PER SERVING: 391 calories, 9 g protein, 21 g fat, 45 g carbohydrate, 99 mg sodium, 107 mg cholesterol

The Ultimate Brownie

Preparation time: 15 minutes
Cooking time: 35 to 40 minutes

Parenting *Senior Editor Nan Wiener received this recipe from her mother, who claims to have gotten it from Katharine Hepburn. Well, not directly. Apparently, Hepburn revealed this gem to her interviewer in a magazine article. "This is truly a classic," claims Wiener, "producing a brownie that's intensely rich and chocolaty, slightly crisp around the edges, and not too cakelike. The key is the scant ¼ cup of flour—just enough to hold the brownies together but not enough to dry them out."*

Instead of unsweetened chocolate, you can also use 2 ounces of sweetened chocolate chips and reduce the sugar to ½ to ¾ cup. The brownies are best if they sit for at least 30 minutes or for several hours before you eat them. As a special treat or in place of a cake, serve these at a birthday party, topped with ice cream, grated coconut, and chopped fruit or berries.

> **1 stick lightly salted butter (½ cup)**
> **2 ounces unsweetened chocolate**
> **1 cup sugar**
> **2 large eggs**
> **1 teaspoon vanilla extract**
> **¼ cup all-purpose flour**

Preheat the oven to 325 degrees. Butter and flour an 8-inch square baking dish.

In a small saucepan over low heat, place the chocolate on top of the butter and heat until melted, stirring occasionally. Alternatively, melt the chocolate and butter in the top of a double boiler.

Transfer the chocolate-butter mixture to a medium bowl, add the sugar, and blend well. Add the eggs and vanilla and blend again. Sift the flour over the mixture and gently fold until blended, being careful not to overmix. Pour into the baking dish and bake for 35 minutes; for slightly cakier brownies, bake for 40 minutes.

YIELD: 12 squares
PER SERVING: 185 calories, 2 g protein, 11 g fat, 21 g carbohydrate, 90 mg sodium, 57 mg cholesterol

Aunt Mary's Squares

Preparation time: 10 minutes
Cooking time: 30 to 40 minutes

Kristen Bruno, Assistant Editor at Parenting, *says these chocolate bar cookies are simple to make and always a crowd pleaser.*

1 stick butter (½ cup), softened
1 large egg yolk
2 teaspoons water
1¼ cups all-purpose flour
1 teaspoon sugar
1 teaspoon baking powder
¼ teaspoon salt
12 ounces chocolate chips or bits

TOPPING:

2 large eggs
1 cup finely chopped nuts
¾ cup sugar
Pinch salt
6 tablespoons butter, melted
1 teaspoon vanilla extract

Preheat the oven to 350 degrees. In a large bowl, mix the butter, egg yolk, and water. Add the flour, sugar, baking powder, and salt. Press into the bottom of a 9-by-13-inch or 7-by-11-inch pan. Bake for 10 minutes (15 minutes if using a 7-by-11-inch pan).

Meanwhile, make the topping. In a bowl, mix the eggs, nuts, sugar, salt, melted butter, and vanilla.

Remove the pan from the oven and scatter the chocolate chips over the crust. Bake another 1 to 2 minutes, or until the chocolate is melted. Using a spatula or flat knife, spread the chocolate evenly over the crust.

Spread the topping on the chocolate and bake another 20 to 25 minutes (25 to 30 minutes if using a 7-by-11-inch pan), or until golden brown. Let cool and cut into 24 squares.

YIELD: 24 squares

PER SERVING: 216 calories, 3 g protein, 14 g fat, 22 g carbohydrate, 123 mg sodium, 45 mg cholesterol

Marble Pumpkin Cheesecake

Preparation time: 30 minutes

Cooking time: 1 hour to bake; 1 hour to sit in the oven

For a festive touch, top this creamy cheesecake with cranberry sauce (see recipe, page 453). Make the cake a day before serving, since it needs to be refrigerated overnight.

1 cup canned pumpkin puree
1½ cups sugar
Pinch salt
2½ teaspoons vanilla extract
2 pounds cream cheese, at room temperature
4 large eggs, at room temperature
1 pint sour cream

Preheat the oven to 275 degrees. Lightly butter and flour a 10-inch springform pan.

Strain the pumpkin puree into a small bowl. Mix in ½ cup of the sugar, the salt, and ½ teaspoon of the vanilla. Set aside.

Using an electric mixer, beat the cream cheese with the remaining 1 cup of sugar and 2 teaspoons of vanilla until smooth. Add the eggs, one at a time, beating until the mixture is smooth. Stir in the sour cream.

Pour half of the cheesecake mixture into the prepared pan. Using a teaspoon, drop half of the pumpkin puree mixture onto the cheesecake batter, leaving 1 to 2 inches between each spoonful. Pour the remaining batter into the pan, then spoon the rest of the pumpkin puree over the batter as before. Using a table knife, cut through the batter in a swirling motion to achieve a marbled effect.

Place the pan on a baking sheet and bake for 1 hour. Turn off the oven and leave the cake in it, without opening the door, for another hour. Remove from the oven and cool thoroughly. Cover the cake with plastic wrap and refrigerate overnight before serving.

Yield: 8 to 10 servings

Per serving: 639 calories, 12 g protein, 49 g fat, 41 g carbohydrate, 359 mg sodium, 229 mg cholesterol

Becky's Pumpkin Roll

Preparation time: 25 minutes
Cooking time: 15 minutes
Cooling time: 1 hour

This is an elegant-looking dessert that actually requires very little effort. The recipe comes from my good friend Becky Schultze. A simple cake batter is made with pumpkin puree, ground cinnamon, ginger, and nutmeg. After baking, the cake is spread with a cream cheese filling and rolled into a fat cigar shape. It's the perfect finale to any autumn meal and is also ideal for the holidays.

CAKE:

Confectioners' sugar

3 large eggs

1 cup granulated sugar

⅔ cup canned pumpkin puree

1 teaspoon lemon juice

¾ cup sifted all-purpose flour

1 teaspoon baking powder

2 teaspoons ground cinnamon

1 teaspoon ground ginger

½ teaspoon ground nutmeg

½ teaspoon salt

1 cup finely chopped walnuts or other nuts

FILLING:

8 ounces cream cheese, softened at room temperature

5 tablespoons butter

1 cup confectioners' sugar

½ teaspoon vanilla extract

Preheat the oven to 375 degrees. Lightly grease and flour a jelly roll pan. Sprinkle confectioners' sugar on a clean tea towel and set aside.

In a large bowl, beat the eggs with a mixer at high speed for 5 minutes or whisk vigorously by hand. Gradually add the granulated sugar and continue beating until smooth.

Stir in the pumpkin puree and lemon juice and beat until smooth. In a separate bowl, mix the flour, baking powder, cinnamon, ginger, nutmeg, and salt, then gently fold into the pumpkin-egg mixture. Pour the batter into the prepared pan and sprinkle the top with the nuts. Bake for 15 minutes.

Remove the pan from the oven and gently tap the cake out onto the sugared tea towel. (You may need to use a flat-edged knife to loosen the cake from the pan.) Sprinkle the top side of the cake with additional confectioners' sugar and roll the cake up with the tea towel into a fat cigar shape. Cool in the refrigerator for at least 1 hour.

Meanwhile, prepare the filling. In a medium bowl, beat the cream cheese and butter until smooth. Add the sugar and vanilla and beat until smooth.

Unroll the chilled cake and remove the tea towel. Spread with the filling. Reroll the cake into another fat cigar shape and serve.

YIELD: 8 servings
PER SERVING: 515 calories, 8 g protein, 29 g fat, 59 g carbohydrate, 387 mg sodium, 132 mg cholesterol

Peach-Honey Sauce for Cakes

Preparation time: 10 minutes
Marinating time: 5 minutes to several hours
Cooking time: about 15 seconds

This is a quick sauce that makes a store-bought pound cake taste homemade. You can use orange juice in the sauce if you're serving it to young kids or substitute dark rum if it's an adults-only party. For an elegant touch, surround the cake and sauce with a mixture of fresh berries.

4 large ripe peaches
¼ cup honey
¼ cup fresh orange juice or dark rum
1 drop of vanilla extract
8 slices pound cake
Fresh mint leaves

Bring a large saucepan of water to a boil. Add the peaches, blanch for 15 seconds, and place in a bowl of ice cold water. Peel the peaches and cut into thin slices.

In a bowl, mix the honey, juice or rum, and vanilla. Stir in the peach slices, cover, and refrigerate for 5 minutes to about 2 hours.

Arrange thin slices of pound cake on serving plates and spoon the peach sauce on top. Garnish with a mint leaf and serve.

YIELD: 8 servings
PER SERVING: 181 calories, 2 g protein, 6 g fat, 32 g carbohydrate, 113 mg sodium, 63 mg cholesterol

Rhubarb-Strawberry Cake

Preparation time: 15 minutes
Cooking time: 45 minutes to 1 hour

This is a favorite recipe in our house in late May, when the rhubarb is tall and the stalks are a bright pinkish red. Maybe it's the color of the rhubarb that makes this cake so appealing to children, or maybe it's the sweet taste (which offsets the sourness of the fruit). Whichever it is, this cake is always demolished quickly. The recipe comes from Becky Schultze, one of the best home cooks I've ever met. Serve it for dessert, snacks, tea time, or even an unusual birthday cake. Top with Rhubarb-Strawberry Sauce (recipe follows).

4 cups small fresh rhubarb chunks (about 8 stalks)
2 teaspoons vanilla extract
1½ cups sugar
½ cup butter
1 large egg
2 cups all-purpose flour
1 teaspoon baking soda
Pinch salt
1 cup buttermilk
1 teaspoon ground cinnamon
Confectioners' sugar (optional)
2 cups ripe strawberries, cut in half

Preheat the oven to 350 degrees. Grease and flour a 9-by-13-inch baking pan.

In a medium bowl, mix the rhubarb, 1 teaspoon of the vanilla extract, and ½ cup of the sugar.

In a large bowl, cream the butter and the remaining 1 cup sugar. Add the egg and beat until smooth and creamy. In another bowl or on wax paper, combine the flour, baking soda, and salt. Sift the dry ingredients over the butter mixture a bit at a time and fold in, alternating with the buttermilk. Stir in the rhubarb mixture, then the cinnamon and remaining vanilla extract.

Pour the batter into the prepared pan and bake for 45 minutes to an hour, or until a toothpick inserted in the middle comes out clean. Let the cake cool for about 5 minutes before removing from the pan. Place on a platter, sprinkle with confectioners' sugar if desired, and decorate with the strawberries.

YIELD: 6 to 8 servings

PER SERVING: 478 calories, 7 g protein, 15 g fat, 80g carbohydrate, 389 mg sodium, 69 mg cholesterol

Rhubarb-Strawberry Sauce

Preparation time: 10 minutes
Cooking time: 15 minutes

Use this easy-to-prepare sauce to top the Rhubarb-Strawberry Cake on page 324 or butter cookies, pound cake, waffles, or yogurt—or just eat it by the spoonful.

1 cup chopped fresh rhubarb
½ cup sugar
¼ cup cold water
1 cup sliced fresh strawberries
¼ teaspoon vanilla extract

Combine the rhubarb and sugar with the cold water in a small saucepan. Simmer over moderate heat, stirring occasionally, until the rhubarb is tender and almost falling apart, about 10 minutes. Remove from the heat and stir in the strawberries and vanilla. Transfer the sauce to a food processor or blender and puree.

YIELD: 6 to 8 servings
PER SERVING: 92 calories, 0 g protein, 0 g fat, 23 g carbohydrate, 1 mg sodium, 0 mg cholesterol

Peanut Butter Fondue

Preparation time: 20 minutes

Peanut butter, sweetened with honey and cinnamon, is served in a bowl surrounded by tidbits for dipping. What better way for children to get their fill of a genuine kid's classic? Since no heat is needed, this is a great way to let your kids cook for themselves.

1½ cups smooth or chunky peanut butter, at room temperature
1 cup low-fat milk
1 to 3 tablespoons honey
½ teaspoon vanilla extract
Pinch of ground cinnamon
Assortment of fresh fruit, cut into bite-size pieces
Graham crackers, mini pretzels, and butter cookies

Place the peanut butter in a medium bowl. Gradually blend in about ¾ cup of the milk, stirring until thoroughly incorporated. Add more milk if necessary; the consistency should be thin enough for dipping but not so thin that it drips right off the fruit. Stir in 1 tablespoon of the honey and taste for sweetness. Add the vanilla and cinnamon and stir again until blended.

Transfer the peanut butter mixture to a small fondue pot or an attractive bowl and surround with the fruit, cookies, graham crackers, and pretzels.

YIELD: 4 to 6 servings
PER SERVING: 505 calories, 24 g protein, 40 g fat, 22 g carbohydrate, 388 mg sodium, 2 mg cholesterol

Vanilla Pudding

Preparation time: 20 to 25 minutes
Chilling time: 2 to 3 hours

Few kids can resist the soothing texture and mild flavor of this dessert. You can reduce the sugar amount to ½ cup and the pudding will still be good.

¾ **cup sugar**
3 **tablespoons cornstarch**
Pinch salt
3 **cups low-fat milk**
4 **large egg yolks**
1½ **teaspoons vanilla extract**

Mix the sugar, cornstarch, and salt in a medium saucepan. Slowly whisk in the milk and bring to a boil, whisking frequently over moderate heat until thickened, about 5 to 8 minutes.

In a medium bowl, beat the egg yolks well. Gradually add 1 cup of the thickened milk to the eggs, then pour the egg-milk mixture back into the saucepan. Bring to a boil, stirring constantly, and simmer for about 1 to 3 minutes. Remove from the heat and stir in the vanilla. Pour the pudding into a large serving bowl or individual pudding cups. Cover and chill for several hours.

YIELD: 6 servings
PER SERVING: 216 calories, 6 g protein, 6 g fat, 35 g carbohydrate, 66 mg sodium, 152 mg cholesterol

Orange and Ginger Rice Pudding

Preparation time: 25 minutes
Cooking time: 15 minutes

Ahhh, rice pudding, the ultimate comfort food. To transform it into a grown-up dessert, soak the raisins in Grand Marnier and add a dash of the liqueur to the egg mixture.

½ **cup raisins**
¼ **cup orange juice or Grand Marnier**
2 **large eggs**
1 **cup milk**
⅓ **cup maple syrup or honey**
1 **teaspoon vanilla extract**
1 **teaspoon ground ginger**
1 **teaspoon grated orange zest**
½ **teaspoon ground cinnamon**
⅛ **teaspoon ground nutmeg**
2 **cups cooked white rice, warm or cold**
2 **tablespoons brown sugar mixed with 1 teaspoon ground cinnamon**
1 **cup heavy cream (optional)**

Preheat the oven to 350 degrees. Generously butter an 8-inch square baking pan. In a small bowl, soak the raisins in the orange juice or Grand Marnier for 20 minutes.

In a large bowl, vigorously whisk the eggs with the milk, maple syrup or honey, and vanilla.

Drain the raisins and add them to the mixture along with the ginger, orange zest, cinnamon, and nutmeg. Mix in the rice, stirring well to break up any clumps. Pour into the prepared pan and bake for 15 minutes.

Sprinkle the brown sugar and cinnamon on the pudding and bake another 10 minutes, or until set. Serve hot, warm, or cold. If desired, pour heavy cream on top.

YIELD: 4 to 6 servings
PER SERVING: 304 calories, 7 g protein, 5 g fat, 59 g carbohydrate, 65 mg sodium, 94 mg cholesterol

Impossible Pie

Preparation time: 10 minutes
Cooking time: about 45 minutes

Liza Gross, Senior Copy Editor at Parenting, *says her grandmother used to make this co-coconut custard pie at least once a month. Not only is it delicious and easy to remember (you use about ½ cup of almost every ingredient), but it also uses only one bowl.*

½ cup shredded coconut
½ cup milk
½ cup sugar
½ cup butter, softened
4 large eggs
1 teaspoon vanilla extract

Preheat the oven to 350 degrees. Grease a 9-inch pie pan. Set aside ¼ cup of the coconut.

In a large bowl, mix all the remaining ingredients with an electric mixer or by hand. Pour the mixture into the greased pan and top with the remaining coconut. Bake for 45 minutes, or until the top is well browned.

YIELD: 8 servings
PER SERVING: 220 calories, 4 g protein, 16 g fat, 16 g carbohydrate, 168 mg sodium, 139 mg cholesterol

Apple Pie

Preparation time: 40 to 50 minutes (plus 2 hours to refrigerate the dough)
Cooking time: 50 to 60 minutes

This classic dish tastes best when you combine a variety of tart apples. Top with ice cream or thin slices of Cheddar cheese.

CRUST:

2 cups all-purpose flour
Pinch salt
2 tablespoons sugar
1½ sticks cold unsalted butter (¾ cup), cut into small pieces
¼ cup ice-cold water

FILLING:

5 to 7 tart apples, peeled, cored, and thinly sliced
½ cup brown sugar
½ teaspoon ground cinnamon
¼ teaspoon ground nutmeg or allspice
¼ cup apple cider
1 tablespoon unsalted butter, cut into small cubes

To make the crust, sift the flour and salt into a large bowl. Stir in the sugar. Using your hands, work in the butter until it resembles coarse bread crumbs. Add the water, a little at a time, and stir until the dough holds together. Wrap and refrigerate for about 2 hours.

When the dough is chilled, cut off two-thirds and return the rest to the refrigerator. Roll out the big piece of dough on a lightly floured surface and then fit it into a 9-inch pie pan. Trim any overhang (add it to the piece in the refrigerator) and crimp the edges with your fingertips. Refrigerate.

Preheat the oven to 350 degrees. To make the filling, toss the apples, sugar, cinnamon, and nutmeg or allspice in a large bowl. Moisten with the cider. Transfer the apple filling to the prepared crust and top with the butter. Roll out the remaining dough and cut it into thin strips. Arrange the strips over the filling in a lattice pattern. Bake until the pie bubbles and the apples are tender, about 50 to 60 minutes.

YIELD: 6 servings
PER SERVING: 539 calories, 5 g protein, 26 g fat, 74 g carbohydrate, 34 mg sodium, 68 mg cholesterol

Caramel Apples

Preparation time: 25 minutes
Cooking time: about 5 minutes
Chilling time: at least 20 minutes

Instead of cooking caramel sauce from scratch, melt store-bought caramels. Plan on dipping the apples 20 minutes before serving.

8 small tart apples
1 cup chopped pecans, walnuts, or peanuts (optional)
1 cup caramel candy
1½ tablespoons water

Wash, dry, and stem the apples. Push a wooden stick into the core of each apple. Lightly butter a sheet of wax paper, lay it on a baking sheet, and set aside. Place the nuts on another piece of wax paper and set aside.

In a medium saucepan, melt the caramels and 1 tablespoon of the water over low heat, stirring constantly until smooth. If the mixture seems too thick to coat the apples, add the remaining ½ tablespoon of water; if it seems too runny, remove from the heat and let stand a few minutes.

Dip the apples in the warm caramel until thoroughly coated, then roll in the nuts. Place on the buttered wax paper, stick side up. Refrigerate for about 20 minutes to set. Remove and let stand 5 minutes before serving.

YIELD: 8 servings
PER SERVING: 127 calories, 1 g protein, 2 g fat, 28 g carbohydrate, 37 mg sodium, 0 mg cholesterol

Cranberry Applesauce

Preparation time: 20 minutes
Cooking time: 15 to 20 minutes

If you like applesauce and you like cranberries, you will absolutely love this flavor combi-nation. This sauce is sweet and tart and has a spectacular rosy pink color. Instead of sweet-ening the applesauce with sugar, I like to stir in real maple syrup and add a touch of ground ginger for an intriguing flavor.

In the fall, if you have the opportunity to go apple picking (or to buy a large amount of fresh apples), this is one of the easiest and tastiest ways to preserve them. Double or triple the recipe and freeze or can the rest to give as holiday gifts. The applesauce can be served alone as a dessert or snack, but it also is a great side for everything from roast pork and chicken dishes to potato pancakes and waffles.

**8½ cups peeled and chopped apples (about 3 pounds), preferably a
   combination of sweet and tart varieties**
2½ cups water
2 cups fresh cranberries
½ cup maple syrup, granulated sugar, or honey
1½ teaspoons ground ginger

Combine all the ingredients in a large heavy-bottomed pot. Bring to a boil over high heat, reduce the heat to a rolling simmer, and stir well. Cover and cook for 15 to 20 min-utes, or until the apples and cranberries have cooked down. Let cool.

Serve as is, or if you prefer a smooth applesauce, transfer to a food processor or blender puree until almost smooth but still a bit chunky, depending on what texture you prefer. Place in glass jars and refrigerate. The applesauce will keep for about 7 to 10 days in the refrigerator.

YIELD: about 1½ quarts
PER QUART: 99 calories, 0.2 g protein, 0.34 g fat, 25 g carbohydrate, 1 mg sodium, 0 mg
   cholesterol

Cranberry-Apple Crisp

Preparation time: 15 minutes
Cooking time: 45 minutes

Try this simple dish in the fall when cranberries are in season.

FRUIT MIXTURE:

> **2 cups fresh cranberries**
> **1½ cups peeled and chopped apples**
> **⅓ cup sugar**
> **2 tablespoons flour**
> **1 tablespoon lemon juice**

TOPPING:

> **½ cup all-purpose flour**
> **½ cup granola**
> **½ cup light brown sugar**
> **½ teaspoon ground cinnamon**
> **1 stick butter (½ cup), cut into small pieces**

Preheat the oven to 350 degrees. Combine the fruit ingredients and place in a pie plate or shallow casserole. For the topping, combine the flour, granola, brown sugar, and cinnamon. Using a pastry cutter or your hands, work in the butter. Sprinkle the topping over the fruit and bake for about 45 minutes, or until the top is golden.

YIELD: 6 servings
PER SERVING: 374 calories, 3 g protein, 17 g fat, 54 g carbohydrate, 167 mg sodium, 41 mg cholesterol

Quick Apple Crumble

Preparation time: 15 minutes
Cooking time: 30 to 35 minutes

This is a great last-minute dessert because it takes only 45 minutes to make—simply peel and season the apples, make the crumble topping, bake, and serve. Whip a cup of heavy cream (lightly sweetened with sugar and a touch of vanilla) or serve with vanilla ice cream.

Butter to grease pan
5 large apples, peeled, cored, and cut into thick slices
1 teaspoon ground allspice
½ teaspoon ground cloves
½ cup all-purpose flour
½ cup granola
⅛ cup sugar
4 tablespoons unsalted butter, cut into small cubes
⅛ cup apple cider

Preheat the oven to 350 degrees. Butter the bottom of a large ovenproof skillet or baking dish. Place the apples in the dish and toss with half of the allspice and cloves.

In a medium bowl, mix the flour, granola, sugar, and remaining allspice and cloves. Using your hands or 2 knives, work the butter into the flour mixture until it resembles small peas. Spoon the mixture over the apples and pour the cider on top. Bake for about 30 to 35 minutes, or until the apples are tender and the topping is golden brown.

YIELD: 6 servings
PER SERVING: 277 calories, 2 g protein, 11 g fat, 45 g carbohydrate, 7 mg sodium, 22 mg cholesterol

Peach Cobbler

Preparation time: 15 minutes
Cooking time: 45 minutes

You can substitute nectarines for the peaches if you prefer, or combine four peaches with a pint of blueberries or raspberries for a peach-berry cobbler.

FRUIT MIXTURE:

> 6 ripe peaches or nectarines, pitted and thinly sliced
> 3 tablespoons brown sugar
> Pinch ground cinnamon
> Butter to grease pan

TOPPING:

> 1 cup all-purpose flour
> 1 teaspoon ground cinnamon
> 1 stick unsalted butter (½ cup), cut into small pieces
> ½ cup brown sugar
> ½ cup granola

Preheat the oven to 350 degrees. Mix the peaches with the brown sugar and cinnamon in a medium bowl. Set aside.

To make the topping, sift the flour into a medium bowl and stir in the cinnamon. Using your hands or 2 knives, work the butter into the flour until the mixture resembles bread crumbs. Gently mix in the brown sugar and granola.

Place the fruit mixture in a buttered pie pan, ovenproof skillet, or small shallow casserole. Spoon on the topping. Bake for about 45 minutes or until the fruit is bubbling and the topping turns golden brown. Serve hot, warm, or at room temperature.

YIELD: 4 to 6 servings
PER SERVING: 497 calories, 5 g protein, 22 g fat, 74 g carbohydrate, 28 mg sodium, 52 mg cholesterol

Fruit Kebabs with Yogurt Sauce

Preparation time: about 20 minutes

Kids love fresh fruit and they love to eat food on a stick. This is the perfect dessert for a birthday party or large gathering. Everything can be assembled ahead of time and kept in the refrigerator until you need it. Be sure to snap off the sharp ends of the wooden skewers when serving this dish to younger children.

- **1 cantaloupe, cut into 1-inch pieces or balls**
- **1 honeydew melon, cut into 1-inch pieces or balls**
- **1 cup hulled strawberries, cut in half**
- **1 cup seedless grapes, cut in half**
- **4 ripe bananas, cut into ½-inch pieces**

YOGURT SAUCE:
- **2 tablespoons frozen orange or apple juice concentrate**
- **2 cups plain low-fat yogurt**
- **Pinch ground cinnamon**

Thread the fruit onto about 20 small wooden skewers, making sure to include a few types of fruit on each. Place the kebabs on a platter, cover, and refrigerate.

To make the sauce, in a medium bowl, mash the frozen juice concentrate until soft. Add the yogurt and just a touch of cinnamon. Taste and add more cinnamon if desired. Cover and refrigerate until ready to serve. (Parents may want to take the fruit off the skewers for young kids.)

YIELD: 10 to 12 servings

PER SERVING: 142 calories, 4 g protein, 1 g fat, 32 g carbohydrate, 46 mg sodium, 2 mg cholesterol

Two Seasons Ultimate Fruit Salad with Toppings

Preparation time: 15 minutes (with toppings), 5 minutes without

A winter fruit salad can be every bit as good as a summer fruit salad, so long as you use the very freshest ingredients. And the toppings make this salad something truly spectacular. This is really two recipes: one for summer and one for winter. It's best to assemble the salad within 30 minutes of serving. Be sure to cut the fruit over the bowl so you don't lose any precious juices.

The list of toppings is optional—use any or all of them. If serving the salad at a party, place all the toppings in small bowls and let your guests create their own "fruit salad sundae."

SUMMER FRUIT:

 1 **cup blueberries**

 1 **cup raspberries**

 1 **cup sliced ripe strawberries**

 1 **cup sliced ripe peaches**

 2 **tablespoons fresh orange juice**

WINTER FRUIT:

 1 **cup chopped apples (peeling is optional)**

 1 **cup chopped ripe pears (peeling is optional)**

 1 **cup small orange sections**

 ½ **cup red and/or green grapes**

 ½ **cup sliced banana**

 2 **tablespoons fresh orange juice**

TOPPINGS:

 ¼ **cup grated coconut**

 ¼ **cup very finely chopped walnuts**

 1 **cup plain low-fat yogurt**

 2 **teaspoons grated orange zest**

In a serving bowl, very gently mix either the summer or winter fruit with the orange juice. Serve with the toppings on the side.

YIELD: 4 to 5 servings
PER SERVING: 158 calories, 2 g protein, 1 g fat, 40 g carbohydrate, 3 mg sodium, 0 mg cholesterol

Marinated Oranges with Coconut

Preparation time: 10 minutes
Marinating time: 15 minutes

Serve this with a pot of herb tea for a simple, refreshing end to any meal.

3 tablespoons orange juice
1½ tablespoons good-quality honey
4 oranges, peeled, white pith and seeds removed, and thinly sliced crosswise
½ cup grated coconut

Mix the orange juice and honey in a bowl. Add the orange slices and toss lightly. Marinate for at least 15 minutes. Just before serving, sprinkle the coconut on top.

YIELD: 4 to 6 servings
PER SERVING: 143 calories, 1 g protein, 3 g fat, 30 g carbohydrate, 24 mg sodium, 0 mg cholesterol

Caramelized Maple Banana Slices

Preparation time: about 2 to 3 minutes
Cooking time: 5 to 6 minutes

I first made these sweet, gooey banana slices one snowy morning to top a stack of blueberry pancakes. But this quick dish—less than ten minutes to make from start to finish—is equally good served with ice cream, pound cake, or a fruit salad or used to make an innovative banana split. It also works well served with curries, as a topping for sautéed fish, or on top of a chicken breast.

> **1 teaspoon butter or margarine**
> **1 banana, about ½ inch thick**
> **1 tablespoon maple syrup**

In a medium skillet, heat the butter over moderately high heat. Add the banana slices and cook about 1 to 2 minutes on each side, or until golden brown. Add the maple syrup, stir to coat the banana, and serve hot, warm, or cold.

YIELD: 2 servings
PER SERVING: 95 calories, 1 g protein, 2 g fat, 20 g carbohydrate, 21 mg sodium, 5 mg cholesterol

Chocolate Bananas

Preparation time: 25 minutes
Cooking time: 5 minutes

Here's a treat no kid can resist: a banana coated in chocolate and rolled in nuts. Be sure to snap off the sharp ends of the wooden skewers when serving this dish to younger children.

½ cup slivered or finely chopped almonds, cashews, or walnuts
1 cup semisweet chocolate chips
6 bananas

Lay a sheet of wax paper on a baking sheet and set aside. Spread the chopped nuts on another piece of wax paper and set aside.

Melt the chocolate in a saucepan over very low heat (even moderate heat can cause the chocolate to thicken instead of melt). Peel the bananas and carefully slide them lengthwise onto wooden skewers. Dip each banana in the warm chocolate, coating thoroughly. Gently roll the chocolate-coated bananas in the chopped nuts, lay them on the baking sheet covered with wax paper, and chill them in the freezer for at least 10 minutes or until the chocolate is completely set. If you freeze the bananas overnight, be sure to thaw for at least 5 minutes before serving to your child.

YIELD: 6 servings
PER SERVING: 304 calories, 5 g protein, 14 g fat, 48 g carbohydrate, 3 mg sodium, 0 mg cholesterol

Basic Butter Cookies

Preparation time: 20 minutes
Cooking time: about 10 minutes

This is a rich and buttery dough that can be transformed into just about any kind of cookie. Add chopped nuts, dates, or figs. Or try ground ginger and cinnamon, grated lemon or orange zest, or at holiday time, bits of candied fruit. You can cut the dough into any shape you like or simply place it by the tablespoonful on a baking sheet. Another variation is to make a hollow in each cookie, bake it, and then fill the center with fruit jam or a fruit puree. Sprinkle the cookies with confectioners' sugar, rainbow sprinkles, granola, or candied ginger. The dough can be frozen and the cookies freshly baked within 10 minutes of thawing, or you can freeze the finished, cooled cookies.

> **2½ cups all-purpose flour**
> **⅛ teaspoon salt**
> **2 sticks butter (1 cup), softened**
> **½ cup sugar**
> **1½ teaspoons vanilla or almond extract or a combination**
> **2 large egg yolks**

In a medium bowl or on a sheet of wax paper, sift together the flour and salt. In a large bowl, using an electric mixer, cream the butter. Gradually add the sugar and beat until the mixture is fluffy. Beat in the extract and egg yolks. Add the flour mixture and beat until the dough is smooth. If you want to roll out the dough and cut out shapes, you need to chill it for at least an hour.

Preheat the oven to 350 degrees. Place single tablespoonfuls (or cut-outs) of cookie dough about 1 inch apart on an ungreased baking sheet and bake about 10 minutes, being careful not to let the cookies brown. Remove from the baking sheet and let cool.

YIELD: 3 to 4 dozen
PER COOKIE: 78 calories, 1 g protein, 5 g fat, 8 g carbohydrate, 52 mg sodium, 22 mg cholesterol

Gluck's Old-Fashioned Molasses Cookies

Preparation time: about 10 minutes
Chilling time: at least 30 minutes
Cooking time: about 8 minutes

John Gluck, a Senior Associate Editor at Parenting, *says this is one of his mother's best recipes.*

Butter and flour for the pan
1 stick butter (½ cup)
1 cup brown sugar
2 large eggs
1 cup dark molasses
½ teaspoon salt
1 teaspoon ground ginger
½ teaspoon ground nutmeg
½ teaspoon ground cloves
4 cups all-purpose flour
2 teaspoons baking soda
1 teaspoon ground cinnamon
1 teaspoon vanilla extract
Double recipe Simple Frosting (see page 367)

Preheat the oven to 400 degrees. Lightly butter and flour a baking sheet.

In a large bowl, cream the butter with the sugar. Add the eggs, one at a time, and beat until creamy. Add the molasses and mix thoroughly. Add the salt, ginger, nutmeg, and cloves. Sift the flour, baking soda, and cinnamon over the mixture and gently mix in. Add 1 cup hot (not boiling) water and the vanilla and mix well. Chill for at least 30 minutes.

Drop the mixture by the teaspoonful onto the prepared baking sheet and bake about 8 minutes. Remove from the baking sheet and let cool before icing.

YIELD: about 8 dozen
PER COOKIE: 47 calories, 1 g protein, 1 g fat, 8 g carbohydrate, 52 mg sodium, 7 mg cholesterol

Andi's Coffee Tortoni

Preparation time: 10 minutes
Freezing time: 1½ to 2 hours

My sister-in-law Andrea Gunst is a gifted baker. Every holiday season she produces spectacular cookies, pies, and chocolates. She was introduced to this melt-in-your-mouth coffee tortoni by her mother, Barbara Deasy, who in turn was introduced to it by her mother, Helen Cosby. The tortoni must be frozen for several hours, so plan your time accordingly. They should be eaten within 24 to 48 hours, however, as they tend to lose their fresh coffee flavor otherwise.

    For an extra treat, serve the tortoni with whipped cream flavored with a touch of vanilla or almond extract or a dash of Kahlua.

> **1 large egg white**
> **1 tablespoon instant coffee granules**
> **⅛ teaspoon salt**
> **¼ cup plus 2 tablespoons sugar**
> **1 cup heavy cream**
> **1 teaspoon vanilla extract**
> **⅛ teaspoon almond extract**
> **¼ cup slivered or chopped toasted almonds**

In a large bowl, combine the egg white, coffee granules, and salt. Beat until stiff but not dry. Gradually add 2 tablespoons of the sugar and beat until stiff and satiny.

In a separate bowl, beat the cream, remaining ¼ cup sugar, and both extracts until peaks form. Fold the whipped cream into the egg white mixture and then gently fold in the nuts. Spoon into paper muffin cups and freeze about 1½ to 2 hours, or until ready to serve. If the tortoni will be in the freezer for more than a few hours, cover with wax paper or aluminum foil or place in a cookie tin or airtight plastic container.

YIELD: 9 servings
PER SERVING: 150 calories, 2 g protein, 12 g fat, 10 g carbohydrate, 47 mg sodium, 36 mg cholesterol

Andi's Coconut-Date Balls

Preparation time: 15 minutes
Cooking time: about 8 minutes

Chewy and sweet, these cookies are delicious served with cocoa at Christmas or any time of year.

   1 stick butter (½ cup)
   1 cup sugar
   1 cup chopped dates
   1 large egg, well beaten
   1 teaspoon vanilla extract
   2 cups Rice Krispies
   1 cup chopped walnuts
   About 2 cups flaked coconut

Combine the butter, sugar, dates, and egg in a saucepan and cook over moderate heat until the mixture starts to bubble. Reduce the heat and stir constantly for 5 minutes.

Remove from the heat and stir in the vanilla, Rice Krispies, and walnuts. Form the mixture into small balls (about ½ tablespoon each) and roll in the coconut to coat.

YIELD: about 3 dozen
PER DATE BALL: 106 calories, 1 g protein, 6 g fat, 13g carbohydrate, 53 mg sodium, 13 mg cholesterol

Lemon Drop Cookies

Preparation time: about 15 minutes (without icing)
Cooking time: about 10 minutes per batch of cookies

Another favorite from Mrs. Elizabeth Gluck, these lemony cookies are delicious with tea or as an after-school snack. The amount of lemon zest and extract depends on how lemony you want the cookies to be.

Butter and flour for the pan
1 stick butter (½ cup)
½ cup sugar
½ teaspoon salt
1 to 2 tablespoons grated lemon zest
2 large eggs
1 cup sour cream
1 to 2 teaspoons lemon extract
1 teaspoon baking soda
2½ cups all-purpose flour
1 recipe Simple Frosting (see page 367)

Preheat the oven to 350 degrees. Lightly grease and flour a baking sheet.

In a large bowl, cream the butter and sugar. Add the salt and lemon zest. Stir in the eggs, sour cream, and lemon extract until smooth. Add the baking soda and flour and gently incorporate.

Drop the mixture by the teaspoonful onto the prepared baking sheet and bake for about 10 minutes. Frost with the icing while the cookies are still slightly warm if desired or when cooled.

YIELD: about 4 dozen
PER COOKIE: 85 calories, 1 g protein, 5 g fat, 9 g carbohydrate, 77 mg sodium, 21 mg cholesterol

SOME THOUGHTS ABOUT . . .
Making Homemade Frozen Fruit Pops

Freshly made frozen fruit pops are one of the easiest and most refreshing snacks you can put together for your kids. Made from juices, fresh summer fruits, yogurt, and a few other ingredients, popsicles can cool everyone off—and make a great summer project for kids. Even the littlest guy can help spoon fruit into cups and top them off with a stick.

These frozen fruit pops are made in small 3-ounce cups with wooden sticks. You'll find sticks in most grocery stores or hobby shops, but if you have trouble locating them, ask your pediatrician for a few of those famous "Say *aaah*" sticks. (You can also use freezer pop molds, which most hardware stores carry.) To unmold the popsicle, simply invert the cup under warm water and carefully peel it away from the frozen treat. Plan on letting the frozen fruit pops freeze for a minimum of 2 hours.

Basic Frozen Fruit Juice Pops

Preparation time: 5 minutes
Freezing time: 2 hours or more

Use any type of juice you like to make this popsicle. Or for a tutti-frutti pop, fill the cup halfway, freeze for an hour, and top with another type of juice. Other variations are listed below.

1¾ cup fruit juice

Divide the juice among six 3-ounce paper cups and freeze for about 30 minutes. Place a stick in the middle of each cup and freeze until hard.

YIELD: 6 pops
PER SERVING: 34 calories, 0 g protein, 0.07 g fat, 8 g carbohydrate, 2 mg sodium, 0 mg cholesterol

Pop Variations

- *Pineapple Crush Pops:* Mix 1 cup pineapple juice and 1 cup finely chopped fresh or canned (drained) pineapple and proceed as directed above.
- *Apple-Raspberry Pops:* Mix 1 cup apple juice or apple-raspberry juice with ½ cup coarsely chopped fresh or frozen raspberries and proceed as directed above.

Strawberry Yogurt Pops

Preparation time: 10 minutes
Freezer time: 2 hours or more

A slightly richer, tangier popsicle.

**1½ cups very ripe fresh strawberries, hulled, or 12 ounces frozen
  berries (no sugar added)**
½ cup plain low-fat yogurt
2 tablespoons sugar (optional)

Place the berries in a blender or food processor and puree just until the fruit is still slightly chunky. Stir in the yogurt and sugar if using, and divide among six 3-ounce cups. Place sticks in the middle of each cup (the mixture will be thick enough to hold the sticks at this point) and freeze until hard.

YIELD: 6 pops

PER SERVING: 23 calories, 1 g protein, 0.43 g fat, 4 g carbohydrate, 14 mg sodium, 1 mg cholesterol

Creamy Frozen Fruit Pops

Preparation time: 5 minutes
Freezer time: 2 hours or more

A childhood classic that never falls out of favor.

1½ cups juice, any flavor
6 tablespoons heavy cream

Fill six 3-ounce cups halfway with the juice and freeze for about 1 hour. Place 1 tablespoon of cream in each cup and freeze for 30 minutes more. Top with the remaining juice, insert sticks in the middle, and freeze until hard.

YIELD: 6 pops
PER SERVING: 79 calories, 1 g protein, 6 g fat, 7 g carbohydrate, 6 mg sodium, 20 mg cholesterol

Chocolate-Covered Pudding Pops

Preparation time: 10 minutes
Cooking time: 5 minutes
Freezer time: 2 hours or more

This pop combines two favorites—pudding and chocolate.

   1¾ cups vanilla pudding
   8 ounces semisweet or milk chocolate, broken into small pieces
   Chopped nuts (optional)

Divide the pudding among six 3-ounce cups. Place a stick in the middle of each cup and freeze until hard.

Melt the chocolate in the top of a double boiler over simmering water or in a small heavy saucepan over *very low* heat, stirring frequently.

Peel the paper off each pop (or unmold it) and dip it into the melted chocolate until thoroughly coated. Scatter chopped nuts on the top and sides of each pop if desired. Place the pops on a sheet of wax paper or aluminum foil and freeze until the chocolate hardens.

YIELD: 6 pops
PER SERVING: 271 calories, 4 g protein, 14 g fat, 39 g carbohydrate, 135 mg sodium, 10 mg cholesterol

SOME THOUGHTS ABOUT . . .
Making Your Own Ice Cream

Next time the kids scream for ice cream, why not let them make their own? It's an ideal activity for a lazy summer afternoon and much simpler than what you may remember from your own childhood. Gone are the days of sprinkling rock salt over ice inside a huge canister and cranking and churning for hours—modern ice-cream makers are a breeze to operate. Some frosty treats, such as ices and frozen yogurt, don't even require a special machine.

With recipes that call for an ice-cream maker, I recommend one of the lightweight models that have a removable freeze-ahead canister insert. I've found that these relatively inexpensive machines ($30 to $60) work as well as the pricier electric ones. Young helpers simply pour the prepared mixture into the chilled canister and gently turn the crank every few minutes. The ice cream thickens in 15 to 20 minutes.

Read through a new recipe ahead of time to avoid unexpected delays. Some recipes involve cooking a custard-like mixture first, then thoroughly chilling it before putting it into the canister (any ice-cream recipe works in any type of machine). Others require no ice-cream machine at all.

Because they lack stabilizers, homemade ice creams and ices don't keep as long as store-bought varieties. For peak flavor and texture, plan on eating your frozen dessert within 24 hours. The kids will be glad to volunteer for that chore.

French Vanilla Ice Cream

Preparation time: 25 minutes plus 4 hours chilling time
Freezing time: varies

This is the real thing, rich and full of vanilla.

    1 cup low-fat milk
    ½ cup sugar
    2 teaspoons vanilla extract
    4 large egg yolks
    2½ cups heavy cream

OPTIONAL INGREDIENTS:
    1 cup chopped mixed nuts
    1 cup chopped chocolate or chocolate chips
    1 cup chopped candy bars
    1 cup chopped fresh cherries
    1 cup raisins mixed with 1 tablespoon honey
    **½ cup orange, lemon, or lime juice plus grated zest from 3 oranges,
       lemons, or limes**

In a medium saucepan, heat the milk, sugar, and 1 teaspoon of the vanilla over moderate heat until simmering. Remove from the heat.

Beat the egg yolks in a small bowl. Whisk in a few tablespoons of the hot milk mixture. Slowly add the warmed egg mixture to the saucepan and cook for about 10 minutes over moderate heat, whisking constantly, until the custard is thick enough to coat the back of a spoon. Don't let it boil.

When the custard reaches the desired thickness, whisk in the cream and remaining teaspoon of vanilla. Pour into a bowl, cover loosely, and chill for at least 4 hours, preferably overnight.

Transfer the custard to an ice-cream machine and freeze according to the manufacturer's instructions. If you're using one of the optional ingredients, add it 3 minutes be-

fore the recommended time limit. Mix well. Continue freezing until the ice cream is
thick. Serve in dessert bowls.

YIELD: 5 servings
PER SERVING: 566 calories, 6 g protein, 49 g fat, 26 g carbohydrate, 76 mg sodium, 337
   mg cholesterol

Frozen Cocoa

Preparation time: 5 minutes
Cooking time: 10 minutes
Freezing time: 1 hour 15 minutes

Make a pot of cocoa, freeze it in a cake pan, and break up the ice crystals every 15 minutes, and you have one of the most refreshing, chocolaty treats imaginable.

¼ cup sifted unsweetened cocoa powder
½ cup sugar or vanilla sugar (page 473)
Pinch salt
2 cups milk
1 teaspoon vanilla extract
Whipped cream (optional)

In a medium saucepan, mix the cocoa, sugar, and salt. Slowly whisk in the milk until smooth. Place the pan over moderately high heat and bring to a simmer, stirring often. Remove from the heat, stir in the vanilla, and pour into an 8-inch cake pan. Chill in the refrigerator until cold, 1 hour or more. Transfer to the freezer and freeze for 30 minutes. Mix with a fork, breaking up the ice crystals. Freeze another 15 minutes and break up the ice crystals again. Continue to freeze for 15 minutes at a time, breaking up the ice crystals, for about 30 minutes. Serve immediately, topped with whipped cream if desired. If you want to serve the frozen cocoa at a later time, remove from the freezer and refrigerate for about 20 minutes before serving. Stir with a fork and serve.

YIELD: 4 servings
PER SERVING: 187 calories, 5 g protein, 5 g fat, 34 g carbohydrate, 94 mg sodium, 17 mg cholesterol

Strawberry Yogurt Frappé

Preparation time: 10 minutes
Freezing time: 30 minutes to 1 hour

You can substitute any type of berry, fresh or frozen, in this frosty concoction.

> 1½ cups thinly sliced strawberries or 12 ounces frozen berries (with no sugar)
> 2 cups small ice cubes (or larger cubes crushed with a rolling pin)
> 1½ cups plain or vanilla low-fat yogurt
> ⅛ teaspoon vanilla extract
> 1 to 2 tablespoons sugar or strawberry jam
> 6 ripe strawberries (optional)

Place the berries, ice, yogurt, vanilla, and 1 tablespoon of the sugar or jam in a food processor or blender. Process at low speed until the ice begins to crush. Taste for sweetness and add another teaspoon or two of sugar or jam if needed.

Blend at high speed until the frappé is smooth and thick. Pour into 6 small glasses and freeze for 30 minutes to 1 hour. Top with a fresh berry if desired and add a long spoon.

YIELD: 6 servings
PER SERVING: 89 calories, 5 g protein, 2 g fat, 15 g carbohydrate, 60 mg sodium, 5 mg cholesterol

Orange-Lemon Ice

Preparation time: 20 minutes
Freezing time: 4 hours

An easy-to-make, refreshing ice for a hot day.

> ½ **cup freshly squeezed orange juice**
> 1 **tablespoon lemon juice**
> ¼ **cup sugar**
> 1½ **cups water**
> 1 **tablespoon grated orange zest (optional)**

In a nonaluminum pan, bring the orange and lemon juices, sugar, and water to a boil. Simmer until the sugar is thoroughly dissolved. Remove from the heat and let cool.

Pour the mixture into a shallow metal cake pan or 2 metal ice-cube trays (without dividers). Carefully place in the freezer. After 30 minutes, use a fork to break up the ice crystals and any lumps. Freeze another 30 minutes and repeat. Freeze for a total of 4 hours, breaking up the crystals every 30 minutes or so. Beat in the orange zest if desired during the last hour.

YIELD: 4 to 6 servings
PER SERVING: 50 calories, 0 g protein, 0 g fat, 13 g carbohydrate, 1 mg sodium, 0 mg cholesterol

Frozen Peach Swirl

Preparation time: 10 minutes
Freezing time: 30 minutes

Here is one of the best ways to use juicy summer peaches. For a frozen treat that's bursting with flavor, make sure the fruit is really ripe.

4 ripe peaches, peeled, pitted, and thinly sliced
2½ cups small ice cubes (or large cubes crushed with a rolling pin)
1 cup low-fat milk
1 tablespoon honey
Pinch ground cinnamon (optional)

Place 3 of the peaches and the ice cubes, milk, honey, and cinnamon in a food processor or blender, and process at low speed. Once the ice cubes are completely crushed, mix at high speed until thick and smooth.

Pour into 4 to 6 cups and freeze for 30 minutes. Top each with a thin slice of the remaining peach.

YIELD: 4 to 6 servings
PER SERVING: 71 calories, 2 g protein, 1 g fat, 15 g carbohydrate, 25 mg sodium, 4 mg cholesterol

Nut and Orange Zest Sauté

Preparation time: 5 minutes
Cooking time: about 6 minutes

The sautéed nuts and grated orange zest take on a buttery flavor that is irresistible, especially when they are served on top of a scoop of ice cream.

1 tablespoon butter
1 cup chopped walnuts, almonds, or other nuts
1 teaspoon grated orange zest

In a medium skillet, heat the butter over moderate heat. Add the nuts and sauté for about 4 minutes, stirring constantly to prevent burning. The nuts should become a light golden color. Remove from the heat and stir in the orange zest. Let cool before serving.

YIELD: 4 servings
PER SERVING: 874 calories, 17 g protein, 86 g fat, 23 g carbohydrate, 129 mg sodium, 31 mg cholesterol

Berry, Berry Good Sauce

Preparation time: 5 minutes

Kids love this sauce because it's fruity and sweet. Serve on fruit salad, yogurt, or ice cream. It's also delicious drizzled over a slice of pound cake.

¼ cup no-sugar-added jam, any flavor
3 to 4 tablespoons apple, cranberry, or cherry juice

In a bowl, mix the jam with the juice until fully blended. The sauce can be as thick or thin as you like, depending on how much juice you add. Serve at room temperature.

YIELD: 4 servings
PER SERVING: 48 calories, 0 g protein, 0 g fat, 12 g carbohydrate, 0 mg sodium, 0 mg cholesterol

Maple-Yogurt Sauce

Preparation time: 5 minutes

Spoon a generous dollop of this simple sauce over a bowl of mixed berries or chunks of fruit.

1 cup plain low-fat yogurt
2 tablespoons maple syrup

Mix the yogurt and maple syrup together. Serve cold.

YIELD: 4 servings
PER SERVING: 62 calories, 3 g protein, 9 g fat, 11 g carbohydrate, 41 mg sodium, 3 mg cholesterol

Chocolate-Orange Sauce

Preparation time: about 2 minutes
Cooking time: about 5 minutes

A chocolate lover's fantasy. Serve with ice cream or use as a dip with butter cookies.

> ½ **cup semisweet chocolate chips**
> 2 **tablespoons orange juice**
> 1 **tablespoon heavy cream or milk**

In a small saucepan, melt the chocolate over the lowest heat possible (too much heat will cause lumps to form). When the chocolate has melted, slowly whisk in the orange juice and cream; mix until smooth. Serve warm.

YIELD: 4 servings
PER SERVING: 118 calories, 1 g protein, 8 g fat, 14 g carbohydrate, 4 mg sodium, 5 mg cholesterol

Roasted Coconut and Raisin Sprinkle

Preparation time: 5 minutes
Cooking time: 5 minutes

Toasting shredded coconut in the oven for a few minutes gives it a rich, sweet flavor. Sprinkle it over fresh fruit salad, wedges of melon or pineapple, or on top of ice cream or yogurt.

¾ cup shredded unsweetened coconut
¼ cup raisins

Preheat the oven to 350 degrees. Spread the shredded coconut evenly on a baking sheet. Toast for 4 to 5 minutes, until lightly browned. Remove and let cool. Mix with the raisins.

YIELD: 4 servings

PER SERVING: 426 calories, 5 g protein, 31 g fat, 40 g carbohydrate, 22 mg sodium, 0 mg cholesterol

Chocolate Buttercream

Preparation time: about 5 minutes
Cooking time: 5 minutes

This recipe makes just the right amount of frosting for the Devil's Food Cake on page 313. If making cupcakes, cut the recipe in half or freeze half of it in an airtight container. The buttercream keeps well frozen for about 6 months.

4 ounces unsweetened chocolate
2 sticks unsalted butter (1 cup), softened
2 cups confectioners' sugar, sifted
¼ teaspoon salt
1 teaspoon vanilla extract

Place the chocolate in a small bowl or double boiler and place over simmering water to melt, stirring occasionally. Set aside to cool.

In a medium bowl, cream the butter, sugar, and salt until light, about 5 minutes. Add the vanilla and the melted chocolate. Mix until smooth.

YIELD: about 2 cups, or 32 servings
PER SERVING: 99 calories, 0.4 g protein, 8 g fat, 9 g carbohydrate, 18 mg sodium, 16 mg cholesterol

Simple Frosting

Preparation time: 5 minutes

Here is a totally straightforward icing for cookies, cupcakes, cakes, and muffins. You can add a drop of food coloring to make the icing any color you like.

1 stick unsalted butter (1 cup), softened
½ cup confectioners' sugar, sifted
Pinch salt

Place all the ingredients in a small bowl and blend thoroughly with a fork.

YIELD: about ½ cup
PER ½ CUP: 1,046 calories, 1 g protein, 92 g fat, 60 g carbohydrate, 145 mg sodium, 248 mg cholesterol

———————— ❧ ————————

Cooking with Kids: It May Be Messy But It Can Teach Them a Lot About Food and Life

It was raining, and the car was in the shop being fixed. It looked like my two-and-a-half-year-old daughter and I were home for a very long day. I knew I would lose my mind if we watched the *Peter Pan* video one more time, so I suggested that we bake a carrot cake. She happily put on my apron, which covered her entire body and trailed along the floor. I pulled up her sleeves, and we got to work.

While I grated carrots, she mixed the flour, eggs, and milk in a big plastic bowl. She spilled 2 tablespoons of vanilla extract into the bowl instead of one, but I wasn't worried. When the cake was done, she sloppily spread cream cheese icing across the top and sides. And while it didn't look like a cover shot for *Gourmet*, the two of us produced a pretty decent-tasting cake. That night, when dessert was served, my daughter declared it to be "the best day" of her life. She was so proud to have baked something so "yummy," something that everyone in the family enjoyed. It's a cake she remembers to this day.

One of the things I recall most vividly about that episode was the way my kitchen looked—like it had been hit by a tornado. Dishes were piled high in the sink, and a thin film of white flour made the kitchen floor look like the beach. But there was my daughter, grinning from ear to ear, saying, "I made it all by myself."

Cooking with kids can be incredibly messy and slow-going. It can even lead to culinary disasters. But these drawbacks are outweighed by the strong sense of accomplishment that many children feel when they prepare food for themselves and others. Once you see the sense of pride on your child's face, you will understand that it's well worth the mess and the patience required to cook with your kids. Allowing your child to help out in the kitchen also sends a powerful message: you are important, you can master this creative process, and you are capable of helping out. Through cooking, your child also learns where food comes from and how her favorite dishes are made.

I know many parents who are terrified to let their children into the kitchen. Not only is there the mess to deal with, but there are also questions of safety. What about knives, boiling water, and a hot stove?

Liz Strahle, who teaches children's cooking classes in Encinitas, California, says parents have to use common sense and discourage children's involvement with obviously dangerous things, like deep-frying, huge pots of boiling liquid, and many electrical appliances. Strahle says that all cooking needs to be supervised by adults. In her classes for seven- to twelve-year-olds, she uses plastic knives with serrated edges. "You wouldn't believe how many things you can cut effectively using a plastic knife," she claims.

Of course, not everyone would agree. Ken Haedrich, the father of three children and author of *Home for the Holidays* (Bantam Books), says, "I think it's a mistake to say 'no' to knives. Kids are fascinated by knives, and if you make them totally off-limits, then they'll only be more fascinated by them. It's the first thing they'll go for when you're not looking." Instead, Haedrich advises parents to teach their children (ideally school age) how to hold a knife properly and start out chopping something simple, like a piece of celery. "When I cook with younger kids," he explains, "I like to guide their hands and show them the right way to do it."

One way to make cooking with kids simpler and safer is to read each recipe through from beginning to end before you start. If a dangerous technique is called for, you might want to consider choosing a different recipe or do some preparation before you get your child involved. Chopping vegetables or boiling water in advance can make the process a lot smoother.

When you're cooking with younger children, let them work at a low table or set them on high stools where everything will be within easy reach. When more than one child is involved, split up the chores so that each of them can work on something that interests him or her. In Liz Strahle's classes the kids sing special songs as a way of making the sharing process a little easier: "Stirring and stirring and stirring the pot, pass it down, ready or not." Or "Grating, grating, grating the cheese, pass it down, hurry please."

The cooperative spirit can also apply to the least loved aspect of cooking—cleaning up. Let your child know, from the very start, that cleaning up is a part of cooking. He can help wash dishes, load the dishwasher, or sponge down a counter. Older children can also sweep or vacuum. Remember that cleaning up is important, but it is only one aspect of cooking and not the part you want to stress most. "If you're hung up about the mess," says Ken Haedrich, "then you're not going to be having fun, and chances are good that your child won't be particularly interested in cooking."

Restaurant owner Alice Waters believes that kids must be part of the eating and cooking experience. "How are they going to be educated about food if we don't include them in the kitchen?" she asks.

The whole idea of inviting your kids to help with the cooking is to spend time together, have fun, and perhaps teach them something about good food. Try to relax and stay open about the experience. This is a time when family traditions are passed on ("These are the cookies that my great-grandmother taught me to make") and lasting memories made. The kitchen can be a place that is warm, delicious smelling, and filled with good things to eat. Letting your kids in on the action only increases the pleasure.

Tips for Cooking with Kids

- Start out with a simple favorite recipe: lemonade, scrambled eggs, cookies, brownies, cupcakes, dips, English muffin pizzas, simple breads, and the like.

- Avoid recipes that require great accuracy. Making buttercream frosting or a soufflé with young children is asking for trouble.

- Always supervise children in the kitchen, particularly around hot stoves, boiling liquid, or sharp knives.

- Always read a recipe through before you begin cooking. Sometimes it's a good idea to do prep work, such as chopping parsley or boiling water, so you can keep the momentum going once you start cooking.

- Set up all your ingredients before you start cooking.

- Never let a young child put her hands in a hot oven. Make a firm rule that the adult always puts things in and takes things out of the oven.

- Kids as young as two can learn simple cooking techniques like squeezing lemons for lemonade or sprinkling grated cheese on a taco or spreading cream cheese on a bagel.

- A few tips on keeping the kitchen clean: Spread an old sheet or a piece of canvas under your worktable. When you're finished cooking, simply shake the sheet out. Or place an inexpensive plastic tablecloth on your worktable and wipe it down when you're done. Let your child wear an apron or an old T-shirt so you won't have to worry about dirty clothes.

- Make cooking fun, and praise your child's efforts so that it's something he wants to do again and again.

Chapter Nine

Snacks

꡴

Many children consider snacks the most important "meal" of the day. Instead of simply worrying about unhealthy snacks, parents can direct their kids to more healthy foods. This chapter places special emphasis on quick, make-ahead snacks kids can serve themselves, such as roasted sweet potato and vegetable chips, peanut butter dip with fruit, muffins, and more.

Yogurt-Cucumber Dip

Nutty Bean Dip

Green Herb Dip

Peanut Butter–Orange Dip

Pineapple Yogurt Dip

Sweet Potato Chips

Parsnip Chips with Sesame Seeds

Tamari-Glazed Eggplant Chips

Dilled Beet Chips

Trail Mix

Roasted Pumpkin Seeds

Pumpkin Seed Flavorings

Some Thoughts About . . . *The Snack Pack:*
  What to Bring When You're on the Road

Yogurt-Cucumber Dip

Preparation time: 10 minutes
Sitting time: 20 minutes or more

Dip raw vegetables, crackers, or warm triangles of pita bread into this fresh-tasting mixture. Or serve it with roast chicken, fish, or lamb. You can also add 2 chopped scallions and ¼ cup chopped fresh dill to this dip.

1½ cups peeled and grated cucumber
1 cup plain low-fat yogurt
2 tablespoons chopped fresh mint or 1 teaspoon dried

Place the grated cucumber in a large bowl and let sit for about 20 minutes. Drain off all the liquid (bitter juices) that has gathered in the bottom of the bowl.

Mix the cucumbers with the yogurt and mint. Serve cold. This dip will keep in the refrigerator for up to 6 hours, after which time it will become watery.

YIELD: about 1½ cups
PER 1½ CUPS: 25 calories, 2 g protein, 0.5 g fat, 3 g carbohydrate, 24 mg sodium, 2 mg cholesterol

Nutty Bean Dip

Preparation time: about 5 minutes

This dip looks beautiful in a large bowl, surrounded by chopped tomatoes, black olives, and cubed cucumbers or avocado. Any type of bean will do, but cannellini or black beans work particularly well. Accompany with tortilla chips or raw vegetables.

1½ cups cooked dried beans or 1 can (20 ounces), drained
2 small cloves garlic, chopped
2 tablespoons olive oil
⅓ cup chopped walnuts, almonds, or pine nuts
Pinch of cayenne pepper (optional)

Place the beans, garlic, oil, and nuts in a blender or food processor and blend until almost smooth. Remove to a serving bowl and, if you like spicy food, sprinkle with the cayenne.

YIELD: about 1 cup
PER 1 CUP: 119 calories, 4 g protein, 7 g fat, 10 g carbohydrate, 1 mg sodium, 0 mg cholesterol

Green Herb Dip

Preparation time: about 5 minutes

Raw or cooked vegetables, crackers, or toast triangles are perfect accompaniments for this dip. Fresh herbs make all the difference in the world, but in a pinch, dried will do.

1 cup low-fat ricotta cheese
½ cup feta cheese
¼ cup chopped fresh dill or 1 tablespoon dried
2 tablespoons chopped fresh thyme or 1 teaspoon dried
½ cup chopped fresh parsley
2 scallions or 1 small onion, chopped
1½ tablespoons olive oil
Salt and freshly ground black pepper

Place all the ingredients except the salt and pepper in a blender or a food processor and blend thoroughly until all the lumps are gone. Season to taste with salt and pepper.

YIELD: about 1½ cups

PER 1½ CUPS: 96 calories, 6 g protein, 7 g fat, 2 g carbohydrate, 151 mg sodium, 14 mg cholesterol

Peanut Butter-Orange Dip

Preparation time: 5 minutes

Dip slices of banana or apple into this sweet sauce, or serve with butter cookies or crackers.

½ cup smooth or chunky peanut butter
2 tablespoons frozen orange juice concentrate
1 tablespoon light brown sugar
About ⅓ cup low-fat milk or orange juice

In a small bowl, mix the peanut butter, orange juice concentrate, and sugar. Add enough milk or orange juice to thin the sauce to dipping consistency.

YIELD: 4 servings

PER SERVING: 129 calories, 6 g protein, 10 g fat, 7 g carbohydrate, 93 mg sodium, 0.5 mg cholesterol

Pineapple Yogurt Dip

Preparation time: 5 minutes

For a fast, healthy after-school snack, scoop up this dip with chopped fresh fruit or cookies. It's also delicious spooned over French toast or pancakes.

2 tablespoons frozen pineapple juice concentrate
1 cup plain low-fat yogurt
⅛ teaspoon vanilla extract
⅓ cup finely chopped canned pineapple, drained

Mix all the ingredients together in a small bowl and serve cold.

YIELD: 4 to 6 servings

PER SERVING: 31 calories, 2 g protein, 0.5 g fat, 5 g carbohydrate, 23 mg sodium, 2 mg cholesterol

Sweet Potato Chips

Preparation time: 10 minutes
Cooking time: about 13 minutes

Want your kids to eat more vegetables? Try thinly slicing sweet potatoes, eggplant, parsnips, or beets and baking them (see pages 379–81). The result will be crisp, sweet chips—more delicious than anything that comes in a bag. For chips that are sweet, "meaty," and positively addictive, give sweet potatoes a try.

1 large sweet potato, peeled and thinly sliced
2 tablespoons vegetable oil
Salt and freshly ground black pepper

Preheat the oven to 350 degrees. Brush a very light coating of oil on a baking sheet. Lay the potato slices on the sheet, being careful not to overlap them. Using a pastry brush or the back of a spoon, brush the slices lightly with oil. Sprinkle with salt and pepper and roast for 8 minutes. Flip the slices with a spatula and brush the other side lightly with oil. Sprinkle with more salt and pepper. Roast the chips another 5 minutes, or until they are cooked throughout and slightly crispy. Drain well on paper towels. Serve the chips hot or at room temperature within an hour of roasting.

YIELD: 4 servings
PER SERVING: 146 calories, 1 g protein, 7 g fat, 20 g carbohydrate, 11 mg sodium, 0 mg
   cholesterol

Parsnip Chips with Sesame Seeds

Preparation time: 10 minutes
Cooking time: 10 to 13 minutes

Parsnips have a naturally sweet flavor that makes them ideal candidates for roasting.

4 small parsnips, peeled and sliced about ¼ inch thick
2 tablespoons olive oil
Salt and freshly ground black pepper
3 tablespoons sesame seeds

Preheat the oven to 350 degrees. Lightly oil a baking sheet and lay the parsnip slices on the sheet, making sure they don't overlap. Using a pastry brush or the back of a spoon, brush the slices lightly with oil. Sprinkle with a little salt and pepper and roast for 5 minutes. Flip the slices with a spatula and very lightly brush the other side with oil. Sprinkle with more salt and pepper and the sesame seeds. Roast for another 5 to 8 minutes, or until tender. Be careful not to let the sesame seeds burn. Drain on paper towels. Serve the chips hot or at room temperature within an hour of roasting.

YIELD: 4 servings
PER SERVING: 152 calories, 2 g protein, 10 g fat, 14 g carbohydrate, 8 mg sodium, 0 mg cholesterol

Tamari-Glazed Eggplant Chips

Preparation time: 10 minutes
Cooking time: about 15 minutes

The tamari imparts a salty flavor and a beautiful mahogany color. Use the smaller Italian or Japanese eggplants for this recipe.

2 small eggplants
Salt
1 teaspoon vegetable oil
¼ cup tamari or low-sodium soy sauce

Thinly slice the eggplants and place the slices in a colander. Sprinkle liberally with salt and let sit for 20 minutes to leach out the bitter juices. Rinse the slices thoroughly under cold running water and let dry on paper towels.

Preheat the oven to 350 degrees. Lightly grease a baking sheet with oil and lay the eggplant slices on the sheet, making sure that they don't overlap. Using a pastry brush or the back of a spoon, lightly brush the slices with half of the tamari. Roast for 5 minutes. Flip the slices and brush the other side with the remaining tamari. Roast another 9 to 10 minutes, being careful not to let the edges burn. Drain on paper towels. Serve the chips hot or at room temperature within an hour of roasting.

YIELD: 4 servings
PER SERVING: 37 calories, 3 g protein, 1 g fat, 5 g carbohydrate, 1,143 mg sodium, 0 mg
   cholesterol

Dilled Beet Chips

Preparation time: 10 minutes
Cooking time: about 18 minutes

As they roast, these chips take on a bright pink color.

2 medium beets, scrubbed, peeled, and sliced ¼ inch thick
2 tablespoons olive oil
2 tablespoons chopped fresh dill
Salt and freshly ground black pepper

Preheat the oven to 350 degrees. Lightly oil a baking sheet. Place the beet slices on the sheet, being careful not to let them overlap. Using a pastry brush or the back of a spoon, very lightly brush the slices with oil. Sprinkle with half of the dill and the salt and pepper. Roast for 10 minutes. Flip the slices, brush the other side lightly with oil, and season with the remaining dill and more salt and pepper. Roast for an additional 8 minutes, or until the chips are tender throughout. Drain on paper towels. Serve the chips hot or at room temperature within an hour of roasting.

YIELD: 4 servings
PER SERVING: 80 calories, 1 g protein, 7 g fat, 5 g carbohydrate, 32 mg sodium, 0 mg cholesterol

Trail Mix

Preparation time: about 5 minutes

Prepare a batch of this high-energy snack and keep it on hand for kids to sprinkle on fresh fruit salad, frozen yogurt, or ice cream, or just to munch on.

¾ **cup granola**
¼ **cup chopped nuts**
¼ **cup raisins**
¼ **cup chopped dried apricots or other dried fruit**

In a medium bowl, mix all the ingredients. Store in an airtight container.

YIELD: 4 servings

PER SERVING: 196 calories, 4 g protein, 9 g fat, 27 g carbohydrate, 12 mg sodium, 0 mg cholesterol

Roasted Pumpkin Seeds

Every October, as children all over the country carve out their Halloween pumpkins, the insides of these large round orange squashes are thrown out and wasted. Next fall, don't miss the opportunity to roast your own pumpkin seeds—a wonderfully addictive snack that is high in fiber. The process is easy, though it takes some patience and adult supervision.

Cut off the top of the pumpkin to make a hole large enough to carve out the insides. Using a metal spoon, scoop out the pumpkin flesh, separating the seeds from the stringy fibers. Don't be concerned if you can't separate them all. Place the seeds (and any adjoining fibers) into a large bowl of cold water. The seeds will float to the surface, while the pulp will sink. (You may need to help separate any remaining pulp by simply pulling it off with your fingers.) Scoop the seeds off the surface of the water and place on a clean tea towel to dry. The seeds should dry overnight.

Preheat the oven to 350 degrees. Lay the seeds on a lightly oiled (vegetable oil is best) baking sheet in a single layer. Sprinkle with salt and any other spices you like (see suggestions below) and flip the seeds over using a spatula or your hands to coat them on both sides with the seasoning and oil. Bake about 5 to 8 minutes, flip the seeds over with a spatula, and bake another 5 to 10 minutes, or until golden brown on each side. Check the seeds frequently to make sure they're not burning. Remove from the oven and let cool thoroughly before placing in an airtight container.

Pumpkin Seed Flavorings

- Instead of salt, sprinkle a very small amount of low-sodium soy sauce on the seeds.
- Make a spicy mixture by adding cayenne pepper to the seeds.
- Sprinkle curry powder and/or cumin on the seeds.
- Sprinkle with ground ginger and a touch of cinnamon.

SOME THOUGHTS ABOUT . . .

The Snack Pack: What to Bring When You're on the Road

It's bad enough being trapped in a car or a plane with a cranky child. But if she is also hungry—watch out. Hunger meltdown ranks up there with video withdrawal. It's not a pretty sight.

Classic take-along fare—crackers, cookies, fruit chews—satisfies just fine, but the recipes that follow will add a little spice to your adventure. These finger foods require only 5 to 10 minutes to prepare. The ones that include cheese (except the popcorn) or chocolate should be kept in a cooler or thermos pack.

To make the snacks even more of a treat, tuck each one into its own colorful container, wrap it in fanciful paper to make it look like a present, or package a new little travel toy with it. Snacking then becomes more than just a way to get from meal to meal; it turns into an activity that makes some of those long, boring travel hours pass more quickly. Each recipe makes enough for two children.

Pita Spirals: Peel and grate 1 large carrot and half a large cucumber. Mix the vegetables with ¾ cup low-fat cream cheese and your child's favorite seasonings (garlic, parsley, cinnamon, pepper). Slice open 2 large pita pockets and spread the cream cheese over each round. Roll each up like a fat cigar, then cut into 1-inch pieces.

French Picnic: Cut some Muenster and Cheddar cheese (or your child's favorite) into small cubes. Select a variety of fruits that won't turn brown—melon, strawberries, oranges—and cut into pieces that are the same size as the cheese. Thread the fruit and cheese pieces onto bamboo skewers (snip off the sharp tips) and pack in small plastic bags. Bring along some bread or rolls to eat with the fruit and cheese.

Chocolate Pretzels: Melt 1½ cups chocolate chips over *very* low heat or in the top of a double boiler until smooth. Using tongs, dip each pretzel into the chocolate, letting the excess drip back into the pan. Place the pretzels on a plate covered with wax paper and refrigerate until ready to pack for the trip.

Lemon-Lime Slush: In a pitcher, mix ½ cup combined lemon and lime juice with 4 teaspoons sugar and 2 cups cold water. Add more sugar to taste. Stir well and divide the mixture between 2 small thermoses that are plastic, not glass-lined. Freeze overnight, or until solid. Depending on the weather, the slush will take between 1 and 2 hours to thaw enough to eat with a spoon or drink through a straw. After that, you'll have cold lemon-limeade for several hours.

Cheese Popcorn: Make a batch of fresh popcorn. While it's still warm, sprinkle generously with sweet paprika and Parmesan cheese (cooking the popcorn in oil will create a more "stickable" surface). Pack in a clean brown-paper bag and bring along plenty of disposable wipes. (Popcorn is not recommended for children under the age of four.)

Other Snack Ideas:

Chapter Ten

Drinks

🎵

"Mom, can I have a glass of juice?" "Dad, can I have a glass of milk?" Instead of simply pouring a glass of milk or juice (particularly since so many brands have sugar added to them), why not offer your child something different for a change, like a Fruity Spritzer, a Lime Rickey, or Kids' Fruity Tea Punch? This chapter also has recipes for classics like Hot Cocoa and Hot Spiced Cider, as well as soothing ideas for a Hot Lemonade and a Chamomile-Lemon Soother to take the chill out of a cold winter's day.

Fruity Spritzer

Lime Rickey

Lime Rickey Variations

Kids' Fruity Tea Punch

Pineapple-Coconut Slush

Hot Spiced Cider

Hot Cocoa

Hot Cocoa Variations

Chamomile-Lemon Soother

Hot Lemonade

Fruity Spritzer

Preparation time: 5 minutes

A fresh fruity flavor makes this drink irresistible. Serve as is for kids, or add a splash of vodka or rum for adults.

½ cup seltzer
⅓ cup cranberry juice (with minimal sugar added)
2 tablespoons orange juice, preferably fresh-squeezed
Ice cubes
2 tablespoons fresh raspberries
1 thin slice fresh orange

In a large glass, mix the seltzer, cranberry juice, and orange juice. Add ice cubes and mix well. Add the raspberries and place the orange slice along the edge of the glass.

YIELD: 1 serving
PER SERVING: 45 calories, 0.47 g protein, 0.18 g fat, 11 g carbohydrate, 3 mg sodium, 0 mg cholesterol

Lime Rickey

Preparation time: 5 minutes

This is a thoroughly refreshing drink, a kind of alternative lemonade.

3 tablespoons fresh lime juice (1 large lime)
1 cup seltzer
1 to 1½ tablespoons sugar
Ice cubes
1 thin slice lime

In a large glass, mix the lime juice, seltzer, and sugar to taste. Add the ice cubes and place the lime slice on the edge of the glass.

YIELD: 1 serving
PER SERVING: 76 calories, 0.26 g protein, 0.05 g fat, 21 g carbohydrate, 1 mg sodium, 0 mg cholesterol

Lime Rickey Variations

- Use an orange or lime-flavored seltzer for an even fruitier taste.
- Add a handful of fresh berries.
- Use a mixture of lemon and lime juice for a Lemon-Lime Rickey.
- Add a tablespoon or two of your favorite fruit juice to give the drink good color and a fruity flavor.
- Add a teaspoon or two of fruit syrup.

Kids' Fruity Tea Punch

Preparation time: 5 minutes
Cooking and steeping time: 10 minutes
Chilling time: several hours

Punch is always a hit with kids at parties, and this herb-tea- and fruit-based drink is no exception. Be sure to leave enough time to chill properly. For an extra-special touch, freeze fresh mint leaves into ice cubes and add to the punch.

3 bags all-natural mint tea (no caffeine)
7 cups boiling water
¼ cup honey, or to taste
3 cups orange juice
1 orange, peeled, seeded, and cut into very small cubes
1 cup fresh berries (optional)

Place the tea bags in a large pot. Pour in the boiling water and stir in the honey. Let steep for 5 minutes and remove the tea bags. When the tea has cooled to room temperature, pour it into a large pitcher. Add the orange juice, small cubes of orange, and berries and stir well. Taste for sweetness, adding more orange juice or honey if needed. Chill until cold.

YIELD: about 10 cups
PER ½ CUP SERVING: 33 calories, 0.31 g protein, 0.03 g fat, 9 g carbohydrate, 2 mg sodium, 0 mg cholesterol

Pineapple-Coconut Slush

Preparation time: 10 minutes

This thick milkshake-like drink relies on fresh pineapple and coconut milk for its refreshing sweetness. Be sure to buy a brand of coconut milk that is not loaded with sugar and preservatives; check Asian food markets for unsweetened varieties.

1 cup cubed fresh pineapple or canned crushed pineapple, drained
½ cup coconut milk
½ cup crushed ice
Pinch sugar (optional)
Slice fresh pineapple

In a blender or food processor, puree the pineapple, coconut milk, and crushed ice. (To crush the ice, simply wrap 2 to 3 large cubes in a clean tea towel and smash with a rolling pin.) Taste for seasoning and add a pinch of sugar if needed. Place the pineapple slice along the edge of the glass.

YIELD: 2 servings
PER SERVING: 163 calories, 2 g protein, 13 g fat, 15 g carbohydrate, 8 mg sodium, 0 mg cholesterol

Hot Spiced Cider

Preparation time: 5 minutes
Cooking time: 5 minutes

This soothing mixture goes well with breakfast, lunch, a snack, or dinner. It's also an ideal accompaniment to apple pie. Serve with cinnamon stick "straws."

2 cups apple cider
2 cups cranberry juice
Cinnamon sticks
1 clove
Pinch ground nutmeg

Place the cider, cranberry juice, 1 cinnamon stick, 1 clove, and the nutmeg in a saucepan and warm over moderate heat. When hot, strain the liquid into 4 mugs. Place a cinnamon stick in each mug if desired.

YIELD: 4 servings
PER SERVING: 131 calories, 0.07 g protein, 0.26 g fat, 33 g carbohydrate, 6 mg sodium, 0 mg cholesterol

Hot Cocoa

Cooking time: 5 minutes

There is no drink that is more comforting on a cold, snowy day than cocoa. Top it with tiny marshmallows, whipped cream, or a grating of chocolate for an extra-special treat.

4 cups low-fat milk
6 tablespoons high-quality unsweetened cocoa
About 8 teaspoons sugar

In a small saucepan, heat the milk over low heat. Mix 1½ tablespoons of cocoa and about 2 teaspoons sugar in each of 4 mugs and fill with the hot milk. Stir or whisk until the cocoa is fully blended.

YIELD: 4 servings
PER SERVING: 153 calories, 10 g protein, 4 g fat, 24 g carbohydrate, 124 mg sodium, 10 mg cholesterol

Hot Cocoa Variations

To make Mexican Hot Chocolate, add a cinnamon stick to the milk while it is heating and sprinkle ground cinnamon on top of the cocoa before serving.

To make Vanilla Hot Chocolate, add ⅛ teaspoon vanilla extract to the milk when heating.

Chamomile-Lemon Soother

Cooking time: 5 minutes
Steeping time: 5 minutes

Here's a mild, natural way to let kids drink tea without getting hyper on caffeine.

> **2 chamomile tea bags**
> **4 cups boiling water**
> **4 teaspoons honey**
> **4 teaspoons lemon juice**

Place the tea bags in a teapot and fill with the boiling water. Let steep for about 5 minutes. Put a teaspoon of honey and lemon juice into each of 4 mugs and fill with the hot tea.

YIELD: 4 servings
PER SERVING: 25 calories, 0 g protein, 0 g fat, 7 g carbohydrate, 8 mg sodium, 0 mg cholesterol

Hot Lemonade

Preparation time: 5 minutes
Cooking time: 5 minutes

While hardly medicinal, this soothing drink can take the edge off a sore throat. You can also make a delicious hot limeade or orangeade by substituting fresh lime or orange juice.

8 tablespoons freshly squeezed lemon juice
8 tablespoons honey or sugar
4 cups boiling water
4 thin slices lemon

Place 2 tablespoons of lemon juice and 2 tablespoons honey into each of 4 mugs. Fill with boiling water and add a lemon slice.

YIELD: 4 servings
PER SERVING: 138 calories, 0.31 g protein, 0.02 g fat, 38 g carbohydrate, 2 mg sodium, 0 mg cholesterol

Chapter Eleven

Microwave Recipes

&a.

The microwave oven is a reality of the American kitchen. Statistics change monthly, but recent reports indicate that more than nine out of ten households in this country now have a microwave oven. And while most people don't rely on it as their primary cooking oven, the microwave oven is frequently used for reheating foods, popping popcorn, and thawing frozen foods.

Microwave cooking has become increasingly popular in recent years. There are certain foods that lend themselves to being microwaved, while others just don't seem to do as well. You won't find a recipe for roast leg of lamb in this chapter, but there are many recipes for vegetable and fish dishes, soups and snacks. These are foods that actually stay as moist and fresh-tasting when cooked in a microwave as they are when cooked in a conventional oven.

Microwave ovens are also a great way to make quick homemade soups and sauces in about half the time they take on a traditional stove. And baking potatoes couldn't be easier or faster—even when they're topped with a simple cheese sauce or a vegetable filling. Be sure to try the Low-Fat Nachos, the Stone Fruit Sauce (for pouring over yogurt or ice cream), and the very quick chicken and turkey cutlet dishes in this chapter, and you'll see how you can use your microwave to its best advantage.

Minestrone

Pasta and Bean Soup

Chicken Breasts with Apricot Sauce

Turkey Cutlets with Mustard and Capers

Poached Fish Fillets with Cucumber Sauce

Fish Smothered in Vegetables

Microwave Baked Potatoes with Toppings

Baked Stuffed Potatoes with a Ham and Jack Cheese Filling

Chili Popcorn

Low-Fat Nachos

Spinach with Raisins and Almonds

Stewed Tomatoes

Steamed Asparagus with Lemon

Applesauce with Ginger and Lemon

Stone Fruit Sauce

Chocolate Sauce in a Flash

Minestrone

Preparation time: 30 minutes
Microwave time: about 50 minutes
Sitting time: 10 minutes

If any soup invites variation and personal interpretation, minestrone is it. Zucchini and string beans are a must, along with potatoes and white beans, but the rest is variable. For instance, all the vegetables listed here are interchangeable: cabbage can be substituted with chard, spinach, or kale. Don't let the long list of ingredients scare you off: the soup is very simple to put together and will last for several meals.

This soup takes about an hour to make, but it would easily take twice that long if cooked conventionally on a stove.

¼ cup olive oil or bacon drippings
¼ cup chopped fresh parsley
2 cloves garlic, finely chopped
1 onion, chopped
1 carrot, diced
1 stalk celery, diced
2 cups diced zucchini
1½ cups green beans cut into 1-inch pieces
4 cups shredded cabbage (about 1 pound trimmed weight)
1 cup diced potato
1 can (19 ounces) cannellini (white kidney beans), drained and rinsed
1 cup diced canned Italian tomatoes
8 cups chicken broth or 4 cups chicken broth and 4 cups water
½ cup short-grain rice
Salt and freshly ground black pepper
Grated Parmesan cheese

Place the oil in a 3- to 4-quart microwave-proof bowl, cover with microwave plastic wrap, and cook on high (100%) for 30 seconds. Add the parsley and garlic and stir to coat with the oil. Cook, uncovered, for 1 minute. Add the onion, carrot, and celery and cook, uncovered, for 5 minutes, tossing halfway through the cooking time. Add the remaining ingredients except the rice, salt, pepper, and cheese. Stir and cover with microwave plastic wrap. Cook 20 minutes, stirring after every 5 minutes of cooking time. Add the rice and cook another 25 minutes, covered, stirring every 5 minutes. Let sit, covered, for 10 minutes. Season with salt and pepper. Serve with Parmesan cheese.

YIELD: 8 servings as a meal; 10 as a first course

PER SERVING: 237 calories, 9 g protein, 9 g fat, 30 g carbohydrate, 1,151 mg sodium, 0 mg cholesterol

Pasta and Bean Soup

Preparation time: 15 minutes
Microwave time: about 35 minutes
Standing time: 10 minutes

You might not expect this well-loved Italian pasta and bean soup to work well in the micro-wave, but it does. There is no need to cook the pasta separately, as it will cook in the broth.

¼ **cup olive oil**
1 **onion, chopped**
1 **carrot, diced**
1 **celery, diced**
4 **cloves garlic, finely chopped**
1 **cup diced canned tomatoes**
2 **cans (19 ounces each) cannellini (white kidney beans), drained and**
   rinsed
1 **teaspoon dried rosemary**
¼ **cup chopped fresh parsley**
4 **cups beef broth**
2 **cups water**
¼ **pound small pasta, such as orzo, baby shells, or ditalini**
Freshly ground black pepper or hot red pepper flakes
Grated Parmesan cheese

Place the oil in a 3- to 4-quart microwave-proof bowl, cover with microwave plastic wrap or a lid, and heat for 30 seconds on high (100%). Add the onion, carrot, celery, and garlic and toss to coat with the oil. Cook 5 minutes, uncovered, tossing halfway through the cooking time. Add the tomatoes, beans, rosemary, parsley, broth, and water. Cook, covered, for 5 minutes. Add the pasta, stir, cover again, and cook until tender, about 20 to 25 minutes, stirring after every 5 minutes or so. Season with the pepper. Remove and let sit, covered, about 10 minutes. The soup should be thick. Serve with cheese on the side.

YIELD: 8 servings
PER SERVING: 239 calories, 10 g protein, 8 g fat, 31 g carbohydrate, 1,046 mg sodium, 0 mg cholesterol

Chicken Breasts with Apricot Sauce

Preparation time: 5 minutes
Microwave time: about 5½ minutes

Skinless, boneless chicken breasts cook perfectly in the microwave; they remain moist and tender. This is a master recipe for cooking chicken breasts in the microwave, so feel free to add other flavorings to the sauce: mustard, basil, and tarragon work particularly well. You can also serve the chicken with the cucumber sauce from the Poached Fish Fillets with Cucumber Sauce on page 403.

If you want to reduce the amount of chicken you cook to one whole breast (2 pieces), microwave for only 3 minutes.

½ cup apricot preserves
1 tablespoon fresh lemon juice
1 tablespoon soy sauce
1 clove garlic, finely chopped (optional)
2 whole skinless, boneless chicken breasts (4 pieces)
Salt and freshly ground black pepper

In a small microwave-proof bowl, mix the preserves, lemon juice, soy sauce, and garlic if using. Cover with microwave plastic wrap, and heat on high (100%) for 30 seconds. Whisk the sauce until well mixed and set aside.

Place the chicken breasts in one layer in a microwave-proof pie plate or baking dish. Cover with microwave plastic wrap and cook on high (100%) for 5 minutes. Remove from the oven and arrange on plates. Sprinkle the chicken with salt and pepper and spoon on the reserved sauce.

YIELD: 4 servings
PER SERVING: 230 calories, 28 g protein, 2 g fat, 26 g carbohydrate, 350 mg sodium, 68 mg cholesterol

Turkey Cutlets with Mustard and Capers

Preparation time: 5 minutes
Microwave time: 6 minutes

Turkey cutlets are now readily available in most supermarkets. They are low in fat and make a great alternative to pork or beef. These turkey cutlets are poached in a touch of chicken broth, and a simple sauce is made from the pan juices. You can vary the herbs to suit your taste.

¾ pound turkey cutlets
3 tablespoons chicken broth
½ teaspoon dried thyme or tarragon
2 teaspoons Dijon mustard
1 tablespoon drained capers
Freshly ground black pepper

Place the cutlets in a microwave-proof baking dish in one layer. Spoon the broth over them and scatter the thyme or tarragon on top. Cover with microwave plastic wrap and cook on high (100%) for 5 minutes. Remove the cutlets to a plate. Whisk the mustard into the baking dish, stir in the capers, and cook on high (100%) for 1 minute, uncovered. Sprinkle the cutlets with pepper and spoon the sauce on top.

YIELD: 2 servings
PER SERVING: 198 calories, 42 g protein, 1 g fat, 0.22 g carbohydrate, 407 mg sodium, 106 mg cholesterol

Poached Fish Fillets with Cucumber Sauce

Preparation time: 5 to 10 minutes
Microwave time: 3 to 5 minutes

The texture of microwave fish is moist and tender. It's best to choose a 1-inch fillet (not a steak), such as salmon, flounder, hake, scrod, or haddock.

½ **cup plain yogurt**
½ **cup diced cucumber**
1 **clove garlic, finely chopped**
2 **tablespoons chopped fresh dill**
Salt and freshly ground black pepper
1½ **pounds skinless fish fillets, about 1 inch thick**

In a small bowl, mix the yogurt, cucumber, garlic, dill, and salt and pepper and set aside.

Place the fish in a microwave-proof baking dish. If any fillet has a thin tail piece, fold it under so that the fish is of uniform thickness. Cover with microwave plastic wrap and cook on high (100%) for 3 to 5 minutes. If your fish is thinner, cook for only about 3 minutes. Transfer the fish to 4 plates, season with salt and pepper, and spoon the sauce on top.

YIELD: 4 servings
PER SERVING: 263 calories, 35 g protein, 11 g fat, 3 g carbohydrate, 96 mg sodium, 95 mg cholesterol

Fish Smothered in Vegetables

Preparation time: 10 minutes
Microwave time: 5 to 7 minutes

This is a simple colorful dish that takes only minutes to make. Use a fresh, firm fish such as swordfish, haddock, halibut, or cod.

1 red, orange, or yellow bell pepper, cored and sliced
1 red onion, thinly sliced
1 tomato, thinly sliced
Salt and freshly ground black pepper
2 tablespoons olive oil
1 tablespoon fresh lemon juice
1 tablespoon chopped fresh basil or 1 teaspoon dried (optional)
1½ pounds fish fillets or steaks, about 1 inch thick
2 tablespoons chopped fresh parsley

Place the bell pepper, onion, tomato, salt, pepper, olive oil, lemon juice, and basil in a bowl and toss well. (Don't be concerned if the tomato slices fall apart somewhat.)

Place the fish in a microwave-proof baking dish. If using fillets with a thin tail piece, fold it under so that the fish is of uniform thickness. Spread the vegetable mixture over the fish to cover completely and cover the baking dish with microwave plastic wrap. Cook on high (100%) for 5 minutes. Check for doneness; the fish should be flaky and cooked through when tested with a fork. Cook another 1 to 2 minutes if necessary. Sprinkle with parsley and transfer to 4 plates and serve.

YIELD: 4 servings
PER SERVING: 296 calories, 35 g protein, 14 g fat, 7 g carbohydrate, 162 mg sodium, 66 mg cholesterol

Microwave Baked Potatoes with Toppi

Preparation time: about 5 minute.
Microwave time: 10 to 25 minutes

There are few foods as versatile as the baked potato, and the microwave is the fastest, most effective way to bake it. These potatoes can be served as a snack, side dish, or main course with one or more toppings. Listed below are two simple toppings, but use your imagination to create your own.

This recipe uses large baking potatoes weighing around 8 to 10 ounces. Instructions are also given for substituting sweet potatoes. The toppings make enough for 4 potatoes.

4 large baking potatoes or sweet potatoes (see note above)

WALNUT–PARMESAN CHEESE BUTTER TOPPING:
4 tablespoons unsalted butter, softened
2 tablespoons finely chopped walnuts
2 tablespoons grated Parmesan cheese
Freshly ground black pepper
1 tablespoon chopped fresh parsley (optional)

SOUR CREAM AND SCALLIONS:
½ cup sour cream
¼ cup sliced scallion greens (about 2)
Salt and freshly ground black pepper

Scrub the potatoes and prick with a fork. Place in the microwave and cook on high (100%) for the following time (based on a 10-ounce potato), turning the potatoes over halfway through the cooking time: 1 potato—10 minutes for white and 8 to 10 minutes for sweet; 2 potatoes—15 to 17 minutes for white and 13 to 15 minutes for sweet; 4 potatoes—20 to 25 minutes for white and 18 to 20 minutes for sweet. Adjust the cooking time if your potatoes are smaller or larger. Remove from the microwave and let cool about 2 to 3 minutes before adding a topping.

To make the walnut and Parmesan butter, place the butter, walnuts, cheese, pepper, and parsley on a small plate. Mix with a fork until well combined. Set aside until the potatoes are cooked. Spread the butter on the cooked potatoes.

To make the sour cream and scallion topping, mix the sour cream, scallions, salt, and pepper in a small bowl. Set aside until the potatoes are cooked.

YIELD: 4 servings

PER SERVING with *walnut and Parmesan butter*: 343 calories, 6 g protein, 15 g fat, 48 g carbohydrate, 64 mg sodium, 33 mg cholesterol

PER SERVING with *sour cream and scallion topping*: 271 calories, 5 g protein, 6 g fat, 50 g carbohydrate, 31 mg sodium, 13 mg cholesterol

Baked Stuffed Potatoes with a Ham and Jack Cheese Filling

Preparation time: about 10 minutes
Microwave time: about 10 to 25 minutes

A delicious stuffed potato that makes a quick main course.

4 large baking potatoes or sweet potatoes
½ cup milk
1 cup diced ham
1 cup diced Monterey Jack cheese
4 tablespoons unsalted butter
Freshly ground black pepper
Ground nutmeg

Bake the potatoes in the microwave according to the instructions on page 405.

Place the milk in a glass measure, cover with microwave plastic wrap, and heat on high (100%) for 1 minute. Place the ham, cheese, butter, pepper, and nutmeg in a medium bowl and add the hot milk. Stir to mix and melt the butter.

Split the baked potatoes in half lengthwise. Scoop out the hot potato flesh, reserving the shells, and mash in a bowl. Mix with the ham and milk mixture. Stuff the filling back into the potato shells and serve hot. (This dish can be made several hours ahead of time and refrigerated. To reheat, cover the potatoes with plastic wrap and cook on high for 2 to 4 minutes, or until the stuffing is hot throughout.)

YIELD: 4 servings
PER SERVING: 498 calories, 19 g protein, 25 g fat, 51 g carbohydrate, 650 mg sodium, 86 mg cholesterol

Chili Popcorn

Preparation time: 5 minutes
Microwave time: about 5½ minutes

Your best bet for making popcorn in the microwave is to use the prepackaged variety. Popping your own popcorn in a paper bag is not recommended because the bag could easily burst and the contents are very hot. You can make this popcorn as mild or spicy as you like.

2 tablespoons unsalted butter
2 tablespoons olive oil
2 teaspoons dried oregano
1 teaspoon chili powder
1 large clove garlic, finely chopped (optional)
1 package (3½ ounces) unseasoned microwave popcorn
½ cup grated Parmesan cheese
Cayenne pepper

In a small microwave-proof bowl, mix the butter, olive oil, oregano, chili powder, and garlic if using. Cover with microwave plastic wrap and heat the mixture for 30 seconds on high (100%) to melt the butter. Remove from the oven, whisk the sauce until smooth, and set aside.

Pop the popcorn according to the manufacturer's directions. When done, carefully open and transfer the popcorn to a large bowl. Pour the reserved butter mixture over the popcorn, scatter the cheese over the top, and sprinkle with as much cayenne as you like (or none at all). Toss the mixture together until the popcorn is evenly coated.

YIELD: about 2 to 3 quarts, or 4 servings
PER SERVING: 277 calories, 6 g protein, 24 g fat, 13 g carbohydrate, 393 mg sodium, 23
    mg cholesterol

Low-Fat Nachos

Preparation time: 10 minutes
Microwave time: 2 to 3 minutes

These nachos are loaded with salsa, scallions, and jalapeño peppers for crunch and flavor. You can make them as spicy or mild as you like. Try any mixture of cheeses, but look for low-fat varieties. This recipe serves 2 but can easily be doubled or tripled.

2 handfuls tortilla chips (approximately 2 ounces), preferably a low-fat variety
½ cup mild, medium, or hot salsa
1 cup grated low-fat cheese or mixture of low-fat cheeses
2 tablespoons sliced olives
1 tablespoon finely chopped green chili peppers with the seeds removed (optional)
1 scallion, sliced

Place half the chips on a large microwave-safe plate. Spoon on half the salsa. Scatter half of the cheese on top. Arrange the remaining chips over the cheese. Spoon on the remaining salsa and cheese. Place the olives, chilies, and scallion on top. Microwave, uncovered, on high (100%) for 2 minutes. Check to make sure all the cheese is melted. If not, microwave for about 30 seconds more. Let cool a minute, then serve.

YIELD: 2 servings
PER SERVING: 286 calories, 17 g protein, 11 g fat, 28 g carbohydrate, 979 mg sodium, 33 mg cholesterol

Spinach with Raisins and Almonds

Preparation time: 5 minutes
Baking time: 5 minutes
Microwave time: 5 minutes

For the most flavorful results, use a good-quality olive oil with this sweet-and-sour spinach.

2 tablespoons sliced almonds
10 ounces fresh spinach, washed
1 clove garlic, finely chopped
¼ cup packed raisins
2 tablespoons good quality olive oil
1 tablespoon fresh lemon juice
Salt and freshly ground black pepper

Preheat the oven to 350 degrees. Place the almonds on a baking sheet and bake for 5 minutes. Let cool.

Place the spinach with water still clinging to the leaves in a 2-quart microwave-proof container. Add the garlic and raisins and cover with a lid or microwave plastic wrap. Cook on high (100%) for 5 minutes, tossing the mixture halfway through the cooking time. Remove from the oven, add the olive oil, lemon juice, salt, and pepper, and mix well. Sprinkle with the almonds and serve.

YIELD: 4 servings
PER SERVING: 126 calories, 3 g protein, 9 g fat, 12 g carbohydrate, 58 mg sodium, 0 mg cholesterol

Stewed Tomatoes

Preparation time: 10 minutes
Microwave time: 10 to 12 minutes

This old-fashioned dish can be served alongside just about any entrée—roast chicken or pork, fish, pasta, or rice. The tomatoes can be made plain or jazzed up with a number of flavorings, such as those listed below.

1 tablespoon unsalted butter
1 onion, finely chopped
Salt and freshly ground black pepper
2 pounds fresh tomatoes, cored, seeded, and cut into chunks
3 tablespoons finely chopped fresh basil
1 to 2 teaspoons sugar

Place the butter in an 8-cup microwave-safe dish, cover with microwave plastic wrap, and heat for 15 seconds on high (100%). Add the onion, sprinkle with salt and pepper, and toss to coat the onion with the butter. Cook, uncovered, for 3 minutes, tossing once after 1½ minutes.

Add the tomatoes, basil, 1 teaspoon of the sugar, and more salt and pepper. Toss together to mix well. Cover tightly with microwave plastic wrap and cook for 6 to 8 minutes, stirring every 2 minutes. Taste for seasoning and add more salt, pepper, or sugar if needed. If the tomatoes are not vine-ripened, they will probably need the extra sugar. Serve hot.

YIELD: 4 to 6 servings
PER SERVING: 74 calories, 2 g protein, 3 g fat, 12 g carbohydrate, 16 mg sodium, 6 mg cholesterol

Other flavorings:

1 clove garlic, finely chopped, added with the onion
¼ cup finely chopped celery, added with the onion
¼ cup finely chopped green or red bell pepper, added with the onion
1 teaspoon grated lemon zest, added with the tomatoes
1 teaspoon dried oregano, added with the tomatoes
2 tablespoons finely chopped fresh parsley, added with the tomatoes

Steamed Asparagus with Lemon

Preparation time: 5 minutes
Microwave time: 3 to 4 minutes

One of the things that is most appealing about cooking vegetables in a microwave oven is that they retain their fresh taste and texture instead of going limp or soft. This recipe is also delicious with orange juice and orange zest substituted for the lemon.

1 tablespoon butter, softened
1 teaspoon lemon juice
¼ teaspoon grated lemon zest
Salt and freshly ground black pepper
1 pound fresh asparagus

In a small bowl, cream together the butter, lemon juice, and lemon zest. Season with salt and pepper and set aside.

Rinse the asparagus in cold water and snap off the bottom of the stems. Leave the water that is clinging to the asparagus and arrange them on a microwave-safe plate in 2 layers. Cover with microwave plastic wrap. Microwave on high (100%) for 3 minutes for slender stalks and 4 minutes for medium or average-size stalks.

Remove from the oven and uncover immediately so that the asparagus don't continue to cook. Toss with the lemon butter and serve hot.

YIELD: 4 servings
PER SERVING: 39 calories, 2 g protein, 3 g fat, 2 g carbohydrate, 31 mg sodium, 8 mg cholesterol

Applesauce with Ginger and Lemon

Preparation time: 15 minutes
Microwave time: 15 to 20 minutes

This is one of those dishes that define the convenience of owning a microwave. How else can you make delicious homemade applesauce in less than 30 minutes?

For a beautiful rosy color, leave the peel on the apples. You can strain the sauce through a food mill or a regular strainer to remove the peel after cooking the sauce, or you can leave it on for a chunkier, more rustic dish.

3 pounds McIntosh or other tart apples, peeled (if desired), cored, and cut into chunks
½ cup sugar
2 tablespoons fresh lemon juice
2 teaspoons ground ginger

Place the apple chunks in a 3-quart microwave-proof bowl. Add the sugar, lemon juice, and ginger and toss the apples to coat with the mixture. Cover with a lid or microwave plastic wrap and cook on high (100%) for 5 minutes. Stir the apples. Cook for another 10 to 15 minutes, tossing the apples every 5 minutes. The total cooking time depends on whether or not the peels were left on; the peels require a longer cooking time. When the apples are soft, mash with a potato masher or fork. Strain if you left the skins on and want them removed. Serve warm or chilled.

YIELD: about 4 to 5 cups
PER ½ CUP SERVING: 119 calories, 0.23 g protein, 0.41 g fat, 31 g carbohydrate, 0.26 mg sodium, 0 mg cholesterol

Stone Fruit Sauce

Preparation time: 5 minutes
Microwave time: 10 minutes

Serve this tasty sauce over frozen yogurt, ice cream, pudding, bread pudding, or yogurt. Cardamom is a distinct flavor that may not appeal to everyone; other flavoring possibilities are listed below.

2 pounds medium-ripe peaches, nectarines, or plums
½ cup sugar
2 tablespoons lemon juice
1 teaspoon ground ginger or cardamom
Pinch salt

Pit but do not peel the fruit. Cut into ½- to 1-inch chunks and place in an 8-cup microwave-proof dish. Add the sugar, lemon juice, ginger or cardamom, and pinch of salt. Stir the mixture to combine. Cover with microwave plastic wrap and cook on high (100%) for 5 minutes. Stir and cover again. Cook for another 5 minutes on high. Uncover and let sit to cool slightly.

YIELD: 6 to 8 servings
PER SERVING: 99 calories, 1 g protein, 0.10 g fat, 26 g carbohydrate, 20 mg sodium, 0 mg cholesterol

Other flavoring ideas

1 to 2 teaspoons grated orange or lemon zest
1 teaspoon anise or fennel seeds
1 teaspoon whole allspice
1 stick cinnamon and ½ teaspoon whole cloves
⅓ cup raisins, currants, or golden raisins

Chocolate Sauce in a Flash

Preparation time: 5 minutes
Microwave time: 1 minute

Here is the perfect sauce to make for those late-night cravings for ice cream. You can make it richer by substituting light cream for the water. Serve drizzled over ice cream, cookies, pound cake, orange slices, fruit salad, whatever you like. There are several variations listed at the end of the recipe.

⅔ cup semisweet chocolate chips
3 tablespoons water
Pinch salt
¼ teaspoon orange extract

Place the chocolate, water, and salt in a 2-cup glass measure or microwave-proof bowl. Cover with microwave plastic wrap and cook on high (100%) for 1 minute. Remove from the oven. Whisk the sauce until smooth, then whisk in the extract. Serve warm or at room temperature.

YIELD: ¾ cup sauce
PER 1 TABLESPOON SERVING: 45 calories, 0.38 g protein, 3 g fat, 6 g carbohydrate, 11 mg sodium, 0.07 mg cholesterol

Chocolate Sauce Variations

- Use light cream in place of the water, increasing the amount to 4 tablespoons.
- Use room-temperature coffee in place of the water.
- Use vanilla or almond extract in place of the orange extract.
- Add 1 tablespoon Grand Marnier, rum, or brandy with the extract.
- Add 2 tablespoons butter with the chocolate and water for added richness.

Chapter Twelve

Birthday Parties

🐦

Birthdays are a time of mixed emotions. Your child is a year older, growing up so fast you can hardly believe it. There are so many memories of the past year—she started kindergarten, learned to ride a two-wheeler and to use a computer, and mastered jump roping. She wants to celebrate with a big party—friends, balloons, lunch, a clown, and cake and ice cream.

Watching your child grow up is a joyous thing, but planning her birthday party can be an anxiety-provoking experience. Many parents dread birthday parties as much as children look forward to them. This chapter will help you get organized for your child's party, offer tips for keeping things simple yet fun, and include many food ideas that kids of all ages will find irresistible.

Whether you're hosting a small slumber party or a pull-out-all-the-stops carnival, the last thing you need to worry about is the food. The truth is that most kids don't really care what food is served at their party, so long as there is a huge sugar-filled cake or cupcakes at the end.

The general rule of thumb with party food is to keep it as simple as possible. Ideal birthday party food can be prepared entirely (or almost entirely) before the big day. This chapter provides many ideas for party themes and recipes that are simple and straightforward but offer a refreshing change of pace from hot dogs, hamburgers, and pizza. All the recipes can be found in other chapters.

> *Birthday Desserts*
> *Birthday Party Menus*
> SOME THOUGHTS ABOUT . . . *General Rules to Keep in Mind*
>   *When Throwing a Kid's Birthday Party*
> *Theme Parties*

Birthday Desserts

I once spent two days making a gorgeous chocolate cake for my daughter's birthday, and on the day of the big event she looked at the cake and said, "Mom, why couldn't we just get the ballerina cake we saw at the grocery store?"

As parents, we tend to get carried away with our own ideas of what makes the perfect birthday party. Be sure to discuss what kind of cake your child wants *before* you start baking *your* fantasy cake. The recipes listed below, all of which appear in other chapters, make great birthday desserts:

Rhubarb-Strawberry Cake with Rhubarb-Strawberry Sauce, pages 324 and page 326

Becky's Pumpkin Roll, page 321

Caramel Apples, page 333

Homemade ice cream, pages 354–56

Michael and Donna's Magic Muffins, page 30, topped with icing and decorations

Strawberry Muffins, page 53, topped with icing and decorations

The Ultimate Brownie, page 317, topped with ice cream, chopped fruit, and grated coconut

Devil's Food Cake, page 313

Devil's Food Cupcakes, page 314

Chocolate Buttercream, page 366

Birthday Party Menus

PARTY MENU FOR TODDLERS:

Confetti Pasta Salad, page 82

Cheese cubes, pitted olives, and cherry tomato halves on a skewer

(To prevent accidents, be sure to cut off the sharp ends of the skewers,

and don't let kids run around with the sticks.)

Bread or dinner rolls and Strawberry Butter, page 33

Juice

Fruit Kebabs with Yogurt Sauce, page 338

Devil's Food Cake or Devil's Food Cupcakes, pages 313 and 314

PARTY MENU FOR SCHOOL-AGE KIDS:

Assorted sandwiches, recipe ideas on pages 72–81

Ham and Cream Cheese Swirls, page 114

Peanut Butter Fondue, page 327

Carrot and celery sticks

Deviled Eggs, page 69

Pitted olives and gherkin pickles

Kids' Fruity Tea Punch, page 390

Fruit Kebabs with Yogurt Sauce, page 338

Cupcakes or birthday cake

PARTY FOOD FOR PRE-TEENS AND TEENS:

Pizza, recipe ideas on pages 87–90

Maya's Chicken Fingers with Two Dips, page 185

Garlic Cheese Bread, page 208

Lime Rickey, page 389, or Fruity Spritzer, page 388

Birthday cake

OTHER IDEAS FOR PARTY FOOD:

Quiche, pages 159–62

Baked Potatoes with Broccoli-Cheese Topping, page 204

Tamale Pie, page 132

Peanut Butter–Orange Dip, page 376

Pineapple Yogurt Dip, page 377

Minestrone soup, page 398

Basic Quesadillas with Toppings, page 164

Chili Popcorn, page 408

Salsa Dipping Sauce, page 445, with chips and raw vegetables

Ground Meat, Spinach, and Ricotta Lasagna, page 280

Emma's Pistachio Bagel Faces, page 75

Roast ham, see Easter Ham, page 270, for a big crowd

Some Thoughts About . . .

General Rules to Keep in Mind
When Throwing a Kid's Birthday Party

• Keep it simple. This is not the time to pretend you're Martha Stewart and throw the perfect party to end all parties. Kids just want to see their friends, have fun, and open presents.

• Plan around your child's party ideas, not yours. Sit down with your child and listen to his ideas. Some kids have visions of elaborate, day-long events. Talk about keeping things realistic, and try to agree to include at least a few of your child's top ideas.

• Involve your child as much as possible in the preparations. Let her choose a theme, make (or pick out) invitations, and choose the games, party paraphernalia, goodie bag treats, and such.

• Always make sure to write the time the party starts and ends on the invitation. Be clear about what time parents should pick up their kids.

• Be sure to put an RSVP on the invitation so you'll know exactly how many children are coming and can plan accordingly.

• When throwing a party for younger kids, be sure to let parents know if they should stay and help take care of their own kids or if you'll be responsible for them.

• In general, try not to invite other parents (unless they're really close friends or relatives) because it gives you the added pressure of having to entertain the grown-ups too.

• Consider asking a friend or favorite babysitter to help out with organized games and activities.

• Make sure to have plenty of film or videotape on hand and check the batteries in your camera or video camera well before the party begins.

• Weather permitting, let the kids spend as much time outside as possible. It's a great way for them to release energy and be noisy and wild without your worrying that your house will look like a war zone.

• Try to keep sugar-filled foods and candies to a minimum. Of course, a birthday isn't a birthday without a cake or cupcakes, but make sure to serve it at the end of the party so you don't have a house filled with sugar-crazed children.

• Another way to control the amount of sugar kids eat is to avoid putting out bowls of candy. If your child insists on giving out candy, make sure to hand it out to the children in a goodie bag as they are *leaving* the party.

• When it's time to open presents, there tends to be a lot of chaos (particularly with younger children). It's not unusual to have half a dozen kids yelling "Open mine first" and crowding the birthday girl into a small corner. Ask the kids to sit in a circle and let the birthday girl decide which present she will open first. Another way of dealing with the "Open mine first" syndrome is to put everyone's name on a piece of paper, place it in a hat or bowl, and let the birthday girl pick a piece of paper and open that child's gift first. It can take the tension off the birthday girl and make a little game out of opening gifts.

Theme Parties

PASTA FOR A PARTY

Pasta is an ideal candidate for party food because it is so well loved by all generations. This party lets your guests create their own pasta dish—choosing their favorite type of pasta, sauce, and toppings. A pasta party is ideal for older kids (it works well with younger kids also but needs to be simplified) or for a gathering with a wide range of ages and tastes. Think of it as a savory version of a Make-Your-Own-Ice-Cream-Sundae Party.

For a party of ten you'll want to offer a few different types of fresh or dried pasta—penne, linguine, fettuccine, cappellini, or wagon wheels. You'll need a minimum of 3 pounds of pasta and up to 5 pounds, depending on what else you're offering. Have a few pots of boiling lightly salted water ready to go so you can add the pasta to order. (Remember that fresh pasta takes only about 3 to 5 minutes to cook, whereas dried pasta can take 12 to 15 minutes.) Once the pasta has been cooked, drain it and immediately toss it with a touch of olive oil to keep it from sticking together.

For sauces, you can simply offer tomato sauce (see recipe, page 155), but it's much more interesting also to have a pan of olive oil and garlic on hand (heat 2 chopped cloves garlic with about ¾ cup olive oil), as well as pesto (see recipe, page 438). For other sauce ideas, see the recipes on pages 91, 92, 149, and 154.

There are endless possibilities for toppings because just about anything works well with pasta. Pick and choose from the list below, and add your favorites. Remember that the more toppings you offer, the more festive the party.

Pitted whole or chopped black and green olives

Chopped fresh tomatoes

Capers

Roasted garlic (place a few heads of garlic in a small, ovenproof skillet and roast at 350 degrees for about 45 minutes; peel the garlic or squeeze out of its skin and serve!)

Anchovies

Sautéed mushrooms

Pepperoni or thinly sliced cooked sweet or hot sausage

Chopped fresh herbs

Roasted bell peppers (see recipe, page 442)

Sun-dried tomatoes

Chopped ham or prosciutto

Assorted grated cheeses (mozzarella, Parmesan, and Cheddar, for example)

Pine nuts or chopped walnuts

Honey-Glazed pecans or walnuts (see recipe, pages 288, 299)

Artichoke hearts

Sautéed onions and garlic

Red pepper flakes

Cooked spinach (see recipe, page 283)

Shelled fresh peas

A CUPCAKE CELEBRATION

It's not often that we permit children to prepare food without a whole litany of precautions and "don'ts." My favorite birthday bash ever was thrown by my friend Judy in third grade: I remember a dozen of us lined up outside at a picnic table, aprons wrapped around our waists, ready to slather bowlfuls of different colored icing all over the cupcakes that Judy's mom had baked.

What was it about that party? Then, as now, there was magic in breaking the rules, making a mess, and otherwise being allowed to have our cake and play with it, too.

Since this kind of party has all the makings of a housecleaning nightmare, if your child's birthday is in a warm-weather month, take it outside. Cover a picnic table with a vinyl tablecloth. Alternately, if you want to do this indoors, cover your kitchen table with a plastic tablecloth. Spread a sheet of plastic or garbage bags on the floor. When you invite your child's friends over, advise parents what you're up to, so they can dress their children in play clothes or send along aprons. (Or better yet, find—or make—some inexpensive children's aprons to give out as party favors.)

As with all good birthday party activities, keep the event simple. Make a cupcake recipe (see recipe on page 314), muffin recipe (see recipes on pages 30, 53, and 55), or use a cake mix, and be sure to make enough for at least 3 cupcakes per child. Whip up several types of frosting using a minimum of sugar—lemon, cream cheese, chocolate—

and put them in separate bowls. (You can also make a few batches of basic white frosting, divide them into three bowls, and color them with food coloring. The wilder the colors, the better.) Then set out an assortment of favorite toppings, such as sprinkles, chocolate chips, granola, nuts, raisins, fresh berries, or slices of fresh fruit. Using spoons, rubber spatulas, and dull knives, the kids can go wild creating edible treats with faces, fanciful patterns, and varied textures. Before they gobble them up, have a cupcake gallery show, where everyone gets to view their friends' "creations." Long after the desserts are devoured, memories of the sweet fun will live on.

SUGAR-IN-SNOW FEAST

One of the oldest, and most popular, winter traditions in New England is a "sugaring off" party. Toward the end of maple syrup season, children are invited to local sugar farms for a winter feast. Everyone is given a plate of fresh, clean snow onto which boiling hot maple syrup is poured. The syrup instantly hardens into one of the most appealing candies imaginable—icy cold, syrupy sweet, with a wonderful, taffy-like consistency.

For kids with a winter birthday, enjoy this old tradition at your house after a blanket of fresh, clean white snow has fallen. Simmer up some pure maple syrup; for best results, it should register 232 degrees on a candy thermometer, or it won't crystallize. (Make sure to keep younger kids away from the boiling hot syrup.) Scoop clean fresh snow onto plates (or make cones out of rolled up paper) and pour the hot syrup on top. Bizarre as it may sound, old-time New England "sugar-in-snow" feasts were always accompanied by sour pickles and doughnuts!

TEA PARTY

For most of us, a birthday tea party still conjures up outdated images of dainty little girls in frilly dresses chatting demurely as they sip tea and nibble on crumpets. But these celebrations actually appeal to all kinds of preschoolers, even Power Ranger–loving rough-housers. Why? A tea party offers what most young kids love more than anything: a game of make-believe, permission to play with their food, and a chance to inhabit the mysterious world of adults.

This is an ideal party idea for four- to seven-year-olds. Send out handmade invitations with a tea bag tucked inside the envelope and ask them to dress up. For food, serve an assortment of tea sandwiches, tea, and punch and let the kids decorate their own cupcakes.

Make sure the tea you make is herbal (mint, chamomile, and berry flavors are good bets) to avoid caffeine, and let an older child or adult serve it from a teapot. To give the party a feeling of elegance, serve the tea with small plates of fresh mint leaves and thin slices of lemon. Instead of plain white sugar, try to find some brightly colored sugar crystals (many supermarkets include these among their cake-decorating supplies). For another special touch, place a few berries or fresh mint sprigs into each of the compartments in an ice cube tray, cover with water, and freeze. The fancy cubes are a fun way to cool off the hot tea.

A proper tea sandwich should be crustless and cut into triangles or cookie-cutter shapes. Many preschoolers are fussy eaters, so limit the fillings to a few sure favorites: peanut butter and jelly, thin slices of mild cheese and cucumber, or plain ham or roast beef spread with unsalted butter; use different types of bread to add color and texture to the selection. Sandwiches should be made two to three hours ahead of time, covered tightly, and refrigerated.

Tea Party Menu

Ham and Cream Cheese Swirls, page 114

Assorted tea sandwiches

Cream Cheese, Raisin, and Nut Sandwiches, page 74

Celery sticks and miniature gherkins

Kids' Fruity Tea Punch, page 390

Cupcakes or cake (see "A Cupcake Celebration" on page 421 for tips)

Chapter Thirteen

Menus

❧

These menus were put together using recipes gathered from throughout the book. There are suggestions here for everything from quick and easy weeknight dinner menus to more elaborate weekend brunches and dinners that are ideal for entertaining or for special occasions.

Following these ideas, you'll find menus for the major holidays. Of all the cooking we do, holiday food is the most personal. Every family has their own set of traditions and rituals—whether it's making a standing rib roast on Christmas Day, or potato pancakes for Chanukah. And of every American who roasts a stuffed turkey on Thanksgiving Day, who isn't looking for new ideas for side dishes to serve with the traditional holiday bird?

The ideas that follow are meant to help guide you to those recipes in this book that lend themselves to holiday fare. They are dishes that would not be considered everyday food, but are particularly celebratory—rich, time-consuming, or associated with holiday traditions in one way or another. Add them to your own holiday menus, find new favorites, or, perhaps, start a holiday tradition that will continue for years to come.

WEEKDAY DINNER MENUS

Granny's Summer Rice Dish (page 166) with Marinated Green Beans (page 218), garlic bread, and fresh fruit.

Zucchini "Lasagna" (page 222), a mixed salad, crusty bread, and Quick Apple Crumble (page 336) or Peach Cobbler (page 337).

Broiled Scallops with Basil and Lemon (page 201), Tomatoes Provençal (page 225), Edwin Potatoes (page 293), and The Ultimate Brownie (page 317).

Roast Chicken with Zucchini and Peppers (page 189), roast potatoes, Roasted Leeks with Parmesan Cheese (page 226), and Quick Apple Crumble (page 336).

Stuffed Peppers (page 178), a salad, crusty bread, and Marinated Oranges with Coconut (page 341) and cookies.

Broiled Chicken (page 188), White Beans Provençal (page 220), steamed white rice, steamed green vegetables, ice cream topped with Berry, Berry Good Sauce (page 362).

Old-Fashioned Meat Loaf (page 268), mashed potatoes, a steamed green vegetable, and fruit salad topped with Maple-Yogurt Sauce (page 363).

WEEKEND LUNCH MENUS

French-Style Vegetable Soup (page 101), crusty bread, and a salad.

Spanakopita (page 119), a cucumber and yogurt salad, garlic bread, and mixed olives.

The Very Best Beef Potpie (page 130), a mixed green salad, hot cider, and Vanilla Pudding (page 328).

Tamale Pie (page 132), an avocado, tomato, and onion salad, and ice cream topped with Chocolate-Orange Sauce (page 364).

Grilled Marinated Pork Tenderloin (page 134), roast potatoes, sautéed zucchini, and biscuits or rolls.

WEEKEND DINNER MENUS

Coq au Vin (page 242), French Mashed Potatoes (page 292), Tomatoes Provençal (page 225), a salad, and Dark Chocolate Tangerine Crepes (page 315).

Roast Pork with White Beans and Cider (page 272), Edwin Potatoes (page 293), sautéed spinach, crusty bread, and Orange and Ginger Rice Pudding (page 329).

Country-Style Pork in Sweet-and-Sour BBQ Sauce (page 273), Mashed Potatoes (page 462), coleslaw or All-American Potato Salad (page 106), Buttermilk-Scallion Corn Bread (page 305), ice tea, and Apple Pie (page 331).

Ground Meat, Spinach, and Ricotta Lasagna (page 280), Garlic Cheese Bread (page 208), a mixed salad, and Lemon Drop Cookies (page 348).

Chris's Somewhat Low-Fat Louisiana Gumbo (page 274), rice, sweet potatoes, a salad, and Ultimate Summer Fruit Salad with Toppings (page 339).

WEEKEND BRUNCH MENUS

Eggs in the Hole (page 46), Fried Tomatoes (page 52), Sautéed Baked-Potato Slices (page 50).

Raspberry-Almond Pancakes (page 42) or Blueberry and Ricotta Pancakes (page 40) or Apple, Raisin, and Cinnamon Pancakes (page 37), Cranberry Applesauce (page 334), fruit salad, and apple cider.

Vegetable and Cheese Frittata (page 47), Down-Home Home Fries (page 49), Chicken Hash (page 48), Bacon Broiled with Maple Syrup (page 51), toast, and assorted jellies.

Cranberry Muffins (page 55) or Strawberry Muffins (page 53), Sour Cream Coffee Cake (page 56), fruit salad, coffee, and tea.

Holiday Menus

CHRISTMAS/NEW YEAR'S:

Standing Rib Roast, page 264

Creamed Spinach, page 227

French Mashed Potatoes, page 292

Stuffed Acorn Squash, page 126

New Year's Day Roast Beet Salad, page 288

Baked Goat Cheese with Mushrooms, page 108

Ginger Beets, page 128

Winter Vegetable Puree, page 127

Potato and Chestnut Gratin, page 297

Sweet Potatoes with Maple-Nutmeg Butter, page 301

Spinach Soufflé Roll Stuffed with Roasted Red Peppers, page 284

HOLIDAY DESSERTS:

Basic Butter Cookies, page 344

Andi's Coconut-Date Balls, page 347

Andi's Coffee Tortoni, page 346

Apple Pie, page 331

Lemon Drop Cookies, page 348

Gluck's Old-Fashioned Molasses Cookies, page 345

Hot Spiced Cider, page 392

Hot Cocoa, page 393

CHANUKAH:

Brisket with Roasted Vegetables, page 266

Potato Pancakes, page 296

Sweet Potatoes with Maple-Nutmeg Butter, page 301

Cranberry Applesauce, page 334

Beet Pancakes, page 210

Carrot and Ginger Pancakes, page 211

Chinese-Style Scallion Pancakes, page 212

Roasted Eggplant Spread, page 112

THANKSGIVING:

Your favorite turkey and stuffing

Cream of Baked Squash Soup, page 240

Roasted Leeks with Parmesan Cheese, page 226

Baked Leeks with Olive Puree and Goat Cheese, page 287

Edwin Potatoes, page 293

Pumpkin Risotto, page 291

Roasted Potatoes with Caramelized Pears, page 295

Mashed Sweet Potatoes with Honey-Glazed Pecans, page 299

Buttermilk-Scallion Corn Bread, page 305

HALLOWEEN:

Squash Soup with Apples, page 144

Spaghetti and Turkey Meatballs, page 254

Pumpkin Risotto, page 291

Becky's Pumpkin Roll, page 321

Quick Apple Crumble, page 336

Caramel Apples, page 333

Marble Pumpkin Cheesecake, page 320

EASTER:

Easter Ham with a Clove, Rum, and Orange Glaze, page 270

Basic Baked Asparagus, page 213

Creamed Spinach, page 227

Herbed Popovers, page 304

French Mashed Potatoes, page 292

PASSOVER:

Chicken Soup with Matzo Balls, pages 434 and 436

Roast Chicken with Zucchini and Peppers, page 189

Basic Baked Asparagus, page 213

MOTHER'S/FATHER'S DAY

Cream of Asparagus Soup, page 104

Greek-Style Lamb Burgers, page 182

Corn Sauté, page 221

All-American Potato Salad, page 106

French Vanilla Ice Cream, page 355, with fresh berries

FOURTH OF JULY/LABOR DAY

Marinated Green Beans, page 218

Tomatoes Provençal, page 225

Salsa Burgers, page 181

Garden Turkey Burgers, page 183

Greek-Style Lamb Burgers, page 182

Honey-Glazed Chicken Wings, page 192

Corn Sauté, page 221
Homemade Frozen Fruit Juice Pops, pages 349–53
Homemade Ice Cream, pages 354–56
Ultimate Summer Fruit Salad, page 339
Peach Cobbler, page 337

SOME THOUGHTS ABOUT . . .
Giving the Gift of Food

Black clouds are forming overhead, and the wind has kicked up. A mixture of snow, rain, and hail spits from the sky. Despite the weather, you gather the kids for a holiday shopping excursion. Putting on coats, gloves, scarves, mittens, and hats seems to take forever. While you struggle to put a sweater on the baby, your five-year-old looks at you with her most earnest expression. "Mom," she pleads, "why do we have to go out shopping? Can't we just stay right here?" You shoot her an exasperated glance. And then it hits you: she's right. There isn't a reason on earth why you can't just stay home and create the holidays on your own terms.

And so instead of shopping, you cook. You cook all day. You make a pot of cocoa and put on your favorite music. You bake cookies—even a loaf of holiday bread—and simmer a pot of cranberry sauce. As your daughter cuts star shapes out of cookie dough, you smile and realize the holiday spirit doesn't have to be defined by crowded malls and overflowing parking lots.

Cooking with kids can be more than a great tonic for the hectic holiday pace; it can also take the panic out of gift giving. How many ties can Grandpa really wear? Does Aunt Lucy really need another book? When you give a gift of homemade food, particularly something that your children have helped prepare, it means a lot.

There are dozens of recipes scattered throughout this book that make wonderful holiday gifts. Below are just a few suggestions, along with some new ideas for wrapping these foods in style.

- Basic Butter Cookies, page 344
- Cranberry Sauce with Ginger and Maple, page 453
- Honey-Glazed Pecans, pages 288, 299
- One-Hour Baguette, page 463
- Oriental Marinade, page 457
- Pesto, pages 438, 440, and 441
- Quick Refrigerator Pickles, pages 465–67
- Vanilla Sugar, page 473
- A loaf of home-baked bread with Cranberry Butter, page 454
- Roasted red peppers, page 442

Some Thoughts About . . .
Wrapping It Up

- Find a collection of old Mason jars at an antique store or flea market. Use them to store cranberry sauce, nuts, relishes, chutney, and such. Wrap the filled jars with gold and silver ribbons and label them with hand-printed cards.

- Line a straw basket with colorful tissue paper and fill it with a jar of caramelized walnuts or other treats. Have your kids make a Pooh Bear honey label.

- Bring a friend or relative a loaf of home-baked bread wrapped inside a new French bread pan.

- Find a white or single-color cookie tin and let your kids draw a holiday scene on the cover with acrylic paints or markers. Or decorate an old cookie tin with homemade stickers or children's artwork glued on the cover. Fill with cookies and goodies.

- Buy a friend or relative a new casserole and fill it with homemade soup or a casserole that they can put directly into their freezer for a hectic week to come.

- Give bread or cookies on a wooden cutting board wrapped in colorful plastic wrap.

- Have your kids decorate brown paper bags and fill them with colored tissue paper and cookies or jars of homemade relishes or sauce.

- Present holiday cookies in a new deep-dish pie plate or casserole along with whole nutmeg, an old-fashioned nutmeg grinder, and a jar of real maple syrup.

Chapter Fourteen

Cooking Basics

🍲

Basics refers to all those recipes that don't fit neatly into any specific category—fabulous sauces, marinades, barbecue sauces, quick pickles that can be made in the refrigerator, stocks (the base of all good soups and stews), and several salad dressings that take about as long to make as it takes to open a store-bought bottle. They are basic to any working kitchen, can be made any time of day, and can be used in a wide variety of dishes. They are ideal make-ahead dishes.

Basic Chicken Soup

Turkey Broth

Matzo Balls

Fish Stock

Pesto

Pesto Variations

Ideas for Using Pesto

Spinach-Walnut Pesto

Roasted Red Pepper and Garlic Pesto

Roasted Peppers: Master Recipe

Ideas for Using Roasted Peppers

Fresh Salsa

Salsa Dipping Sauce

Pineapple Salsa

Fresh Corn Relish

French Vinaigrette

Blue Cheese Dressing

Chinese-Style Dressing

Orange-Peanut Dressing

Green Goddess Dressing

Cranberry Sauce with Ginger and Maple

Cranberry Butter

Cranberry Puree

Basic Barbecue Sauce

Oriental Marinade

Citrus Sauce

Spicy Moroccan Marinade

Yogurt Marinade

Yogurt Cheese

Basic Mashed Potatoes

One-Hour Baguette

SOME THOUGHTS ABOUT . . . *Quick Refrigerator Pickles*

Quick Zucchini Pickles

Chili and Dill Pickles

Pickled Carrots with Ginger and Rice Wine

Pickled Red Onions

Speedy Dilly Beans

Sweet Bread-and-Butter Pickles

Kim Chee (Korean-Style Pickled Cabbage)

Vanilla Sugar

Pumpkin Puree

Basic Chicken Soup

Preparation time: 20 minutes
Cooking time: 1½ to 2 hours

Chicken soup is often referred to as "Jewish penicillin" because some cooks believe it will cure all that ails you. This master recipe is the base of many dishes, or it can be served as a soup with noodles, rice, or matzo balls (see page 436).

1 large chicken (about 3 to 4 pounds), excess fat removed
4 carrots, cut into thin slices or strips
4 stalks celery, cut into thin slices or strips
4 black peppercorns
4 small onions, quartered
1 bay leaf
½ cup chopped fresh parsley
Salt
2 cups cooked egg noodles or 1 cup cooked rice (optional)

Place the chicken in a large pot and pour in enough cold water to cover three-quarters of the bird. Add the carrots, celery, peppercorns, onions, bay leaf, parsley, and salt and bring to a boil over high heat. Reduce the heat to moderately low and partially cover. Simmer until the chicken is cooked (the drumstick should be very loose) and the broth is flavorful, 1½ to 2 hours.

If the chicken is done but the broth tastes weak, remove the bird from the pot and set aside. Bring the stock to a boil and reduce until it's full of flavor. Refrigerate until the fat solidifies, then lift off the fat (save for matzo balls). Season to taste.

You can serve the soup as is, with a sprinkling of parsley, or remove the chicken meat from the bones, shred it, and add to the soup. Add the noodles or rice if desired. If you want to use the broth or stock only, strain the soup and use as needed. Reserve the chicken for another dish.

YIELD: 6 servings
PER SERVING: 220 calories, 29 g protein, 4 g fat, 16 g carbohydrate, 137 mg sodium, 89 mg cholesterol

Turkey Broth

Preparation time: 10 minutes
Cooking time: 1 to 2 hours

When the last few slices of leftover turkey have been consumed and the holiday feels well behind you, it's time to make soup. For me turkey soup is almost as good as the bird itself. A turkey carcass is still full of good flavor; and a large carcass can make enough soup to last you well into the winter. Make this basic broth and then use it to create a variety of different recipes (see Granny's Turkey-Lemon-Rice Soup on page 239 and the vegetable soup on page 101).

Carcass of a 10- to 25-pound turkey, with any substantial amounts of
    meat removed and reserved
3 onions, quartered
4 carrots, cut into chunks
4 stalks celery, cut into chunks
1 bay leaf
6 black peppercorns
1 cup chopped fresh parsley
Salt

Break the turkey carcass into several pieces and place it and the onions, carrots, celery, bay leaf, peppercorns, parsley, and salt into a large stockpot. Cover with cold water and bring to a boil. Reduce the heat to moderate and let simmer, partially covered, for about 1 to 2 hours, or until the broth is flavorful. If the broth tastes weak, strain all the solid ingredients out and boil the broth vigorously until reduced somewhat and more intensely flavored.

Taste for seasoning, then strain the broth into a large bowl. The broth can now be used to make a variety of soups and stews, or it can be placed in a clean glass jar and refrigerated for up to a week or frozen for several months. If you choose to freeze the broth, let it cool to room temperature, then freeze in several smaller jars or plastic containers so you can use it as needed.

YIELD: about 2½ quarts broth
PER 1 CUP SERVING: 29 calories, 3 g protein, 2 g fat, 3 g carbohydrate, 121 mg sodium, 0
  mg cholesterol

Matzo Balls

Preparation time: 10 minutes (plus 2 hours sitting time)
Cooking time: 25 minutes

It's easy to make these small dumplings, but the secret is to handle them with a light touch and make the "batter" at least 2 hours ahead of time.

    4 large eggs, beaten
    ½ cup chicken soup or broth
    ¼ cup chicken fat (skimmed from Basic Chicken Soup, page 434) or
       solid shortening
    Salt and freshly ground black pepper
    1 cup matzo meal

Mix the eggs, soup, and chicken fat in a medium bowl. Add the salt, pepper, and matzo meal and let sit for about 2 hours. Gently stir the mixture and form it into small to medium-size balls. Bring a large pot of water to a boil, reduce the heat, drop in the balls, and simmer for 15 to 20 minutes, or until firm. Drain and add to hot chicken soup.

YIELD: 6 servings
PER SERVING: 433 calories, 36 g protein, 16 g fat, 35 g carbohydrate, 180 mg sodium, 238 mg cholesterol

Fish Stock

Preparation time: 10 minutes
Cooking time: about 1 hour

Fish stock is one of the easiest of all stocks to make because it doesn't require a long cooking time. It's also inexpensive because fish racks (the skeletons of filleted, large fish) are almost always available free of charge from a reputable fish market.

  **4 fish racks (haddock, halibut, or other fairly mild fish; avoid strong,
    oily fish)**
  1 large onion, quartered
  3 stalks celery, chopped
  1 tablespoon chopped fresh thyme or 1 teaspoon dried
  Sprig fresh parsley
  6 black peppercorns
  Salt

Place all the ingredients in a large stockpot and cover with water, breaking up the fish racks if they are too large. Bring to a boil, reduce the heat, cover partially, and let simmer about an hour, skimming off any foam that rises to the surface of the stock. Strain the stock, discarding the fish and vegetables. If the stock is flavorful, it's ready to use. If the stock tastes weak, let it boil and reduce for about 5 to 10 minutes.

The stock can be used as is, refrigerated for up to a week, or frozen for several months.

YIELD: about 1½ quarts
PER 1 CUP SERVING: 8 calories, 1 g protein, 0 g fat, 1 g carbohydrate, 270 mg sodium, 0 mg cholesterol

Pesto

Preparation time: 15 minutes

This is a classic Italian sauce made by pureeing fresh basil, garlic, olive oil, pine nuts, and Parmesan cheese. Its bright green color and fresh herb taste are traditionally paired with pasta, but it goes well with a wide variety of foods. Listed below are suggestions for using pesto, as well as several variations.

Although pesto always includes grated cheese (Parmesan is the traditional cheese of choice), I've made several batches of pesto without any cheese and found that it's delicious. This is a creamy-tasting sauce that is ideal for dairy-free diets.

> **2 cups fresh basil leaves, stemmed**
> **2 cloves garlic, chopped**
> **⅔ cup good-quality olive oil**
> **⅓ cup pine nuts**
> **About ½ cup grated Parmesan cheese (optional)**
> **Salt and freshly ground black pepper**

Place the basil in the container of a food processor or blender. Add the garlic and puree. Add the oil in a thin stream, whirling the machine until the pesto is somewhat smooth. Add the nuts and puree again. Remove from the machine and gently blend in the cheese if using. Season to taste with salt and pepper.

If you want to make a large batch of pesto in the summer when basil is plentiful, you can freeze it in airtight plastic bags, glass jars, plastic containers, or ice cube trays. Alternatively, you may want to can the pesto in Mason jars in a hot water bath for about 25 minutes. Whatever method you use, be sure to coat the top of the pesto with a very thin layer of olive oil before sealing to prevent freezer burn or discoloration in the refrigerator. Do not add the cheese before freezing or canning. It's best added when you're ready to use the sauce.

YIELD: about 1 cup

PER 1 TABLESPOON SERVING: 101 calories, 1 g protein, 11 g fat, 2 g carbohydrate, 1 mg sodium, 0 mg cholesterol

Pesto Variations

- Substitute 2 cups fresh parsley for the basil.
- Add an herb-flavored olive oil for extra herb taste.
- Substitute 2 cups fresh cilantro for the basil and use in Oriental or Indian dishes.
- Use walnuts, almonds, or other nuts instead of pine nuts.
- Use a combination of cheeses—balancing sharp and mild ones—for added depth of flavor.

Ideas for Using Pesto

- Spread on pizza or toasted English muffins.
- Toss with any shape of pasta.
- Toss a few tablespoons with linguine and a chopped ripe tomato.
- Spoon onto a cooked chicken fillet.
- Stuff a chicken breast with pesto and sauté or grill.
- Add a tablespoon to a vinaigrette.
- Spoon over fresh sliced tomatoes.
- Cut a ripe tomato in half, spread each half with a large spoonful of pesto, and broil until hot.
- Add to a hero sandwich instead of mustard or mayonnaise.
- Spread on a warm biscuit.
- Use as a dip for raw vegetables.
- Spread on raw shrimp or scallops and grill.
- Make a pesto, tomato, and roast beef sandwich.
- Toss a few tablespoons with steamed vegetables.

Spinach-Walnut Pesto

Preparation time: 10 minutes

This pesto is lighter in both color and flavor than traditional pesto. Be sure to use fresh, tender spinach.

¾ cup packed fresh spinach, stemmed, washed, and dried
2 cups walnut halves
3 cloves garlic, peeled
1 cup grated Parmesan or Romano cheese
¾ cup plus 1 tablespoon olive oil

In a food processor or blender, puree all the ingredients except 1 tablespoon of the oil and the cheese. Place in a glass jar and spoon the remaining tablespoon of oil on top. The pesto will keep, refrigerated, for several weeks.

YIELD: about 1½ cups

PER 1 TABLESPOON SERVING: 202 calories, 4 g protein, 20 g fat, 3 g carbohydrate, 99 mg sodium, 4 mg cholesterol

Roasted Red Pepper and Garlic Pesto

Preparation time: 10 minutes
Cooking time: about 20 minutes

Whole sweet red peppers and cloves of garlic are roasted until tender and mellow and then pureed with olive oil, pine nuts, and a clove of raw garlic to give the pesto a garlicky bite. Toss with pasta, serve with grilled or steamed shrimp, or use as a dip for raw vegetables and warm pita bread. If you omit the raw garlic, this beautifully colored pesto is mild enough for even the pickiest eater. Serve with your favorite pasta shape for a quick dinner.

5 cloves garlic, *unpeeled*
½ to ¾ cup olive oil
1 teaspoon chopped fresh thyme or ½ teaspoon dried
2 roasted sweet red peppers (see recipe on page 442), cut into thin strips
1 clove garlic, peeled
½ cup pine nuts
Salt and freshly ground black pepper

Preheat the oven to 400 degrees. Place the 5 unpeeled cloves of garlic in a small ovenproof skillet and toss with 1 tablespoon of oil and the thyme. Roast for about 20 minutes. Remove from the oven, let cool slightly, and squeeze the garlic cloves from their skins, reserving the oil. Set aside.

Place the roasted peppers, roasted garlic, reserved oil, and peeled clove of raw garlic (if you want a very garlicky pesto) into a blender or food processor and puree. Slowly add ½ cup of the oil, blending until smooth. Add the pine nuts, salt, and pepper and process until smooth. If you want a thinner sauce, add the remaining oil and taste for seasoning.

YIELD: about 1 cup
PER 1 CUP: 1,786 calories, 20 g protein, 189 g fat, 26 g carbohydrate, 141 mg sodium, 0 mg cholesterol

Roasted Peppers: Master Recipe

Preparation time: 15 minutes
Cooking time: 15 minutes

If you've ever gone into a gourmet food shop and gazed longingly at rows of roasted red, yellow, and orange peppers glistening in olive oil, you know the appeal of these sweet veg- etables. But then you see the price tag and wonder how anyone can charge so much for something so simple.

This is the dish to make when peppers are plentiful and inexpensive—either from your garden, from a farmer's market, or from your local supermarket when they're on sale. Roasting peppers is an entirely straightforward endeavor—they are broiled until blackened and then wrapped in foil to steam for a few minutes until you can peel them easily. You can then layer them in a glass jar, cover with good olive oil, and add any seasoning you like. I always make a big batch at a time and keep them in the refrigerator to use whenever the need arises. They will keep for several months, and the olive oil takes on a wonderful flavor.

There are endless ways to use roasted peppers. You'll find some ideas at the end of this recipe.

10 red, yellow, and/or orange bell peppers
Olive oil
3 tablespoons capers
6 peppercorns
1 bay leaf

Place a large piece of aluminum foil on the rack closest to the broiler and preheat the broiler. Lay the peppers on the foil and broil about 5 minutes. Turn the peppers over and broil again, until they are blackened on all sides. Remove from the broiler and wrap in the foil for a few minutes. (This steams the peppers and helps to loosen their skins.) Let cool slightly and, using your hands or a small, sharp knife, peel the blackened skins off the peppers. Cut the peppers in half, remove the core and seeds, and cut into thick or thin strips. Place the pepper strips in a glass jar or Mason jar and cover with a good-quality olive oil. Add the capers, peppercorns, bay leaf, and any herbs you desire. Seal tightly and refrigerate. Make sure the peppers are always covered with oil as you use them.

YIELD: about 3 cups

PER 1 STRIP SERVING: 11 calories, 0.1 g protein, 1 g fat, 1 g carbohydrate, 8 mg sodium, 0 mg cholesterol

Ideas for Using Roasted Peppers

- Place a few strips, along with a teaspoon of oil, on top of polenta.
- Add to risotto and other rice dishes.
- Place pepper strips on grilled swordfish or other fish.
- Finely chop and add to homemade mayonnaise.
- Puree with nuts and oil to make a roasted pepper pesto (see recipe page 441).
- Add to antipasto platters.
- Add to egg salad or tuna.
- Add to pizza.
- Top a grilled chicken breast, steak, or pork chop.
- Chop into salsa and other sauces.
- Add to hot or cold pasta dishes.
- Top a grilled cheese sandwich.
- Split an Italian roll or hunk of French bread in half and layer on some roasted peppers, lettuce, shredded cheese, olives, and tomatoes to make a vegetarian hero.

Fresh Salsa

Preparation time: 10 minutes

A staple of Mexican cooking, salsa has become so popular in this country that some reports indicate that it outsells catsup. Making your own salsa couldn't be simpler; make it as spicy or mild as you like. Serve with chips, nachos, tacos, raw vegetables, grilled foods, quesadillas, and more.

> **2 cups coarsely chopped very ripe tomatoes or 2 cups canned
>   chopped tomatoes**
> **¼ cup fresh lime juice**
> **1 onion, coarsely chopped**
> **2 scallions, chopped**
> **Salt to taste**
> **2 to 3 tablespoons finely chopped jalapeño peppers (optional)**
> **¼ cup finely chopped fresh parsley or cilantro**

In a medium bowl, mix all the ingredients together. This sauce is best if used within 6 hours; the longer it sits, the hotter and less crunchy it becomes.

YIELD: about 2 cups
PER ¼ CUP SERVING: 21 calories, 1 g protein, 0.2 g fat, 5 g carbohydrate, 6 mg sodium, 0
   mg cholesterol

Salsa Dipping Sauce

Preparation time: about 5 minutes

You could substitute plain, low-fat yogurt for the sour cream in this dish.

> **1 cup low-fat sour cream**
> **¼ cup mild, medium, or hot salsa (see preceding recipe)**
> **Hot pepper sauce (optional)**

In a bowl, mix the sour cream and salsa. Add the hot pepper sauce if desired. Keep covered and refrigerated until ready to serve.

YIELD: about 1 cup
PER 1 CUP: 301 calories, 9 g protein, 16 g fat, 37 g carbohydrate, 246 mg sodium, 80 mg
  cholesterol

Pineapple Salsa

Preparation time: about 15 minutes

I first came up with this recipe while visiting friends in south Florida, where I was confronted with one of the biggest, juiciest pineapples I'd ever seen. This is a colorful, very fresh-tasting salsa that wakes up the flavors of any roasted or grilled goods. It's particularly good served with grilled shrimp or swordfish, or try it on a burger or roast chicken sandwich.

> 1 large fresh pineapple or 4 cups canned pineapple chunks, drained
> 1 red bell pepper, cored and cut into small chunks
> 5 scallions, very thinly sliced
> 1 large ripe tomato, cored and cut into small chunks
> ¼ cup finely chopped fresh parsley or cilantro
> Juice of 2 large limes (about ⅓ cup)
> Juice of 1 large lemon (about ¼ cup)
> About 1 jalapeño pepper, cored and finely chopped (and seeded if you
>   like a less spicy salsa), or a few dashes hot pepper sauce

Using a large sharp knife, remove the skin from the pineapple. Working over a large bowl, remove the core and cut the fruit into small chunks, making sure to catch any juices.

Mix the pineapple chunks with the bell pepper, scallions, tomato, parsley, lime and lemon juices, and about half of the jalapeño. Taste for seasoning, making the salsa spicier if need be. If the salsa seems dry (which would mean your pineapple wasn't particularly juicy), add more lemon or lime juice to taste.

YIELD: 6 to 8 servings
PER SERVING: 62 calories, 1 g protein, 1 g fat, 16 g carbohydrate, 7 mg sodium, 0 mg cholesterol

Fresh Corn Relish

Preparation time: 15 minutes

Spoon on burgers, tacos, chicken, or fish.

> 1 cup fresh or frozen corn kernels, uncooked
> 1 cup chopped ripe tomatoes
> ½ cup finely chopped gherkin pickles
> 1 scallion, thinly sliced
> 3½ tablespoons olive oil
> 1½ tablespoons red wine vinegar
> Salt and freshly ground black pepper

Mix all the ingredients in a bowl and season to taste.

YIELD: about 2½ cups, or 4 servings

PER SERVING: 53 calories, 0 g protein, 4 g fat, 6 g carbohydrate, 85 mg sodium, 0 mg cholesterol

French Vinaigrette

Preparation time: 5 minutes

Pour this dressing on everything from mixed greens to cold chicken salad to steamed vegetables.

> 1 tablespoon Dijon mustard
> Salt and freshly ground black pepper
> 3 tablespoons red or white wine vinegar
> 6 tablespoons olive oil
> 1 clove garlic, mashed (optional)
> 1 tablespoon chopped fresh herbs or 1 teaspoon dried (optional)
> 1 or 2 teaspoons honey (optional)

In a small bowl, mix the mustard with a little salt and pepper. Spoon in the vinegar and then the oil, whisking to form a smooth dressing. Add any of the remaining ingredients as desired. Taste for seasoning and add more vinegar if the dressing tastes too oily, or a touch of oil if it's too tart.

YIELD: about ½ cup, or 4 servings

PER SERVING: 185 calories, 0 g protein, 20 g fat, 1 g carbohydrate, 113 mg sodium, 0 mg cholesterol

Blue Cheese Dressing

Preparation time: 5 minutes

Spoon this thick, cheesy dressing over salads or use as a dipping sauce for raw or steamed vegetables.

¼ **cup plain low-fat yogurt**
¼ **cup low-fat milk**
Salt and freshly ground black pepper
½ **cup crumbled blue cheese**

Place the yogurt, milk, salt, pepper, and ¼ cup of the blue cheese in a blender or a food processor and puree until smooth. Adjust the consistency by either thinning with a few more teaspoons of milk or thickening by pureeing a few more teaspoons of cheese. Pour into a bowl and stir in the remaining crumbled cheese.

YIELD: about ½ cup, or 4 servings
PER SERVING: 76 calories, 5 g protein, 5 g fat, 2 g carbohydrate, 253 mg sodium, 15 mg
  cholesterol

Chinese-Style Dressing

Preparation time: 10 minutes

This delicious dressing adds a distinctive flavor to green salads, steamed vegetables, or diced cooked chicken.

> 1 teaspoon finely chopped fresh ginger or ½ teaspoon ground
> 1 tablespoon tahini (sesame seed paste) or chunky peanut butter
> 1 teaspoon soy sauce
> 1 tablespoon low-fat milk or plain yogurt
> 1 teaspoon dark sesame oil
> 2 tablespoons red wine vinegar or lemon juice
> ¼ cup safflower oil
> Freshly ground black pepper

In a small bowl, mix the ginger and tahini until blended. Stir in the soy sauce, milk or yogurt, and sesame oil. Slowly stir in the vinegar and safflower oil until smooth. Add pepper to taste.

YIELD: about ½ cup, or 4 servings

PER SERVING: 157 calories, 1 g protein, 17 g fat, 1 g carbohydrate, 92 mg sodium, 0 mg cholesterol

Orange-Peanut Dressing

Preparation time: about 5 minutes

Add a crunchy texture to salads with this tangy topping.

¼ **cup olive or vegetable oil**
2 **tablespoons orange juice**
1 **teaspoon grated orange zest**
¼ **cup chopped peanuts**
¼ **cup chopped scallions (optional)**
Salt and freshly ground black pepper

In a small bowl, whisk together all the ingredients until well blended. Taste for seasoning. If made with salted peanuts, it won't need any additional salt.

YIELD: about ½ cup, or 4 servings
PER SERVING: 177 calories, 2 g protein, 18 g fat, 3 g carbohydrate, 1 mg sodium, 0 mg cholesterol

Green Goddess Dressing

Preparation time: about 5 minutes

This oil-free salad dressing doubles as a dip.

   ¼ **cup chopped fresh parsley**
   ¼ **cup chopped scallions**
   1 **clove garlic, chopped**
   ½ **cup plain low-fat yogurt**
   2 **tablespoons low-fat milk**
   1½ **teaspoons fresh lemon juice**

   Place the parsley, scallions, garlic, yogurt, 1 tablespoon of the milk, and half of the lemon juice into a blender or food processor and blend until smooth. Taste for seasoning and add salt, pepper, and additional lemon juice if needed. For a thinner dressing, add the remaining milk and blend until smooth.

YIELD: about ½ cup, or 4 servings
PER SERVING: 27 calories, 2 g protein, 1 g fat, 3 g carbohydrate, 26 mg sodium, 0 mg cholesterol

Cranberry Sauce with Ginger and Maple

Preparation time: 10 minutes
Cooking time: about 15 minutes

This cranberry sauce can be used to top turkey, goose, chicken, and ham, as well as ice cream, pound cake, or vanilla cookies.

1½ **cups sugar**
2 **cups water**
4 **cups cranberries**
⅓ **cup orange juice, preferably fresh**
⅓ **cup maple syrup**
1 **tablespoon grated orange zest**
1 **tablespoon finely chopped fresh ginger**
½ **teaspoon vanilla extract**

In a large saucepan, mix the sugar and water and bring to a boil. Let boil for 8 minutes, or until slightly syrupy. Add the cranberries and simmer about 5 minutes, until they begin to pop. Add the orange juice, maple syrup, orange zest, ginger, and vanilla, and simmer 2 minutes more. Remove from the heat and let the sauce cool (it may appear thin at this point, but it thickens as it cools). Store in the refrigerator for up to 2 weeks.

YIELD: about 5 cups, or 10 servings
PER SERVING: 162 calories, 0 g protein, 0 g fat, 42 g carbohydrate, 2 mg sodium, 0 mg cholesterol

Cranberry Butter

Preparation time: about 8 minutes

A maroon-colored butter, this sweet treat adds an extra-special touch to muffins, pancakes, corn bread, or French toast.

1 stick butter or margarine (½ cup), at room temperature
3 tablespoons cranberry puree (see recipe, page 455)
1 teaspoon vanilla sugar (see recipe, page 473), or plain sugar
Pinch ground nutmeg

In a small bowl, soften the butter with a flat knife or the back of spoon. Mix in the cranberry puree, sugar, and nutmeg until well incorporated. (This can also be done in a food processor, but be careful not to overprocess. You simply want to incorporate all the ingredients into a smooth butter.) Place in a ramekin or small attractive bowl and serve.

YIELD: about ½ cup

PER 1 TABLESPOON SERVING: 114 calories, 0.15g protein, 12 g fat, 3 g carbohydrate, 117 mg sodium, 31 mg cholesterol

Cranberry Puree

Preparation time: about 10 minutes
Cooking time: about 10 minutes

This is a simple puree made from fresh cranberries, water, and a touch of sugar. It is used to make the cranberry butter on page 454, or it can be added to pancake and muffin mixtures or spooned over ice cream, yogurt, or pound cake. The puree also adds a sweet-tart flavor to savory sauces.

1 bag (12 ounces) fresh cranberries
¾ cup water
⅓ cup Vanilla Sugar (see recipe, page 473) or plain sugar

Place the cranberries and water in a small saucepan and bring to a boil. Reduce the heat and let simmer about 10 minutes, or until the mixture has reduced to about 1¼ cups. Remove from the heat and add the sugar. Strain the puree through a sieve. Let cool before serving.

YIELD: about 1 cup
PER 1 TABLESPOON SERVING: 27 calories, 0.08 g protein, 0 g fat, 7 g carbohydrate, 0.25 mg sodium, 0 mg cholesterol

Basic Barbecue Sauce

Preparation time: 5 minutes

Feel free to add any chopped fresh herbs that you like or a spoonful of Chinese chili paste for a hotter sauce. This recipe makes enough for 3½ pounds of country-style ribs or a large chicken cut into small pieces.

2½ cups catsup
⅓ cup orange juice
1 tablespoon ground cinnamon
1 tablespoon maple syrup or honey
1½ tablespoons soy sauce
1½ tablespoons Worcestershire sauce

In a medium bowl, mix all the ingredients and taste for seasoning, adding more cinnamon if desired. Use to marinate meat; brush on additional sauce during cooking.

YIELD: about 3 cups, or 4 servings
PER SERVING: 216 calories, 3 g protein, 0 g fat, 49 g carbohydrate, 2,249 mg sodium, 0 mg cholesterol

Oriental Marinade

Preparation time: 10 minutes

Use this aromatic sauce on 1½ pounds of fish, chicken breasts, or pork.

1 cup reduced-sodium soy sauce
3 tablespoons grated fresh ginger
2 teaspoons dark sesame oil

Mix all the ingredients and pour over the fish or meat. Toss to coat. Let marinate for at least 30 minutes before grilling.

YIELD: 1 cup, or 4 servings
PER SERVING: 62 calories, 4 g protein, 2 g fat, 7 g carbohydrate, 2,400 mg sodium, 0 mg cholesterol

Citrus Sauce

Preparation time: 10 minutes

This light, refreshing sauce complements shrimp, chicken breasts, pork, or any thick, firm-fleshed fish, such as swordfish. Makes enough for 1 pound of fish, poultry, or meat.

⅔ **cup fresh lemon or lime juice or a combination**
2 cloves garlic, finely chopped
¼ **cup very finely chopped fresh cilantro or parsley**
Freshly ground black pepper

Mix all the ingredients and pour over the fish or meat. Toss to coat. Let marinate for at least 30 minutes before grilling.

YIELD: about ⅔ cup, or 4 servings
PER SERVING: 13 calories, 0 g protein, 0 g fat, 4 g carbohydrate, 1 mg sodium, 0 mg cholesterol

Spicy Moroccan Marinade

Preparation time: 15 minutes
Cooking time: about 3 minutes

For adventurous eaters only—it's spicy! A little of this marinade will add a lot of flavor. It's particularly good served with lamb, chicken, and grilled vegetables.

½ teaspoon cayenne
1 teaspoon peanut oil
2 cloves garlic, chopped
½ small fresh chili pepper, cored and seeded
1½ tablespoons chopped fresh cilantro or parsley
1 tablespoon ground cumin
1½ teaspoons paprika
½ teaspoon salt
2 tablespoons red wine vinegar
2½ tablespoons olive oil

Mix the cayenne and peanut oil in a small bowl.

Place the garlic, chili pepper, cilantro or parsley, cumin, paprika, salt, vinegar, and 1½ tablespoons of water in a blender or food processor and blend until smooth. Drizzle in the cayenne and peanut oil mixture and the olive oil and blend until the sauce is smooth.

Transfer the marinade to a medium saucepan and simmer for 3 minutes before pouring over the food. Marinate for at least one hour in the refrigerator.

YIELD: about ½ cup, or 4 servings
PER SERVING: 99 calories, 1 g protein, 10 g fat, 3 g carbohydrate, 277 mg sodium, 0 mg cholesterol

Yogurt Marinade

Preparation time: 5 minutes

The yogurt in this sauce acts as a tenderizer and also adds an unforgettable creamy flavor. It's especially good with chicken or lamb; try it on half a leg of lamb or skewered cubes of lamb. Makes enough to coat 2 pounds of meat.

1 cup plain low-fat yogurt
1 teaspoon ground cumin
½ teaspoon ground cinnamon
1½ tablespoons olive oil
2 tablespoons finely chopped scallions or onion
1 tablespoon soy sauce
Freshly ground black pepper

MIX together all the ingredients and toss with the meat to coat; the sauce will be thick. Let marinate for at least 30 minutes before grilling.

YIELD: 1 cup, or 4 servings
PER SERVING: 87 calories, 3 g protein, 6 g fat, 5 g carbohydrate, 298 mg sodium, 4 mg cholesterol

Yogurt Cheese

This is a simple way to transform regular low-fat yogurt into a thickened, low-fat cheese. Place a container of natural low-fat yogurt into a colander or sieve lined with cheesecloth set over a medium bowl. Let drain to remove all the liquid from the yogurt, about 24 hours. Press down on the yogurt to remove as much liquid as possible and place the yogurt cheese into another bowl.

Yogurt cheese can be a healthy substitute for sour cream in dips, sauces, and soups. It's also delicious spread inside a hot baked potato, on a bagel, or tossed with pasta.

YIELD: 16 servings

PER 1 TABLESPOON SERVING: 12 calories, 1 g protein, 0.37 g fat, 1 g carbohydrate, 9 mg sodium, 1 mg cholesterol

Basic Mashed Potatoes

Preparation time: about 5 minutes
Cooking time: about 25 minutes

This is the traditional, straightforward recipe for mashed potatoes, but you can experiment with herbs and spices, add flavored olive oils instead of traditional butter, or stir in a touch of grated Parmesan or a variety of cheeses just before serving.

12 medium boiling potatoes, peeled (or unpeeled) and quartered
1 stick unsalted butter (½ cup)
1 cup low-fat milk
Salt and freshly ground black pepper

Place the potatoes in a large pot of boiling water. Simmer until they are tender but not falling apart, about 15 to 20 minutes. Drain thoroughly. Using a ricer or a potato masher, mash the potatoes in the pan over a low heat. Add half the butter and half the milk and mash well to incorporate. Add the remaining butter and milk and season to taste. Some lumps are desirable.

YIELD: 6 servings
PER SERVING: 287 calories, 5 g protein, 16 g fat, 33 g carbohydrate, 33 mg sodium, 43 mg cholesterol

One-Hour Baguette

Preparation time: 10 minutes
Cooking time: 20 minutes
Sitting time: 20 minutes

You say you don't have the time to make your own bread? This is the recipe that will prove you wrong. It couldn't be simpler, or faster. This herb-and-cheese bread goes well with salads, roasts, or a thick soup. You can use dried herbs, but fresh herbs are preferable. For a heartier bread, add ½ to 1 cup chopped ham, pressing it into the dough along with the cheese. If possible, bake the loaf in a French bread pan.

1½ **cups warm water**
1½ **tablespoons yeast**
1 **tablespoon honey**
4 **cups unbleached all-purpose or whole-wheat flour or a combination**
1 **teaspoon salt**
6 **tablespoons mixed fresh herbs (thyme, sage, rosemary, and basil) or**
   3 **teaspoons dried**
1 **cup grated Parmesan cheese or cheese of choice**
Olive oil

In a large bowl, combine the warm water, yeast, and honey. Let sit in a warm spot for 10 to 15 minutes, or until the yeast has dissolved and starts to bubble. Sift the flour and salt over the yeast mixture, 1 cup at a time, and mix until the dough forms a large ball. Knead for a few minutes until smooth.

Lightly flour a work surface and a rolling pin. Cut the dough in half, and roll out one half to form a rectangle about 15 inches long and 8 inches wide. Scatter half the herbs and cheese over the surface and lightly press them into the dough. Gently roll up the dough lengthwise into the shape of a baguette. Repeat with the other half of the dough. Place the loaves in 2 well-greased French bread pans or on a baking sheet. Drape a clean tea towel over the dough, and set in a warm spot for 20 minutes to rise.

Preheat the oven to 450 degrees. Lightly brush the loaves with olive oil and bake for

20 minutes on the middle rack. Remove and let cool slightly before serving. The bread will keep for several days or can be frozen; cool for an hour before freezing.

YIELD: 2 loaves

PER LOAF: 1,304 calories, 47 g protein, 29 g fat, 211 g carbohydrate, 1,856 mg sodium, 32 mg cholesterol

SOME THOUGHTS ABOUT . . .
Quick Refrigerator Pickles

Pickles are little bundles of concentrated flavor that explode in your mouth with a pleasing crunch. Even kids who shy away from spicy foods love their salty-sour punch. Despite the popularity of pickles, most people don't make their own. That's because the majority of pickles take weeks or months to complete and require the use of home canning equipment. However, I have found that you can make fresh-tasting pickles in just a few hours and still have the crunch and pleasing sour taste of the old-fashioned kind—with a minimum of effort. Imagine picking cucumbers from your garden (or a farmer's market) in the morning and having incredibly fresh-tasting pickles ready to eat by dinnertime!

The quick pickling technique used in the following recipes relies on vinegar as well as other common pickling ingredients such as salt, sugar, and fresh and dried herbs and spices. The difference is that quick pickles are not made to last more than a few days. Instead of going to the trouble of canning your pickles in sterilized jars, you store quick pickles in the refrigerator in a loosely covered jar or even a ceramic bowl covered with plastic food wrap.

The method is quite simple: Fresh vegetables are cut into thin slices or strips in order to allow the vinegar and spices to quickly permeate the flesh. In most cases, a hot vinegar solution is poured on top, which enables the pickling process to begin on impact. An alternative method is to salt the vegetables first to leach out the bitter juices. The salt is rinsed off after an hour or so, and vinegar is then added. As in all other pickling recipes, always use nonreactive (stainless steel, glass, or ceramic) saucepans and containers to heat the vinegar and marinate the pickles.

The quantities for these pickles are small because most of them won't last more than a few days.

Quick Zucchini Pickles

Preparation time: 10 minutes
Pickling time: 3 to 24 hours

The time to make these pickles is when you have an abundance of zucchini flowing from the garden. Mixed with chopped shallots and fresh dill, they make a terrific addition to any grilled or barbecued foods. This recipe can easily be doubled or tripled to feed a crowd.

1 medium zucchini, cut into thick 3-inch-long spears
1 tablespoon chopped fresh dill
1 shallot, finely chopped, or 1½ tablespoons finely chopped onion
½ tablespoon sugar
¼ teaspoon salt
½ cup cider vinegar or enough to cover the vegetables

Place the zucchini spears in a bowl. Mix with the dill and shallots. Add the sugar, salt, and enough vinegar to cover the zucchini. Cover and refrigerate for at least 3 hours before serving.

YIELD: 1½ cups
PER 1½ CUPS: 73 calories, 2 g protein, 0.26 g fat, 20 g carbohydrate, 549 mg sodium, 0 mg
   cholesterol

Chili and Dill Pickles

Preparation time: 10 minutes
Cooking time: 3 minutes
Pickling time: 4 to 24 hours

Be sure to make these in a glass canning jar to show off the beautiful combination of colors and shapes. Mild red chili peppers are layered with slices of pickling cucumbers and seasoned with fresh dill and whole cloves of garlic. Look for a mild variety of chili peppers unless you prefer really spicy pickles.

2 pickling cucumbers, sliced ¼ inch thick
2 mild red chili peppers, seeded and thinly sliced
1 whole mild red or green chili pepper
2 cloves garlic, peeled and left whole
2 tablespoons plus 1 teaspoon chopped fresh dill
1½ cups cider vinegar
1 tablespoon salt

Clean a 1-quart glass canning jar and rinse in hot or boiling water. Layer the cucumbers and sliced chilies in the canning jar, alternating the vegetables. Place the whole chili pepper on top and push the garlic cloves into the jar. Sprinkle with the 2 tablespoons of dill.

In a medium nonreactive saucepan, heat the vinegar, salt, and 1 teaspoon of dill until simmering. Pour the hot vinegar over the other ingredients and let cool. Cover and let marinate for 4 hours or up to 24 hours before eating.

YIELD: 1 quart
PER 1 QUART: 171 calories, 5 g protein, 1 g fat, 49 g carbohydrate, 6,613 mg sodium, 0 mg cholesterol

Pickled Carrots with Ginger and Rice Wine

Preparation time: 10 minutes
Cooking time: 3 minutes
Marinating time: 4 to 24 hours

These thin strips of carrots have a decidedly Oriental flavor. Give them at least 4 hours to pickle, or better yet, let them sit overnight. Serve with rice dishes and stir-fries or serve them alongside sandwiches and salads. They are also an excellent accompaniment to barbecued and grilled foods. Rice vinegar is available in Asian supermarkets and gourmet food shops.

4 medium carrots, cut into thin 3-inch strips
1 tablespoon julienne strips fresh ginger
¼ cup sugar
¾ teaspoon salt
1¼ cups Oriental rice vinegar

Place the carrots in a 1-quart jar, packing them down evenly.

In a medium nonreactive saucepan, mix the ginger, sugar, salt, and vinegar and bring to a boil over high heat. Reduce the heat and let simmer for 3 minutes. Pour the hot vinegar mixture over the carrots, making sure all the carrots are submerged in the liquid. Let cool. Cover and refrigerate for 4 hours or overnight. Drain the vinegar from the carrots and serve cold.

YIELD: 1 quart
PER ¼ CUP SERVING: 23 calories, 0.18 g protein, 0.03 g fat, 6 g carbohydrate, 109 mg sodium, 0 mg cholesterol

Pickled Red Onions

Preparation time: 8 minutes
Cooking time: about 5 minutes
Pickling time: 4 to 24 hours

Thin strips of pickled red onions can transform the most basic sandwich into a full-flavored treat. Layer them on any sandwich, serve with an antipasto or cheese platter, or for true onion lovers, just eat them straight out of the bowl. You can also try this recipe using sweet Vidalia onions, but you'll miss the beautiful rosy red color. The flavor of the onions can be varied by adding other ingredients, such as 1 to 2 teaspoons of peppercorns, mustard seeds, coriander seeds, fennel seeds, or dried chili peppers.

1 red onion
½ cup cider vinegar
⅓ cup water

Peel the onion and slice thinly. Separate the rings and place in a medium bowl. Cover with boiling water, let sit for 1 minute, and drain. Place the onions in a bowl.

In a medium nonreactive saucepan, combine the vinegar and water and boil. Pour over the onions and let cool. Cover and refrigerate for at least 4 hours or overnight. Drain the onions from the pickling liquid before serving. Serve cold.

YIELD: about 1 cup
PER ¼ CUP SERVING: 18 calories, 1 g protein, 0.05 fat, 4 g carbohydrate, 5 mg sodium, 0 mg cholesterol

Speedy Dilly Beans

Preparation time: 10 minutes
Cooking time: 5 minutes
Marinating time: 6 to 24 hours

This is a fast version of dilly beans, one of the most popular garden pickles. Thin green beans are pickled in cider vinegar with chopped dill, slices of pungent garlic, and spicy chili peppers. You can make these pickles as mild or killer-hot as you want, depending on how many chilies you add. Dilly beans are delicious served with a platter of assorted cheeses and crackers, with summer salads, or as a condiment with just about any grilled meat, poultry, or seafood dish.

3 cups cider vinegar
1 pound thin green beans, trimmed
1 clove garlic, peeled and cut in thirds lengthwise
1 to 3 dried red chili peppers
2 tablespoons coarsely chopped fresh dill
½ tablespoon salt

Heat the vinegar over high heat in a nonreactive saucepan.

Meanwhile, place the beans in a medium jar, packing them in side by side. Add the garlic slices, chili pepper(s), dill, and salt and pour the hot vinegar on top. Let cool slightly, cover, and refrigerate for at least 6 hours or overnight.

YIELD: about 3 cups
PER ½ CUP SERVING: 41 calories, 1 g protein, 0.18 g fat, 12 g carbohydrate, 555 mg sodium, 0 mg cholesterol

Sweet Bread-and-Butter Pickles

Preparation time: 10 minutes
Cooking time: about 5 minutes
Pickling time: 4 to 24 hours

A classic sweet pickle, this one goes well with just about any sandwich or grilled dish. Thin slices of pickling cucumbers are layered with sweet Vidalia onions, mustard seeds, and cinnamon sticks, and then pickled in a brown sugar–vinegar solution. The pickles will be ready in about 4 hours, but they taste even better the next day.

2 pickling cucumbers, unpeeled, sliced about ½ inch thick
½ large Vidalia onion, very thinly sliced
1½ teaspoons mustard seeds
1½ cups cider vinegar
1 cup light brown sugar
1 tablespoon salt
2 cinnamon sticks

Layer the cucumber and onion slices in a 1-quart glass canning jar. Sprinkle the mustard seeds on top.

In a medium nonreactive saucepan, heat the vinegar, sugar, and salt, whisking well to thoroughly incorporate the sugar. Let simmer and pour over the cucumber and onions. Place the cinnamon sticks in the jar, pushing them down so they are thoroughly covered by the vinegar. Let cool, then cover and refrigerate for 4 to 24 hours before eating.

YIELD: 1 quart
PER 1 QUART: 1,034 calories, 7 g protein, 2 g fat, 267 g carbohydrate, 6,076 mg sodium, 0 mg cholesterol

Kim Chee (Korean-Style Pickled Cabbage)

Preparation time: 10 minutes
Sitting time: 2 hours
Pickling time: 2 to 24 hours

Kim chee, a traditional Korean dish made from Chinese cabbage and chili peppers, is a fiery pickle that is frequently served with grilled foods and noodle dishes. This quick variation uses Napa or Chinese cabbage layered with chopped garlic and chili peppers. First the cabbage is liberally sprinkled with sea salt or pickling salt to drain away any bitter juices. After about 2 hours the salt is washed off, and vinegar and hot chilies are added. You can make the *kim chee* as mild or spicy as you like, depending on your and your children's tastes.

> **4 cups sliced Chinese or Napa cabbage**
> **2 tablespoons plus about ¼ teaspoon sea salt or pickling salt**
> **1 tablespoon sugar**
> **5 tablespoons white or rice vinegar**
> **1 teaspoon paprika**
> **3 cloves chopped garlic**
> **1 to 3 dried red chili peppers, crumbled, with seeds**

Place the cabbage in a bowl and sprinkle with 2 tablespoons of the salt. Place an inverted plate over the bowl and place a weight (a bag of beans or rice) on top; the idea is to weigh the cabbage down so it releases all its bitter juices. Let sit for about 2 hours at room temperature, or until liquid forms at the bottom of the bowl. Place the cabbage in a colander and rinse thoroughly. Drain and dry on paper towels.

In a bowl, mix the sugar, vinegar, and paprika. Add a pinch of the remaining salt. Stir in the cabbage, garlic, and chili peppers to taste and stir well to coat the vegetables. Cover with the inverted plate and weight and place in the refrigerator for at least 2 hours, stirring once or twice. Taste for seasoning, adding more salt and chili pepper if desired.

YIELD: about 2 cups
PER ¼ CUP SERVING: 17 calories, 1 g protein, 0.17 g fat, 4 g carbohydrate, 142 mg sodium, 0 mg cholesterol

Vanilla Sugar

Preparation time: 5 minutes
Sitting time: 2 to 3 weeks

When a whole vanilla bean is buried in a few cups of sugar, magical things begin to happen. The rich vanilla essence is infused into the sugar, making it a special flavoring to add to cakes, cookies, pastry, hot cocoa, tea, and such.

3 cups white sugar
1 whole vanilla bean, split in half

Place the sugar in a jar with a tight-fitting lid. Bury the vanilla bean halves inside the sugar and let sit in a cool, dark spot for at least 10 days before using. Remove the vanilla bean after 2 to 3 weeks.

YIELD: 3 cups
PER 1 TABLESPOON SERVING: 49 calories, 0 g protein, 0 g fat, 13 g carbohydrate, 0 mg sodium, 0 mg cholesterol

Pumpkin Puree

Preparation time: 15 minutes
Cooking time: 1 hour

Use this recipe for any dish that calls for pureed squash. The puree is delicious by itself, tossed with a little butter, salt, pepper, and grated Parmesan cheese.

1 pumpkin (about 2 pounds)

Preheat the oven to 400 degrees. Cut the pumpkin in half and remove the seeds and fibers. Place the halves on a baking sheet, cut side down, and bake for 45 minutes to 1 hour, or until they are tender when pierced with a fork.

Remove from the oven and let cool. Scoop out the flesh and puree in a blender or a food processor. The puree will keep in the freezer, tightly covered, for a month.

YIELD: about 4 cups
PER ½ CUP SERVING: 21 calories, 1 g protein, 0 g fat, 5 g carbohydrate, 1 mg sodium, 0 mg cholesterol

Index